Roy Williams
Plays: 5

Roy Williams
Plays: 5

Kingston 14
The Firm
Advice for the Young at Heart
Death of England (written with Clint Dyer)
Death of England: Delroy (written with Clint Dyer)

With an introduction by Roy Williams

methuen | drama
LONDON • NEW YORK • OXFORD • NEW DELHI • SYDNEY

METHUEN DRAMA
Bloomsbury Publishing Plc
50 Bedford Square, London, WC1B 3DP, UK
1385 Broadway, New York, NY 10018, USA
29 Earlsfort Terrace, Dublin 2, Ireland

BLOOMSBURY, METHUEN DRAMA and the Methuen Drama logo
are trademarks of Bloomsbury Publishing Plc

First published in Great Britain 2022

Kingston 14 © Roy Williams, 2014
The Firm © Roy Williams, 2017
Advice for the Young at Heart © Roy Williams, 2013
Death of England © Roy Williams and Clint Dyer, 2020
Death of England: Delroy © Roy Williams and Clint Dyer, 2020
Introduction © Roy Williams, 2022

A catalogue record for this book is available from the British Library.

A catalog record for this book is available from the Library of Congress.

ISBN: PB: 978-1-3502-8904-8
ePDF: 978-1-3502-8906-2
eBook: 978-1-3502-8905-5

Series: Contemporary Dramatists

Typeset by Mark Heslington Ltd, Scarborough, North Yorkshire

To find out more about our authors and books visit
www.bloomsbury.com and sign up for our newsletters.

Contents

Roy Williams: Introduction

It was 2012 when the idea came to write *Kingston 14*. It was fifty years since Jamaica got its independence and it has been argued that they are far worse off than they were back in 1962. But whose fault was that? The Jamaicans themselves? The so-called great British Empire? Jamaica was the home of my parents; I was keen to see if I could write a contemporary story about the island seen through the eyes of the police. The National Theatre, who had originally commissioned the play before they passed on it, paid for me to go over there for two weeks; I had interviewed officers, who may have been very young but were wise beyond their years. Their choices for a good life in Jamaica were limited: for them it was either join a gang, or be a police officer. I had explored issues of gang culture in previous plays of mine set in this country. The gang war situation over in Jamaica was far more violent as well as political. There are two main parties in Jamaica, the People's National party, and the Jamaican Labour party. As well as fighting each other over territories, such as the locale of *Kingston 14*, gang members would often follow the banner of either of those parties. And they mean business; I remember observing bullet holes in a wall of the bar where I met the officers, who generously gave their time on what I assumed was their day off. We chatted for hours and I paid them with several rounds of Red Stripe. I remember having to pretend I didn't see a handgun being passed from one guy to another on a neighbouring table. The guys saw it as well but it was not in their interest to do anything about it. This was Jamaica and the police handle things a little different than they do here.

It was *Kingston 14* that indirectly led me to write *The Firm*. The assistant director of *Kingston 14*, Steve Macaulay, who also had a small role in the play, has had quite an interesting life, coming in and out of prison before turning his life around, becoming an actor as well teaching drama to young people. During breaks between rehearsals, he would tell of his life growing up in care with a bunch of white and Black lads, forming their own little crew of criminals, committing small acts of crime: shop-lifting, pickpocketing, fencing stolen goods – the bigger the better. They were doing what they could to survive Thatcher's Britain in the 1980s. The guys all took turns doing stints in prison, but it was who they are now, not what they were, that interested me. Older fatter but wiser? A bunch of those guys came to see *Kingston 14* when it was on at Stratford East. They sat in the front row, and did almost anything to try and make Steve corpse on stage. Anyone who has ever been to Stratford East will know how involved the audience can be with whatever is performed in that theatre – these guys took it to another level. After meeting them in the bar afterwards, witnessing how much they loved each other, I knew I had to write a play about them.

Before writing, I had a brief spell as an actor, working mostly in young people's theatre/TIE. Theatre Centre, arguably the leading young people's theatre in this country, if not the world, have been operating for almost seventy years, and they gave me my first job back in 1988. Working with such amazing writers and beautiful human beings such as Noel Greig, Lin Coghlan and Philip Osment inspired me to follow my true passion, which was not acting but writing. My close relationship with Theatre Centre continues to this day. I was equally proud to have written two plays for them, one of which was *Advice for the Young at Heart* in 2013. The play came about because at the time I had two ideas for two different plays: one set during the race riots that occurred in Notting Hill London in 1958, and the other about the London riots in 2011, brought on by the shooting by the police of Mark Duggan. As part of my research, I read up on the government of the time's public response to the riots of 1958, and their wording was almost like-for-like what our prime minister at the time, David Cameron, had to say about the carnage that was unfolding on the streets of London. That was when I had the idea to blend the two plays together. Telling the story of a young girl, sexually objectified by boys of a similar age, struggling to find her own identity on the night of the riots in South London, and a young teenage Teddy Boy who acts one way about the flux of West Indian immigrants coming into England at the time, and thinks another when he falls in love with one of them. The play reveals both characters, living in different time periods, are related to each other. I remain a passionate supporter of young people's theatre. You will not find a more honest audience in schools and youth centres. If they do not like what you are doing, they will make it apparent to you. But if you are good enough to silence them, on their turf, when you can hear a pin drop, trust me on this, there is no better feeling.

Death of England started off as a short film, a ten-minute film, I was commissioned, along with five other writers, to write a short piece inspired by the *Guardian* newspaper's Saturday sections. Sport, Fashion, Education, Music, Politics and Food. I went for Sport. It was 2014; England had exited the World Cup finals without winning a single game. It was the first time I was starting to hear the word Brexit. The film was centred around a funeral with the main character Michael addressing the congregation, and verbally attacking everyone in a drunken, drug-fuelled state. Michael was angry about everything: not just how bad England were, losing his dad, but about the state of the country as a whole. Clint Dyer, my director, was convinced there was more story there, and together we set about writing a full-length play. More: In 2017 the National Theatre studio gave us a rehearsal room and a whole bunch of lovely actors to play Michael's enlarged white working class family, which would serve as a metaphor for how England sees itself, the good as well as the bad. We improvised some amazing stuff. But the first draft of the play was arguably the biggest and longest play ever. It was so fat that I felt the central character Michael was being lost, but I had a crazy idea. I suggested to Clint that he let me go away and write a new draft as a one-person show; we would not lose anything, but it would be told through Michael's voice. When I came back a few months later, Clint took it away to do further work. Thankfully the National liked where we were going and programmed the piece. Rafe Spall, who played Michael in the original film, was up for playing him again and gave, at least in my humble opinion, one of the greatest performances ever on the London stage. Clint and I found that we had so much more material left over, we could write another piece. Over the long, scary period of the first country-wide lockdown, as well as the incredible world-wide response to the murder of George Floyd, we set about telling almost the same story as *Death of England*, but this time seen through the eyes of Michael's Black best friend Delroy, who is as confused and angry as Michael was in his piece. It was the one line in the first DOE play that was a starting point in writing *Death of England: Delroy* where Michael says to Delroy, '*you may sound like us, but you will never be one of us'.* I had the same comment thrown at me my entire life in so many different ways.

My respect as ever to the amazing company of actors of each of these plays and every single member of the creative teams. Much thanks to Emily McLaughlin, Rufus Norris. Kerry Michael. Steve Macaulay. Edward Hall. Lin Coghlan. Heaps of love to the wonderful Natalie Wilson who directed *Advice for the Young at Heart* and to Denis Lawson, director of *The Firm*, who, by the way, knows how to make the best martinis ever! But my biggest cheer has to be the brilliant Clint Dyer: a fantastic director, a brilliant co-writer and a bloody good friend to boot!

March 2022

Kingston 14

Kingston 14 premiered at Theatre Royal Stratford East on 28 March 2014 with the following cast and creative team:

Marcus	**Brian Bovell**
Neil	**Ashley Chin**
Adrian	**Gamba Cole**
James	**Derek Elroy**
Joker	**Goldie**
Sarge/Manny	**Trevor Laird**
Boss Man	**Tyson Oba**
Carl	**Charles Venn**
Additional Supporting Roles	**Franklin Nwaokolo, Stephen Macaulay**

Writer	Roy Williams
Director	Clint Dyer
Designer	ULTZ
Lighting Designer	Jo Joelson
Composer and Sound Designer	Richard Hammarton
Associate Designer and Scenic Artist	Sadeysa Greenaway-Bailey
Fight Direction	Alison de Burgh
Assistant Director	Stephen Macaulay

Kingston 14

Characters

Carl, *twenty-eight*
James, *forty*
Neil, *twenty-five*
Sarge, *forty-five*
Marcus, *fifty-five*
'**Joker**', *thirty-five*
Adrian, *seventeen*
Manny, *thirty*
Boss Man, *twenty-five*

Setting: Kingston Town Jamaica, 2014. Various locations.

Act One

Denham Police Station, Downtown Kingston

It is early morning. The sun is rising outside. A near riot is going on inside the station. The suspect **Joker** *is fighting off a ream of officers trying to restrain him. He breaks free and tries hard to get one of their guns. More officers come running in, each trying to grab hold of* **Joker***.*

Neil   Backside!

Carl   Yu just go sit deh?

Neil   Right here, him mad.

Joker   Yer fucker yu, all of yu!

Sarge   Bwoi, yu is de fucker!

Neil   Yes Sarge, dat go help.

Sarge   Well look pon him! Smash up mi yard, go mek up noise like sum blasted ejut.

Carl   Yu hear dat Joker, yu hear dat! Sarge pissed, and mi nuh like it when sarge is pissed. Yu best kill yerself now before I catch yu.

Joker *is laughing uncontrollably.*

Sarge   Him tink it funny?

Marcus   Nuh mind, Sarge.

Sarge   I go have him backside den we'll si if it funny, hold him fer mi!

Neil   Leave him, he'll calm down.

Marcus   Him look calm to yu, Neil?

Neil   Alright den, yu lot carry on.

Sarge   Will somebody hold diss fool down.

Carl   Am trying.

Sarge   Is diss a police station or what? Neil, get up from yer behind and help us nuh man!

Joker   Yu tink yu can boss mi.

Marcus   Yes, yer carry on.

Joker   No one boss mi!

Neil   Hey Joker, sit down nuh man!

Joker   Mi go kill all a yu.

Carl   Bring yerself.

Sarge   Hold down diss fucking rass, now!

Joker *manages to disarm* **Carl***, he then grabs him and aims the gun at* **Carl***'s head. Everyone is quiet. This is now a hostage situation.*

Marcus   Aw shit!

Joker   Yeah, come boss mi now, eh?

Sarge   Joker?

Joker   Come boss mi!

Sarge   Why yu nuh put de gun down for mi, eh?

Joker   Why mi want to do dat?

Neil   Ca we have more gun dan yu.

Joker   What him say?

Sarge   Nuh mind him. I'm in charge.

Joker   Yu de boss man?

Sarge   If yu like? Put de gun down so we can talk.

Joker   Yu lie bad.

Sarge   Nuh lie, no shit.

Joker   What mek yu tink mi want talk?

Sarge   So what do yu want? Let's talk 'bout dis.

Joker   Mi want out. Mi want a helicopter.

Sarge   What him say?

Marcus   Mi believe him say him want *helicopter?*

Joker   Right now

Sarge   Yu want *helicopter?*

Joker   Yeah man!

Sarge   Well a' course, sure ting, no problem. Yu want fling down mi wife too? Some one, call my wife fer mi.

Joker   Yu tink now is de time to mek joke? I kill yer man!

Carl   Oh God!

Sarge   Bwoi, shut up.

Carl   What?

Sarge   Stop yur stupidness.

Joker   Him no bwoi, cry like a bitch gal.

Sarge   On dat yu and I are in complete agreement, nuttin but a pussy 'ole dat.

Marcus   Seen.

Sarge   But yu need to put down dat gun.

Joker   Come get it.

Sarge   Joker, look at mi, mi say look. I only mek joke wid yu, ca yu know mi nuh lie, I am always straight wid people.

Joker   So gimme what mi want.

Sarge   Yu si bwoi, dat is what mi talking about, yu say want *helicopter?*

Joker   Now!

Sarge   Ware de hell we going to find *helicopter?*

Joker   Dass yer business.

Sarge   Ware de hell it go land? In de middle a' town? Think it through nuh man?

Joker   Yu go tek mi.

Sarge   Where?

Joker   Airport, cha rass!

Sarge   Yu want cut down on de skunk, bredren.

Joker   Yu want him dead?

Carl (*pleads*)   Hey, Sarge?

Sarge   Sarge, what? Who de hell talking to yu?

Joker   Yeah, who de hell talking to yu?

Carl   But mi . . .

Sarge   Shut yer damn mout!

Joker   Shut up.

Carl   Him have a gun in mi face.

Sarge   I look blind to yu?

Carl   No.

Sarge   Yu nuh hear mi say keep yer tail quiet?

Carl   But mi . . .

Sarge   Yu want die? Not anudda word.

Carl   Diss aint right yu nuh.

Sarge   I change my mind, cha rass. Shoot him.

Carl   Hey!

Sarge   Bwoi nuh listen. And dem who nuh listen, must feel.

Carl   Sarge, mi sorry.

Sarge   Joker, listen right, listen good, cards on de table now, we aint going to bring no *helicopter*, yu know dat. I'm not going to lie; de only way yu go leave dis station, is in a box.

Joker   Yu lie.

Sarge   Didn't yu hear mi just tell yu, mi nuh lie?

Joker   Mi go kill yer man.

Neil   Then we go kill yu.

Joker   Who dis fool?

Neil   Who am I?

Joker   Who are yu?

Neil   I am the anti Christ!

Joker   What him say?

Neil   . . . Yu have mi in a vendetta kind of mood.

Sarge   Oh Lawd!

Carl   Not now, Neil.

Marcus   Yu start him off now, yu si.

Neil   . . . Yu tell the angels in heaven, yu never si evil so personified in the eyes of the face of the man who is about to kill yu, or summin like dat.

Joker   What kind a' shit is dis?

Sarge   His shit.

Neil   Name dat flim? Name dat flim nuh man.

Joker   Mi nuh know.

Neil   Yu nuh know?

Joker   Mi nuh know!

Neil   I should shoot yu right now for not knowing. *Christopher Walken* best flim, since *King of New York*, by far! Even though him only in it for five minutes. Yu still nuh know? Mi go give yu a clue, same man who write it write *Pulp Fiction*.

Joker   *Tarantino!*

Neil   Dat him name, but de name of de flim? It's a classic.

Joker   How it can be classic if mi nuh know it?

Neil   Ca yu stupid?

Joker   Hey!

Neil   Mi tell yu what Joker, mi go give yu de first word . . . *'True'*

Joker   Listen, mi have a gun in him face. Yu go let mi go?

Sarge   No, we are not letting yu go. No, we are not getting yu a helicopter, so put down de gun, and stop yer noise!

Joker   So, wat yu go do fer mi?

Neil   Why should we do anything fer yu, fool nuh even de know de flim?

Joker   How long he go on wid dat?

Sarge   A long time Joker, believe mi. (*Aside.*) Juss go tell him, *True Romance?*

Neil   Rahtid, Sarge, why de hell yu go tell him?

Sarge   Ca mi want dis shit to be over, ca mi want dis fool lying in a pool a' blood in him cell with de mashed up head dat mi 'bout to give him!

Neil   Nuttin compared to what mi go do.

Joker   Yu?

Neil   Yu look *niccee* in dem jeans yu nuh, Joker.

Joker (*panics*)   Him dead!

The officers make a move for **Joker**. **Carl** *is released, but* **Joker** *breaks free and aims his gun at the officers.*

Sarge   Joker, yu lickle fuck!

Marcus   Nice going, Neil.

Neil   Hold on a second.

Sarge   Last chance, Joker.

Neil   Hold on. Think about it.

Joker   Think about what?

Neil *quotes a few lines from* The Presidio.

Joker   What? What him say?

Neil *continues with the lines from the movie.*

Joker   Hold on, Mi know diss one! Mi know dis. *Sean Connery* right? And dat wathimname from *NCIS*. Yes, mi right.

Neil   Yeah, yer right, yu stupid fucker, yu!

The officers finally jump **Joker**. **Marcus** *is knocked back. He looks hurt.* **Sarge** *and the others join in.* **Carl** *and a few others manage to hold him down, and keep him down.*

Neil   So explain diss to mi. After *The Untouchables*, *Sean Connery* make nuttin but poop movie until him mek *The Hunt for Red October*. Nuttin but poop! But yu remember one of him poop film, *The Presidio*, but yu can't remember a classic flim like *True Romance*. Wurtless.

Sarge   Mash up mi yard and act de rass clart fool! (*To* **Joker**.) Before God, yu go clean up diss mess!

Carl   Den mi go work on yer head!

Joker   Mi go kill yu.

Carl   Shut yer mout!

Sarge   Tek him!

A couple of uniformed officers drag the **Joker** *away.* **Neil** *and* **Carl** *scream at each other with delight.*

Carl   Boom!

Neil   Oh yes!

Sarge (*protests*)   Hey!

Carl   Backside nuh man, we have im!

Neil   Yes Sarge, yu move fast!

Sarge   Shut yer damn noise!

Carl   Oh come on.

Neil   But we have him!

Carl   At last!

Neil   Joker nuh man!

Sarge   Shout down my ear again and yu nuh believe what mi go di to yu, mi know who it is, I was deh as well yu nuh, Neil.

Neil   I can't believe dass all mi say.

Sarge   Dat mek two.

Carl   Yu go call the press, Sarge?

Neil   Yu go call the Prime Minister?

Sarge   I go call the Superintendent, dat alright wid yu?

Neil   Then go call the press?

Sarge   Chas rass, boy!

Neil   Dass Campbel wid one L.

Carl   Mitchell wid two!

Sarge   Like it was only the two a yu dat fling him down. Marcus had a hand too as well yu nuh. It him case.

Marcus   It's alright man, let dem enjoy demselves.

Sarge   Yu alright?

Marcus   Mi fine!

Sarge   Den put it in the drawer.

Marcus   Hey, Paul?

Sarge   Now.

Marcus *reluctantly takes a flask of whiskey out from his pocket and puts it on the table.*

Sarge   No one talk to anybody outside till mi hear from the Super, yu understand?

Carl   Never mind press, we go be on TV cha rass!

Sarge   Deh only place yu go be right now is morning parade.

Carl   Parade?

Sarge   Yu deaf?

Carl   We all had a hell of a morning already yer nuh, Sarge.

Sarge   I haven't missed a morning parade for twenty years, mi nuh start now.

Carl   But mi thought . . .

Sarge   Yu thought what?

Carl   Nuh mind.

Sarge   Yu tink ca yu help catch some big man dat mek yer shit smell of perfume all of a sudden? Yu mad?

Neil   But you go mention our name though, tell de relief what we do.

Sarge   Which was what, Neil? Doing yer job?

Neil   Hey we put our life on the line fer yu this morning!

Sarge   Yer fart!

Neil   Me one stare at death in the face.

Carl   Mi too.

Sarge   Yer chat shit, two a yu. All yu do put deh handcuffs on de fool. Marcus one, had to fight him off, wrestle I'm to the ground. Nuh true, Marcus? Marcus!

Marcus *is about to take a swig from his flask when* **Sarge** *snatches it away.*

Marcus   Hey, Sarge, come on.

Sarge *empties the flask into a trash can.*

Sarge   All of which, I might add, without a blind bit of help from the *JDF*. Leave it to dem trigger-happy good fer nuttin, and de go shoot everyone and everyting in sight. What happened this morning was nuttin but de finest example of good old-fashioned police work. Amen!

Carl   I thought you say it was an anonymous call yu have?

Sarge   It don't matter wat it was. We catch de baddest man in *Denham* without firing a single shot! Two a yu remember dat.

Marcus   Sarge, may I please . . .

Sarge   Mi nuh joke now. (*Sees* **Neil** *and* **Carl** *still standing there.*) Yu two still here?

Carl   You say this is Marcus' case?

Sarge   Him Corporal to yu.

Neil   Alright but de Corporal was looking a lickle *bush* out deh.

Marcus   Wat him say?

Neil   No offence.

Marcus   I buss yer rass *'bout no offence!*

Neil   We just want to help, that is all.

Carl   Any time you feel you want some one else, to help shoulder the load, we yer man.

Neil   Men! We yer men.

Carl   Yu can trust us, Marcus . . . Corporal.

Marcus   I wouldn't trust de two yu wid a glass of mi own piss.

Carl   Oh come on man, nuh be like dat.

Marcus   It not up to me anyhow, dat English bwoi want talk to him first.

Carl   Say?

Neil   Hey, Sarge?

Sarge   Don't even bother, don't even start.

Carl   Dat aint right.

Neil   Joker is our catch.

Sarge   It Marcus who catch.

Neil   Joker nuh kill dat man.

Sarge   Yo don't know dat.

Neil   Hotel robbery, it's not his style!

Sarge   I'm done listening to yu! Right, parade in five, den I want you two to check in all de guns we find in Joker's car, right? (*To* **Marcus**.) Yu awright?

Marcus   Dat was a waste of some damn fine scotch yu nuh? Wat it ever do to yu?

Sarge   Are you awright?

Marcus   I'm fine.

Sarge   Well smile nuh man. Yu one catch de *Joker!* Super go plant a big feather up yer backside, cha rass.

Marcus   Mi too old fer dat foolishness, Paul.

Sarge   A lie yu a tell. Alright. Morning parade in five. That mean yu as well yer nuh.

Marcus   I'll be right deh.

Sarge   Nuh let dem two fools boys steal yer glory.

Marcus   Coming.

Sarge   Stop coming and come.

Sarge *goes.*

Marcus *takes a swig from the hip flask in the vain hope there is whiskey left in it but there is nothing left.* **Neil** *motions* **Carl** *to fetch a bottle of whiskey from* **Carl***'s locker.*

Neil (*teasing*)   Hmm, mi love scotch! Mi love it yu si.

Carl   Is it dat right, Neil?

Neil   Yeah, man. Dat warm tingling yu feel when it go down yer neck?

Carl   Oh, yes.

Neil   Yu know what mi say?

Carl   Mi know exactly what yu say.

Neil   Marcus, yu know wat mi say?

Marcus   No.

Neil   Say what?

Marcus   No, as in *I* will not do whatever it is yu want mi to do.

Neil   Marcus, man.

Marcus   Yu muss tink mi a fool.

Neil   No.

Marcus   Yu be right. Mi a fool. An old fool. But I was a young fool once, and diss young fool woulda beat yer wurtless arse all over de street.

Carl   Back in de day.

Marcus   Believe dat. Yu and yer *I love America* chat. Why yu nuh give mi de bockle?

Neil   Why?

Marcus   Ca dass a fine bockle a' scotch, yu have in yer hand, and mi nuh believe yu are dat much of a bastard not to let mi have it.

Carl   We just want a lickle summin from yu, Marcus?

Marcus   No.

Carl   Yu aint heard it yet.

Marcus   Still no. Bockle.

Carl   Five minutes.

Marcus   Carl, yu deaf?

Carl   Just five minutes wid Joker, man.

Marcus   Mi want dat bottle

Neil   Dat fool bwoi go steal our glory.

Marcus   Give him a chance. He might do summin.

Neil   Yer fart.

Marcus   Sarge's orders. Yu have to wait.

Carl   The sarge is old like yu.

Marcus   Say dat to him face, mi dare yu.

Carl   He can't bruc him.

Marcus   Yu can? Couple a fool's wid yer hard man Hollywood movie bullshit. Mad if yu tink otherwise.

Carl   Well at least we nuh soff like yu.

Carl *prods at* **Marcus**'s *fat stomach.*

Carl   Yu want skip a meal, cha rass.

Marcus   I go shoot yu if yu touch mi again.

Neil   Alright bwois, I tink we coming off de point a lickle here.

Carl   Fat fucker yu.

Neil   Carl, ease up, yeah.

Marcus   No budda play good cop, bad cop wid mi.

Neil   Come on.

Marcus   Remember who yu chat to.

Neil   Marcus Blake, bad man!

Carl (*mocks*)   Soff man.

Neil   Alright.

Marcus   Good!

Neil   Come nuh.

Marcus   Yu must wait.

Neil   Let's leave diss fool.

Marcus   Bockle?

Neil   Yu want diss, diss fine bockle a' scotch, yet yu want give nuttin in return?

Marcus   Yes.

Neil   Fuck off.

Carl   Neil, let him have de bockle nuh man.

Neil   Yu know how much diss cost?

Carl   Yeah, I know how much diss cost, ca mi one buy it. Let him have it.

Neil *slams the bottle down on* **Marcus***'s desk.*

Carl   Yu is still a fat fucker.

Neil   Parade?

Marcus   Mi nuh deaf.

They go. **Marcus** *finds a glass from inside his desk and pours himself a glass of whiskey which he down quickly. He holds his head.*

Marcus   Oh lawd Jesus Christ, help mi!

James, *a younger officer, comes in. He is on the phone.*

James (*on the phone*)   No. They got him this morning, first thing. Yes, darling, without me. At the hotel, where else? Coming home no, not yet. Well, I should at least interview the man that is what I came here for, I'm not going until I see him. Say again, what? (*Laughs.*) Yes. Because if you were, you would see what a mess it is. You would never have seen such disorganisation in your life, no wonder they asked for help. Have you heard from Luke, he was supposed to call me? (*Listens.*) No, no, no, no. They have been through everything and more Gina, what more do they want? I was cleared for God's sake, Tell Luke, the answer is no. I don't care. It's been two years, What more do they want to do to me, they sent me here! Yes, yes, then I am coming back. You make it sound like I never want to come back, far from it. I'm not upset, look, let's not do this now, I have work to do. I'll see you. (*Wife hangs up.*) Bye! Sorry.

Marcus   Fer what?

James   My wife. She's always calling me.

Marcus   Mi know all about dat.

James   Know all about what?

Marcus   Women. Wives nuh man.

James   She just misses me.

Marcus   Well dass nice.

James   Nice?

Marcus   To be missed, by somebody.

James   She thinks I'm sunning myself on the beach. I mean, if only.

Marcus   She only say dat ca she worried fer yu.

James   But she shouldn't be.

Marcus   True say, yu nuh know *Kingston*.

James   I have told her a dozen times. She shouldn't be calling. I'm at work, I need to be focussed. Right?

Marcus   Yer focussed.

James   Thank you. Congratulations, I hear.

Marcus   Fer what?

James   I just heard it was you.

Marcus   Thank you.

James   You should do well out of this.

Marcus   You joking mi?

James   I'm sorry?

Marcus   This a English ting? A joke?

James   Not at all. I am just congratulating you, one fellow officer of the law to another.

Marcus   Right.

James   Perhaps you will be kind enough to let me speak with him?

Marcus   What?

James   The Joker that is. With you in attendance of course.

Marcus   Si, dass de shit mi talk 'bout.

James   Sorry, I'm not following.

Marcus   You know damn well yu go speak to him. Ca yer boss tell our boss to do whatever you say.

James   To help and assist in your investigations, Corporal, that is all.

Marcus (*mutters*)   Yer fart.

James   So, will you?

Marcus   What?

James   Let me speak with him?

Marcus   You polite, you si!

James   Is that a yes?

Marcus   Him nuh kill yer man yer nuh.

James   Sorry, but you're speaking a little too fast again.

Marcus   HE. DIDN'T. KILL. YOUR. MAN.

James   He's not my man. I'm just doing my job.

Marcus   Gwan den.

James   So where is he?

Marcus   Lock up in 'im cell.

James   Well?

Marcus   Well what?

James   Shall we?

Marcus   We have morning parade first.

James   I think you will find that it's you who have morning parade, Corporal.

Marcus   Sarge like to run a tight ship.

James   Is that what you call this place, a tight ship?

Marcus   Tell mi summin, do the rest of yu from England carry on so? *Joker* nuh going anywhere, you have time, relax nuh bwoi.

James   Are you coming?

Marcus   Morning parade?

James   Yes.

Marcus   You must be mad.

James   But you just said . . .

Marcus   I am allowed a few minor rebellions.

Marcus *pours himself another glass of whiskey and drinks.*

Marcus   Such as.

James (*pointedly at his watch*)   I see.

Marcus   Keep it dat way.

James *goes to join the others for morning parade.*

Sarge   Alright, now settle down. Let's have a bitta hush, mi say shut up!

Room goes quiet.

Sarge   Better. Right, as you all probably know by now, we finally have de Joker in custody.

The officers cheer loudly.

Sarge   Mi say shut yer damn mout!

The room goes quiet again.

Sarge   Right, now the Super don't want this getting out, not until him have a chance to speak with the Commissioner who then want speak with the Prime Minister's people who will then want speak with the Prime Minister, yu understand? Keep yer mout shut. Yu may have seen him around de last few days but those who don't know or too bone idol to give a rass, dis here is . . .

James *rises from his seat.*

James   . . . *James Richards* from the British Police. Helping us with out with de Hadleigh Hotel murder, yu know. We now have dat fool Joker in custody. We have a witness who swear blind de si Joker running out of de hotel, now we have him . . .

Carl   Tanks to mi.

Neil   Yu mean mi!

Sarge   Two a yu mean, Marcus! Now, as yu know, or should, the victim, Andrew Parker was a retired businessman or summin.

James Pharmaceuticals.

Carl Mi say yu had a wasted trip, we got him. He'll confess.

James For what exactly?

Carl What we tell him to.

James Andrew Parker was killed almost eight weeks ago.

Carl Yer point?

James Your government requested the help of the Metropolitan Police

Carl But deh send yu?

James One murder, one detective.

Carl Yu say we soff?

James I am saying I can help.

Carl Fer what? We have him, deal done, gwan home.

Neil Or sit on a beach.

James Any harm in finding out if he is our man, before I pack my bags?

Carl Him calling us soff, mi know it.

Neil And him our man, not yer man.

Sarge Alright just let de bwoi do him job. And you do your jobs, it's business as usual, mi nuh want hear no more talk about de Joker! Good old fashioned police work is wat mi want chat 'bout from now on. Now, we still got dem lickle youths still robbing people in de park. Now yu telling mi, a bunch a' big grown men such as yourselves can't get hold of a couple of wurtless pickne? A bottle of my finest rum go to de first one a yu dat catch one of de little rass necks. Also, as of yesterday, we still got de same cheeky lickle rass robbing tourists, stealing deh car and money.

Neil What deh doing downtown anyway?

Carl Why can't de just stay on de beach ware de belong?

Sarge   Just find did man fer mi.

Carl   Another bottle a' rum fer us, Sarge?

Sarge   No, dis one yu do fer free, *fer a change*! Now him, (*Reads.*) Black.

Neil   Would he be blue? I mean fer a change?

Sarge   Black, age thirty, six feet, medium build. Wid teet bright yellow.

Carl   Dass half of down town, Sarge!

Sarge   Just do what yu can, find him fer mi.

Carl   Needle in a haystack.

Sarge   Next, gang shootings, yu all know about de one last night, two dead, is Joker and him *Kingston Town Massive* who pull de trigger, so we can expect at least four dead in reprisals by de end of today. If not *the Trench Town boys*, de certainly de Shower posse.

Carl   *Kingston Town Massive* must tink de are brave.

Neil   Just gimme five minutes with de Joker before mi tell him, 'Hey Joker'. (*Grabs his crotch.*) The *PNP* can fuck dis!

Carl   Well dat proves it.

Neil   Prove what?

Carl   *JLP* love up man!

Raucous laughter from everyone.

Neil   Move yerself, only one *chi chi* man in here, and it's mi chatting to him.

Carl   Yu dat.

Sarge   When yu have quite all finished playing de arse wid yerselves, may I finish? Yu nuh hear mi say I don't want to hear no more chat about de Joker? Two more tings.

Carl   Oh yes!

What yu have fer us today, Sarge?

Sarge   A *Bajan* man walks into a bar and him si a very large jar on de counter filled to de brim with ten dollar bills. Bartender say yu pay ten dollar and, if yu pass three tests, yu get all de money. 'First yu have to drink dat entire gallon a' pepper tequila . . . Second, there's a pit bull chained-up out back with a sore tooth. Yu have to remove de tooth with yer bare hands. Third, there's a hundred-year-old woman upstairs who want fuck before she dead'. *Bajan* man grab de gallon and drink. Den he stagger out back where de pit bull is chained-up. De hear de guy screaming, he staggers back into de bar, with him shirt rip up. 'Now,' he say, 'where de old woman dat want she teet tek out?'

More laughter.

Sarge   Alright, go about yer business. Mind yerself, yu hear mi? I will not lose any a' yu. Go do yer job man, and hey! Nuh get dead!

The officers disperse. **Sarge** *approaches* **Carl** *and* **Neil**.

Sarge   Hey?

Carl   Guns, we know.

Sarge   Gwan den. And hey, mind yerself.

Carl   Wat yu mean, Sarge?

Sarge   Nuh mind.

Sarge *shakes his head as they go.*

A Police Cell

Joker *is alone in his cell. Pumped up. You can almost hear his heart beating.*

A while later.

Carl *and* **Neil** *are in a store room checking in the guns.*

Neil (*looks inside*)   Blouse and skirt nuh man.

Carl   My lawd in heaven!

Neil   Him have enuff here to start a war.

Carl   Wid who, de *Bajan*s?

Neil   Sign mi up.

They chuckle.

Neil   Oh yes, look pon diss.

Carl   Put it down nuh, man.

Neil   But look. (*Takes out a gun, aims it.*)

Carl   Watch ware yu aiming dat.

Neil (*mimicking Al Pacino*)   *'Say hello to my little friend'.*

Carl   Dass not de same gun him use fer dat.

Neil   So what?

Carl   Yu done?

Neil   No man, mi enjoying myself.

Carl   Put de shit down.

Neil   Toy, toys, toys!

Carl   Neil, man!

Neil (*holds another gun*)   Him have *Glocks*, him have *Berettas!* *Walthers*! Jesus!

Carl   How yu know so much about weapons?

Neil   Two words, *Steven Seagal*! Well, *Steven Seagal* of old. Him turn soff now. See how old and fat him look?

Carl   I wouldn't know, and mi nuh care.

Neil   Hold on a second.

Carl   Wat yu look fer?

Neil *finds a Magnum 44 pistol.*

Neil   Yes, wa 'appenin', baby?

Carl   Dat a Magnum?

Neil   No collection de same without one.

Carl   Yu carry on like yu want fuck.

Neil *holds the pistol against* **Carl**'*s temple.*

Carl   Hey!

Neil   Yu laughing' at mi?

Carl   Neil, fuck off, man.

Neil   Are yu?

Carl   Someone here wants him rass kicked and it aint mi.

Neil   '*I know what you're thinking. Did he fire six shots or only five?*'

Carl   I go fire sum licks in yer head.

Neil *laughs as he lowers the gun.*

Neil   Yu know yu love mi.

Carl   Move!

Neil   Yu know yu love dat ting mi do fer yu.

Carl   Yer a tease, bitch. Mi mek yer ting go sore fer a month. Like yu got nothing better fe do.

Neil   Yu best believe mi got nuttin better fe do, not wid da fool bwoi in deh, chatting shit to Joker.

Carl   Him might do alright.

Neil   Him chat shit, man. Bring him all de way from England to run tings dat aint right.

Carl   Dat is de way it is.

Neil   Hundred dollar say him fuck up!

Carl   Mi nuh bet wid yu.

Neil   Ca yu know.

Carl   Ca mi bruc.

Neil   Some white man get kill in de hotel. Weeks later, some witness say de si Joker leave de hotel, go drive off in some car. Same car where we find all diss as well as de Joker? Dat nuh mek sense. Too easy man, wa gwan?

Carl   Hey, mind yerself Neil, yu know wat yu sound like?

Neil   What?

Carl   A policeman.

Carl *takes out a spliff from* **Neil**'s *shirt pocket.*

Neil   Hey, go easy, it de only one mi have fe the day.

Carl *lights then inhales. He then spits it out.*

Neil   Carl, wat de fuck!

Carl   Wat yu call diss?

Neil   Mi finest ganja, why wat yu call it?

Carl   Herbs!

Neil   Herbs?

Carl   Herbs! Yer fucking ejut, yu buy herbs.

Neil   Nuh!

Carl   Yes!

Neil   Yu joke!

Carl   Smell dat, wat diss?

Neil   *Oregano.*

Carl   Yer backside! Ware yu buy it?

Neil   Some bwoi in town.

Carl   And ware 'im buy it?

Neil How de blasted hell mi know dat?

Carl Yeah yu do, tink! Only one idiot would try a con like diss.

Neil/Carl Manny!

Neil Come we go find him. Mi go buss his arse, yu si?

Interview Room

James *and* **Marcus** *enter. They both sit down to face the* **Joker**.

James Right, so are you then? Are you alright? Is there anything you need? I'm James, by the way. James Richards. I'm a detective sergeant from England, in case you were wondering.

Joker *sucks his teeth.*

James Sorry, I didn't quite catch that, what was that?

Joker *sucks his teeth again at him.*

James And you are (*Reads from file.*) *Gibson Alchemist Persuad*? That's your name? No wonder you like *Joker*. Age, thirty-seven.

Joker *again sucks his teeth.*

James *Jamaican?*

Marcus *Guyanan.*

James I'm asking him. You are a long way from home, *Gibson*. That makes two of us. What are you doing here?

Marcus Him daddy from *Guyana*, him mudda from here, him born here.

James (*aside*) Like I said Corporal, I am asking him.

Joker (*mutters*) Ah fool dat!

James I'm sorry? Gibson?

Joker *resumes his silence.*

James   Right, I think I can see where this is going. Don't worry, I am hoping this won't take too long. I just have a few questions for you, about Andrew Parker to be precise. Do you know Andrew Parker? Gibson? Alchemist? Persuad? The man, some people say you may have killed. But don't say anything, please do not breathe a word.

Marcus   Bwoi, what?

James   I need to put the tape on record, get you on down for the record, but you probably knew that didn't you, again, don't say anything.

James *puts the tape in an old fashioned tape recorder and presses record.*

James   Shall we begin?

Joker *sucks his teeth again.*

James   For the benefit of the tape, I am Detective Sergeant Richards.

James *waits for* **Marcus** *to give his name.* **Marcus** *looks oblivious.* **Marcus** *realises he is being stared at.*

Marcus   What? What you want?

James   It's for the tape.

Marcus   What is?

James   Name.

Marcus   Name?

James   Yes.

Marcus   You want name?

James   Your name.

Marcus   What about my name?

James *presses pause on the tape recorder.*

James   You are supposed to give your name.

Marcus   Alright.

James *plays the tape to record. He waits again.*

Marcus   Oh sorry. Marcus.

James *presses pause again.*

Marcus   Lawd Jesus, what now, wat yu want?

James   Your full name.

Marcus   Yu nuh say dat.

James   So sorry, I thought it was obvious.

Marcus   Yu want get *renk?*

James   I just want you to say your name.

Marcus   Come nuh!

James *presses the record button once more.*

Marcus   Marcus Blake.

James *presses pause again.*

Marcus   Look bwoi, nuh budda mi.

James   Full name and rank.

Marcus   Dat it?

James   That is it.

Marcus   Yu sure?

James   Please?

Marcus   Nu trouble mi again.

James   Name and rank.

Marcus   Come.

James *press record.*

Marcus   Marcus Blake, Detective. Corporal.

James *looks over at* **Joker** *who remains quiet.*

James   Would you like to give your name?

Joker *sucks his teeth again.*

James   For the benefit of the tape, the suspect *Gibson
Alchemist Persuad* has sucked his teeth and refuses to state his
name. Gibson Alchemist Persuad, it is my duty to inform
you, you do not have to say anything but it may harm your
defence if you do not mention when questioned, something
you may rely on in court. Anything you do say will taken in.

Marcus *and* **Joker** *glance at each other in slight bemusement.*
James *presses pause.*

James   What? What is it? Tell me?

Marcus   Nuttin.

James   Are you saying you have never read a suspect
his rights?

Marcus   Course mi have.

James   You just can't remember?

Marcus   Yeah, dat must be it.

James   Are you drunk?

Marcus   Hey English or no, don't get renk.

James *presses record.*

James   . . . evidence. So, Gibson, would you like to tell us
about Andrew Parker and what happened? For the benefit
of the tape the suspect has looked away. Gibson? Andrew
Parker? Did you know him? You were seen at the hotel, what
were you doing there? Gibson? For the benefit of the tape,
the suspect is smiling? Do you think this is funny, Gibson? I
am here to help, believe it or not? You see Gibson, may I call
you Joker? I am a very patient man. It must be the Jamaican

in me. Shall I bore you with my life, oh well if you insist,
thank you. Funny thing is, until now, I have never been to
the West Indies. Not once. You see, my parents were
divorced when I was six, my dad left England, came back to
live in Jamaica, where he was born. We never saw him again.
He used to write, asking me and my brother to come over,
but I believed, I felt that even thinking about him, was a
betrayal to our mother, and he did leave us, if he loved us he
would have stayed, something in me just couldn't get past
that. He's still alive, somewhere up in Frankfield I believe.
Do you know where that is, I have no idea. Listen up, yeah!
You will speak to me Joker, you will. I was not flown out here
for nothing. If I go home with just a suntan, they are putting
me back in uniform. I don't need that. Did you kill Andrew
Parker? Joker, you were seen at the hotel, what were you
doing there? Checking it out, casing the joint? From what I
understand that is low grade for you? You are into guns,
drugs. Organised crime. That is not my business, so don't
worry. I just want to know who killed Andrew Parker. I want
to know what you know. Tell me about the murder. He was
knighted two years ago. For services to business. Politically
connected if you catch my drift. We will not let this go. That
is why we are here. Tell us something, Joker. Tell us! (*To*
Marcus.) Is this a Jamaican thing?

Marcus *storms out. The stress is getting to him. He heads straight
for his desk, grabs the bottle and goes outside with it, passing* **Neil**,
Carl *and* **Manny** *as they come in.*

Neil   Yu know already, mi nuh like to run, Manny.

Manny   Yeah man.

Carl   Yeah man, what?

Manny   Mi know.

Neil   So, why run?

Carl   What yu have to hide?

Manny   Nuttin.

Neil *slaps* **Manny** *across the head.*

Neil   Not a good start fer yu, Manny.

Carl   Not a good start at all.

Neil   Nuh lie to us so. What mi tell yu about selling shit on our street?

Carl *takes a turn slapping* **Manny**.

Carl   Answer him, nuh!

Neil   What mi say to yu?

Manny   Yu say nuh do it.

Neil   Right! Dass right, yu not as stupid as yu look.

Carl   Or smell, Jesus!

Neil   *Ganja*, Manny. Yu sell the finest *ganja* fer us, not *herbs*, *ganja!*

Manny   Mi nuh know dat.

Neil   Wat yu tink go happen if yu carry on wid yer foolishness, if yu keep sellin' herbs to customers?

Manny   Deh nuh come back.

Neil   Dass right, deh go find anudda street, anudda Manny, one who nuh waste deh time wid diss stupidness and give dem way deh want. Dat is bad fer business.

Manny   Yeah man, Neil, mi know, mi know.

Neil   So, wa gwan? Waiting!

Carl   Hit him again.

Manny   No!

Carl   So wa gwan, den?

Manny   Mi have summin.

Neil   What yu have?

Carl   What yu have fer us?

Manny   Weren't mi.

Neil   Dat is what yu have?

Manny   No listen, I give up selling herbs, yu warned me plenty a' times, mi no fool, mi listen, mi behave myself. Mi Manny sell de finest skunk deh is fer yu in all a' Kingston!

Neil   So, wa gwan Manny, fer the last time.

Manny   Teddy.

Carl   Teddy?

Manny   Dass wa gwan.

Neil   Who?

Carl   Or what?

Neil   Is Teddy?

Manny   Fat Teddy.

Neil   Mi nuh know him.

Manny   Teddy Regis, man!

Neil *slaps him again.*

Neil   Yu nuh hear mi say we nuh know him?

Manny   He come here, six a' him friends, wid guns, deh stick gun in my mout, telling mi deh tekin my street corner.

Neil   My corner.

Carl   Our corner!

Manny   Dass wat mi tell dem. It's is yer corner and dem is asking fer trouble if de think de can trouble yu.

Neil   So why is dis de first time mi hear about it?

Manny   Deh say mi go keep my corner

Neil   Our corner, nuh man!

Carl   But?

Manny   It go be sixty forty in their favour. Brudda mad!

Neil   Hold on a minute. Sixty forty? Dass our arrangement.

Manny   So dat mean, mi kick back yu sixty a' what mi have left.

Neil   I was wondering why tings were getting a little light.

Manny   Deh yu go! So mi hold back a lickle.

Neil *slaps him again repeatedly.*

Carl   Ease up nuh, man.

Neil   Fucking bwoi, hear him chat so. *'Hold back a lickle!'*

Manny   Neil, man!

Neil   Yes, dawg, beg! I want hear yu beg!

Carl   Hold on a minute, Neil!

Neil   Yu is lucky he is here Manny, so fucking lucky.

Manny   Why yu love to hit mi so?

Neil   Ca mi love it!

Manny   Him mad!

Carl   Manny?

Manny   Trying to help, cha rass.

Carl   Manny, why yu nuh come fe us?

Manny   Ca mi afraid. Diss Teddy sick man, like de Joker!

Carl   Him work fer de Joker?

Manny   Him PNP, yu nuh?

Carl   Yu have problem wid de *PNP?*

Manny   No man!

Carl   Mind yerself.

Manny   A' course, we cool. So Neil, we alright?

Neil   Why?

Manny   Ca mi were tinking?

Neil   Yu want be careful wid dat Manny, yu and tinking don't manage so well.

Manny   Yu tek care a' Teddy, we back in business, yes?

Neil   Maybe. Or maybe we have to revise a couple a' tings, like say seventy thirty.

Manny   Seventy thirty? Oh cha rass, Neil?

Neil *slaps him again.*

Neil   Wat yu say? *Cha rass, Neil?* I hear yu right? How yu tink dis go? Come here!

Manny (*to* **Carl**)   Why yu stand there, get him off mi!

Carl (*laughing*)   Neil man, have a heart nuh.

Neil   For dis piece of shit, yu mad? Manny, Manny! Yu is under manners, from birth to earth, shut yer mout!

Carl   I nuh know Neil, dis Joker business.

Neil   So?

Carl   We should call dis in, tell Sarge.

Neil   Mi nuh having anybody calling de shots on our corners, without him ask? Mi nuh business if it's Joker.

Manny   Unlike mi, I ask, yu know where yu stand wid Manny. Mi know where mi stand wid yu.

Carl   Well nuh stand too close, ca yer breat stink.

Neil   Where dis Teddy live?

Manny   Yu have a pencil?

Neil   Nossir, yu tek us.

Manny   Mi?

Neil   Bwoi, don't mek mi hit yu again. Ca next time yu won't be able to stand up. Yu hear mi?

Manny   Alright, alright, mi tek yu.

Carl   Neil, yu sure?

Neil   More dan sure. I aint gonna allow some little rass neck tek my corner!

Carl   Our corner!

Neil   Dass wat mi say man, relax! And don't yu worry about a ting Manny, ca yu si, yu is a bitch. Yu is one nasty, dirty scabby lickle bitch, but . . .

Carl   Yu is our bitch.

Neil   Fer trut.

Carl and **Neil** *grab* **Manny**. *They pass* **Marcus** *coming back in as they leave.* **Marcus** *is speaking on his phone.*

Marcus   So, what yu want now, more money, ca if yu do, yu can ferget it! Yeah, we have him, we have him lock up, well a' course we are blasted well sure. Hey, it's cos of yu is why mi in diss mess. Yu and yer nastiness, Dennis. Yu stay at yer yard, yu nuh come out, yu nuh do nuttin till mi say, yu understand? Wat yu bawlin' fer, stop it, Yu call yerself a man? Nasty, good fer nuttin! Yu let mi deal wid dis right, right? Yu leave deh house. Fer once in yer life, keep yer tail quiet. Mi gone.

Marcus *hangs up.*

A House

Carl and **Neil**, *followed by* **Manny** *arrive at the house.*

Neil   Cal him nuh?

Manny (*calls*)   Teddy? It Manny, open up nuh man? Teddy? Him not here.

Carl   Dat alright.

Carl *kicks the door in.*

Neil   We'll wait inside.

Carl   I'm sure we won't mind.

Manny   Mind? Him go mind, him not go like.

Neil   Him won't like my piece up him batty hole either!

Manny   So, mi go now, right?

Neil   Go?

Manny   Yu go handle Teddy fer mi? Mi can go, yes?

Neil   Hear dat Carl?

Carl   Mi hear dat.

Neil   Him ask if he can go.

Carl   Wat yu want from a pig but a grunt?

Manny   Mi get yu.

Carl   Of course not.

Neil   Ca yu stupid.

Manny   Yu go let mi go or not?

Neil   Stay deh.

Manny   So yu not?

Carl   Bwoi catching on.

Neil   No, yu nuh go. Yu stay which part and keep yer eye out.

Manny   He go know it was mi.

Neil   Nuh worry yerself, mi and Teddy go have a lickle chat when him get here. Move one step, and yu will not believe what is happening to yu, even when it go happen.

Manny   Alright, juss ask a question.

Neil   Mi answer.

Carl   We go do diss?

Neil   Alright!

Neil and **Carl** *go into the house.*

Shots are fired from inside. **Manny** *cowers.* **Carl** *runs out, he trips and falls to the ground. A man (* **Boss Man** *) with his face hidden, wearing a Joker T-shirt comes out carrying a rifle.* **Carl** *reaches for his handgun, but* **Boss Man** *knocks him down with the butt of his rifle. He and two of his accomplices then drag* **Neil** *out.* **Manny** *takes delight in kicking* **Carl**.

Manny   Who stupid now, who? Who den bitch, who de bitch now!

Boss Man   Hey, hey, move away from him, now!

Manny *ignores him and continues to kick at* **Carl** *and then* **Neil**. **Boss Man** *aims his gun at the side of* **Manny**'s *head.*

Boss Man   Yu want diss? Yu want it? When mi say stop, mi mean it.

Manny *backs away.*

Manny   Yu go kill dem now? Come on man, mi want si diss.

Boss Man   Change of plan.

Manny   What you mean change of plan? Teddy say . . .

Boss Man   Mi nuh give a rass wat Teddy say. Him nuh run tings. Gwan nuh!

Manny *runs away.*

Boss Man   Come!

Boss Man *and friends, also wearing Joker T-shirts tie up* **Neil** *and* **Carl** *and drag them off.*

Police Station

A little while later. **Marcus** *enters the interview room, where the* **Joker** *remains.*

Joker   Wa gwan, Marcus?

Marcus   Mi sorry.

Joker   Yer sorry? Mi do fer yu but yu nuh do fer mi, is dat how it go?

Marcus   No.

Joker   Yu have phone?

Marcus   Yes.

Joker   Pass mi it. Quick nuh man!

Marcus *hands him his phone,* **Joker** *dials.*

Joker (*into phone*)   Yeah man, wat yu have fer mi? Yu have who? Two a dem? Good. Good. Alright, mi wait.

Joker *hangs up. He throws the phone back to* **Marcus**.

Marcus   Have who? Two of who?

Joker *grins.*

Marcus   Joker? Is who yu have?

Act Two

A Room

Carl *is alone in a dark room. He has a blindfold covering his eyes.*

Carl Neil? Neil? Where yu deh, yu alright, Neil! Hey! Mi say hey! Mi can't si nuttin. Hey! Anyone there? Is anyone there, can anyone hep mi? So, wat de plan, cha rass? What yu want from mi? Mi can't si shit, yu deaf? Mi want out, yu understand? Come tek diss fucking ting off my head, now. Come on, mi say hey! What yu want wid mi? Answer nuh man, someone answer.

Carl *rocks the chair from side to side until it tilts over.*

Carl Look pon mi? Mi swear Manny, if mi find yu, mi go fucking kill yu, mi no joke! What yu tink dis is? Yu tek my gun away? Is someone there, can yu hear mi, why de fuck yu nuh answer, somebody?

Adrian *comes into the room.*

Carl Who dat? Mi can hear yu, mi say who dat? Yu deaf? Yu better untie now, before yu get into a world of trouble, and yu best do it now, yu understand? Diss foolishness yu playing wid had better stop. Look pon mi nuh? At least help mi up, wat de rass! Come on.

Adrian *helps* **Carl** *back up.*

Carl Tank yu.

Adrian *goes to leave.*

Carl Hey, hey, where yu go? Yu nuh finish. Let mi go nuh man. Come on, untie and let mi go.

Adrian Yu nuh go anywhere.

Carl Say what?

Adrian Yu not going anywhere. So stop yer stupidness.

Carl   Is diss some bwoi talkin' to mi?

Adrian   Mi sound like bwoi to yu?

Carl   Yeah, yu do.

Adrian   It's man yu chat to.

Carl   Wat de fuck? Gwan fetch yer daddy now.

Adrian   Mi daddy dead.

Carl   Mi nuh fucking business, yeah. I want to see Neil. I want chat to de man who is running tings here.

Adrian   Is mi running tings.

Carl   Bwoi, listen. Listen good, yu in whole heap of trouble, if yu want carry on playing bad man.

Adrian   Him say yu can't go.

Carl   Who, de fuck say dat?

Adrian   *Joker.*

Carl   *Joker?*

Adrian   Yes, yu fraid now?

Carl   Yu run wid de *Joker?*

Adrian   Yeah man!

Carl *laughs.*

Adrian   Why yu laugh? Stop it.

Carl   Tell mi summin.

Adrian   What?

Carl   How did a lickle pussy hole of a bwoi like yu, work for de *Joker?*

Adrian   Mi have yer gun yu nuh?

Carl   So what?

Adrian *places the gun at the side of* **Carl**'s *head.*

Adrian So, mind yerself! Before yu find a hole in yer head, yer rass!

Carl Yu only a man if yu know how to use it.

Adrian I'm a man.

Carl Yu nuh sound it.

Adrian I look it.

Carl Let mi si for myself.

Adrian Yu nuh give orders.

Carl Please!

Adrian *Joker* say no.

Carl *Joker*, lock up in de station. Yu understan', yu know what dat means It's over! Listen to mi.

Adrian It's mi one who have de gun, yu listen to mi.

Carl What yur name? It nuh hurt for yu to tell mi yer name, what is it, man? Alright, bwoi, just listen yeah, I beg yu.

Adrian Yes dawg, beg mi!

Carl Yu know mi a policeman, right? Yu know yu have to let mi go, right? Sooner or later. What yu want, what yu friends want?

Adrian Yu find out soon enuff. Open yer mout.

Carl Why?

Adrian Ca mi say so.

Carl *opens his mouth.* **Adrian** *feeds him food and drink.* **Carl** *devours what is being given to him.*

Adrian Yu hungry fer trut. Alright, yu done, yu done!

Adrian *goes to leave.*

Carl Tank yu. Who are yu? Wat yu want? Please?

The Station

James, **Sarge**, **Marcus** *and* **Joker** *are in a room at the station.*

James   He is as quiet as a bloody tomb.

Sarge   Is what yu expect?

James   I never expect anything. I go where the leads take me.

Sarge   Bwoi love himself.

James   For some reason, he believes he has us where he wants us.

Marcus   Well him right.

James   Well then it is our job to flip that over. To have him where we want him, and I will. I mean, us, we will.

Marcus   Him ting get big, Paul!

Sarge (*laughs*)   Assuming him know where him ting is.: Is dat right James, yu know where yer *ting* is? Look, bwoi go bawl. Must be an English ting.

James   It may interest you to know, my family come from *Jamaica*.

Sarge   Oh yes?

James   *Kingston* in fact.

Marcus   Where in *Kingston*?

James   *Rae town*.

Marcus   Yu nuh go si dem?

James   I might.

Marcus   Him might?

James   I do have a job to do.

Sarge   Dat mean no.

James   No, it means I might.

Sarge   It's alright bwoi, none of our business, yes?

James   My parents divorced the same year I was born. My father came back to live here, I don't know him, I never have. Anything else?

Marcus   But you still miss him.

James   I just told you, I do not know him.

Marcus   Why yu judge him so harsh?

James   Judge him? I don't even know him, he's the one who left.

Marcus   Yer fudda is eighty-five years of age, right?

James   Eighty-six, how did you know that?

Marcus   So dat mean he left here in wat, fifty-seven. Yer mudda stayed behind ca she have a pickne wid him awready. Yer older what?

James   Brother.

Marcus   Him work in *England*, factory or summin, till him can afford to send fer she, she come in fifty-nine thereabouts, deh have anudda pickne in sixty-two, right?

James   Sister.

Marcus   Deh three a' dem all cramp up in one room. Yer papa can't hold on to a job, ca dem white people nuh like black people. Yer mudda tell him to find work and a bigger house. Yer fudda nuh happy at work, he nuh happy at home, so him happy here. (*Grabs his own crotch.*) How many brudda and sisters yu have over deh in England dat yu know of?

Sarge (*laughs*)   Marcus, yu bad.

James   That's some imagination you have.

Marcus   Yu nuh deny it.

James   Please continue.

Marcus   Yer mudda and fudda carry on so for a few more years, yer brudda from Jamaica come to stay, but him an' yer fudda nuh get on, yer brudda too Jamaican, yer fudda have no patience fer him. Couple of year later, yer fudda buy a house, but when yer mudda say she pregnant wid yu, him can't tek it nuh more so 'im gone.

James   And this is the man you think I should go and see?

Marcus   Mek yer peace wid him?

James   Why? Why would I want to do that?

Marcus   Ca deh lie to him.

James   Who?

Marcus   England! White man! Yer fudda, my fudda, my bruddas. Deh shoulda stayed which part dem deh, and help out here. Help dis island. Lawd knows it needed it.

James   Can we please talk about something else?

Sarge   Awright, so how it go in England?

James   Go, what do you mean?

Sarge   Policeman, how it go?

James   We are doing alright, thank you.

Sarge   A lie yu a tell! We have internet here yu nuh, bwoi! Google, cha rass! What about that nonsense last summer? London right? Tottenham? Hackney? Yu nuh see dem Marcus, all dem pickne playing the rahtid fool, go mash up everything in front a dem. If it weren't nailed deh teif it.

James   I'm not excusing it.

Sarge   I should hope not.

James   At least no one was killed.

Sarge   A lie yu tell! Did it not all start ca dem policemen shoot up dat black bwoi?

James   So, what is your point Sergeant, your police is better than ours?

Sarge   My point is bring all dem pickne who want play de rass claart fool, over here, we know how to deal wid dem, put them all in dat *special place*.

James   *Special place*, what is that?

Marcus   Coma.

Sarge   Nuh true, Marcus?

Marcus   Don't put me in the middle of this.

Sarge   Lloyd Adkins fer one!

Marcus   Oh shut up, man.

Sarge   Yu know wat mi say.

Marcus   Lloyd Adkins sell *crack* to pickne. He been in jail three times and he come out, carry on wid de same ting! So mi slap him a lickle.

Sarge (*laughs*)   A *lickle*? Hear him say, a *lickle*? Yu fractured the man's skull, cha rass.

James   Yes, nothing like a good dose of police brutality.

Sarge   Bwoi move, like yer shit don't stink.

James   Say what you want, but we've never had what you had at *Tivoli*.

Sarge   Hey, yu nuh know de first thing about *Tivoli*, yu weren't deh.

James   Seventy-six people, dead, all to protect one man, a gangster.

Sarge   Dat is one word fer him.

James   And what would yours be?

Sarge   Fer *Dudus?* President!

James   Drug dealer.

Sarge   Don!

James   Murderer!

Sarge   And yer point yer a mek?

James   There is no point, I am sorry this conversation has even began.

Sarge   You should be sorry you come.

Marcus   Why you come?

James   Your commissioner requested an experienced officer.

Marcus   So, why they send you?

Sarge   They nuh know what to do wid him.

Marcus   Say?

Sarge   Him and policeman friends back in England go on a drug bust, arrest some fool, help de themselves to a little too much of the fool's money dough.

Marcus   Oh I see. James get a lickle greedy, yes?

James   How could you possibly . . .

Sarge   Super tell me. Commissioner tell him.

James   Did they also tell you I was cleared of all charges?

Sarge   Si wat we have here Marcus, is a *bangarang*. Dass wat de give us.

Marcus   You know wat a *bangarang* is, bwoi?

James   Like I said, my family are from here.

Marcus   How much yu tek?

James   I said I was cleared.

Marcus Yeah yeah, how much?

James Right, I think we have waited long enough.

Marcus Ten thousand, twenty thousand?

James We should get back in there.

Marcus It's alright.

James Right now.

Marcus We understand, we in Kingston.

James Understand this. I was cleared. I did nothing wrong. Now?

Sarge Yu nuh have a clue who are yu. Where yu come from.

James Is there really any more of this?

Sarge Just say de word when yu need us.

James If I need you.

Sarge Oh *if I need yu*, yu English fer trut.

James You don't think I can do it?

Sarge Mi nuh say dat.

James You didn't have to.

Marcus We don't know yu, dat is all.

Sarge Why yu care?

James It's my job. I want to do this right.

Marcus How much yu tek?

James Oh for God's sake!

Sarge Him a white man. Only reason you are here. Diss nuh budda yu, not even a lickle? Or are yu all white up inside now?

Marcus White up, him all man up ca of de money 'im teif

James   For the last time, I was cleared. And I wouldn't be here if your own people had trusted you.

Sarge   Now, yer a claart! We arrested him diss morning with not a blind bit of help from yu, how yu like dat?

Marcus   Alright, alright, enuff now. A joke we a mek James, honest. We crack Joker, everything will be sweet, yes?

James   Right.

Sarge *goes.*

Marcus *and* **James** *walk towards the interview room.*

Marcus   James, let mi lead diss.

James   Oh great! You as well.

Marcus   Just relax, bwoi.

James   You believe I can't do this.

Marcus   I believe you are to help us, remember? This is not about yu. We need a new approach.

James   I'm right here.

Marcus   Of course

Marcus *pulls up a chair, he slides up next to* **Joker**.

Marcus   I was five years old when Jamaica get its independence. Daddy come running into de house, screaming 'we is free', he picked mi up over his head like he always do when him happy. '*Jamaica for Jamaicans*' him would say, him would scream. Dat was de best time in de house for us. Mi always looked forward to dem times, ca my Daddy was a fiend. He love drink too much, and he drink, he was a top draw son of a bitch! He would go off on all of us, whenever he feel. He would have belts for each of us, he would save his fists for our mudda. Dat is how much him enjoy hitting us. But when independence come, dat was de good times. Everyone say 'we go do this, we go do dat', Daddy believe all a' dem. For his good mood only lasted a couple of months. Once all of dem English clear out, soon everyone realised what shit we were in, on de account we have nuh money. Same people who say we go dis, soon realise de go nuttin. Daddy nuh think either way about politics, neither did I. All de same he would say. *Edward Seaga*, go fuck himself! *Norman Manley*, go fuck himself! All he would do is stamp round him yard, telling each prime minister to go *fuck himself*. Dat is when he weren't beating de black off mi and my brothers and sisters wid him belt buckle. No matter who was in charge yeah, *PNP, JLP*, we still get licks, we still get beat! *Jamaica for Jamaicans, wat Jamaica? Wat blasted Jamaica, ware it deh?* Ca yu se Joker, this is happens to a people when you're robbed of yer history and your present economy is fucked because deh is no businesses left dat run by Jamaicans. No money, deh money leave de island. And if money gone, people are gone. Wat chance diss island have if everyone leave? Yu understand what mi say? Joker?

Joker *remains silent.*

Marcus   I think yu do. As mean as my daddy was, even he knew, dem fools in power, never mind what party deh in, nuh mean nuttin to him, or to us! So, why yu killing fer dem? Tell mi Joker, why? No one knows, no one remembers, no one fucking cares! All de want is diss shit to stop. Every one ferget what deh fighting about. It's time yu lot gave up, Joker. No one will win. Yu, us. Joker? Joker? Come on man, say something. Something, anything!

Joker   Mi bored now.

James   Excuse mi?

Joker   Yu and da English fool. Yu never shut up. It time.

James   Time for what?

Joker   Mi have dem.

James   Have who?

Joker   Tanks to Marcus here.

James What?

Marcus Him chat shit. Yu have no idea.

James What is going on?

Joker Mi have yer men.

James What do you mean?

Marcus Leave mi alone wid him.

James I want to know what you mean by that.

Joker Gwan get yer boss man, yu will soon si what mi mean.

James Marcus?

Joker Gwan nuh man.

James *goes.*

Marcus Diss is not what we agreed.

Joker Yu tink I business 'bout yu now?

Marcus We had a deal.

Joker Fuck off, man!

The Room

Carl *and* **Adrian** *are in the room.*

Carl Come on bwoi, tek off de blind nuh? Yu want si mi dead, yu want dead mi? If dat was de plan, yu woulda killed mi by now. So, wat de fuck yu want man, eh? Yu go tell mi sooner or later, it might as well be now, yu understand? Come on bwoi, act like a man if yu want play man. What yu say? Bwoi?

Adrian Yu can shout fer trut yu nuh.

Carl Why yu no answer?

Adrian   Yu my mudda?

Carl   Just take off de blind.

Adrian *takes off the blind.*

Carl   Tank yu.

Adrian   Nuh tank mi. Joker's orders.

Carl   Him running tings?

Adrian   Better believe.

Carl   Him running yu?

Adrian   Two a' us run tings.

Carl   Big man, lickle bwoi.

Adrian   Yu mek fun?

Carl   Nuh man.

Adrian   Yu want fer mi to put de blind back over yer eyes?

Carl   Easy, bwoi. Easy.

Adrian   Nuh call mi bwoi.

Carl   What yer name den?

Adrian   Mi nuh tell yu my name, yu mad.

Carl   So what de hell mi supposed to call yu den?

Adrian   Is who yu chatting back to, so?

Adrian *aims his gun at* **Carl**'s *head.*

Carl   Alright, easy yes?

Adrian   Answer de question, mi say who?

Carl   Nobody, mi nuh mean nuttin by it, just calm yerself.

Adrian   Better.

Carl   Just tell mi what yu want mi to call yu, and mi will.

Adrian Good.

Carl So?

Adrian So what?

Carl What yu want mi to call yu?

Adrian Just bwoi to yu.

Carl But mi tought yu want . . .

Adrian Never mind what mi want.

Carl Backside!

Adrian Yu come fresh, policeman?

Carl No man, mi good, mi alright. But yu nuh like being called *bwoi*.

Adrian Mi nuh like being treated like a bwoi, deh's a difference.

Carl Alright. From now on, *bwoi,* mi treat yu like a man. Is dat alright wid yu, *bwoi?*

Adrian Nuh laugh at mi.

Carl Mi nuh laugh.

Adrian Ca mi have gun.

Carl Mi si it.

Adrian Good.

Carl So, bwoi? What we do now?

Adrian We wait.

Carl For Joker?

Adrian Him man want si yu.

Carl So bring him come, si mi.

Adrian Him busy?

Carl (*mutters*)   Playing teif.

Adrian   What was dat?

Carl   It was nuttin, mi say nuttin.

Adrian   Nuh worry, he nuh ferget about yu.

Carl   Where's Neil, ware him deh?

Adrian   Boss man want chat to him.

Carl   'Bout what?

Adrian   'Bout him big mout is wat. Boss man go quiet him mout fer him.

Adrian *stares hard at* **Carl**.

Carl   What, what yu stare at?

Adrian   Yu.

Carl   Like mi am sum duppie, why, why yu staring?

Adrian   Mi know who yu are.

Carl   Oh yes?

Adrian   Yeah, man.

Carl   So, what is it?

Adrian   Carl Mitchell. Right or wrong?

Carl   No, yu are not wrong.

Adrian (*feeling quite pleased with himself*)   Si!

Carl   Bwoi, where yu know my name from?

Adrian   Yu is *Carl Mitchell!*

Carl   Right, so yu know?

Adrian   Yu used to live on my street.

Carl   Yu from Lamont Road?

Adrian   Yeah, so.

Carl   Well, help mi out of diss nuh man, untie my hands.

Adrian   Gw'y!

Carl   If yu from *Lamont Road*, I is from *Lamont Road*, dat mek us bruddas.

Adrian   Mi nuh tink so.

Carl   How? Why? Please?

Adrian   Ca mi say mi know yu. Ca mi know yu live pon east side of Lamont Road.

Carl   Yu from de west side?

Adrian   Yu have a problem wid de south side?

Carl   Not at all, apart yu bin nuttin but a bunch of pussy 'oles.

Adrian   Yu want reminding mi have gun?

Carl   Relax nuh man, mi just chat so. So how yu know mi?

Adrian   My cousin know yu.

Carl   Cousin name?

Adrian   Mi nuh tell yu. He know yu, mi know yu, dat is all yu need to know.

Carl   Yeah, but how he know mi?

Adrian   Him play ball wid yu.

Carl   Mi nuh recall ever playing ball wid a west side pussy, and before yu yer pull gun on mi, a joke mi a mek.

Adrian   Of course yu wouldn't, yu musta erased it from yer head, ca we always beat yu.

Carl   Dat what yu call it?

Adrian   Wat yu call it?

Carl   Cheating, yer rass.

Adrian   Backside, move yerself!

Carl   Yu move yerself!

Adrian   It's we one who own de court.

Carl   Teif de court more like.

Adrian   Yu want explain yerself?

Carl   All de wanna do is play offence. Yu never want pass. De do nuttin but push and shove

Adrian   And score hoops!

Carl   Hey, mi score plenty hoops in my time.

Adrian   Mi know.

Carl   Yu do?

Adrian   Like mi say, mi si yu. So, what yu doing now?

Carl   Mi a policeman a' course.

Adrian   Mi can si dat, mi have eyes.

Carl   So, why ask foolish question?

Adrian   It's one a' dem questions yu know de answer record . . . rhter . . . summin.

Carl   *Rhetorical?*

Adrian   Yeah mi know!

Carl   Of course.

Adrian   Yu mek fun?

Carl   To a bwoi wid a gun, nossir!

Adrian   A what wid a gun?

Carl   *A man*, a big man wid a gun.

Adrian   Fer trut. So, what yu do?

Carl   Mi sorry, but mi nuh understanding de question.

Adrian See if yu understand diss. Yu wa a bad man, *Carl Mitchell* a bad man. Yu one who mash up Reggie Travers's face wid a knife, ca him knock over yer beer. Then yu go fling him gal down on top of de bar, and go fuck her right in front a' him.

Carl Nuh believe everything yu hear, yungsta. First off, it was his beer, and him say mi knock it over. Secondly, it was a fair fight, Reggie Travers is a crazy son of a bitch, him mad! Mi do whatever mi could to survive. Third, Vivienne Hamilton was not his gal. She like to free it up fer man too much to be any man's gal. Dat is one pussy dat want brick up.

Adrian Mi know.

Carl How yu know?

Adrian Same way as yu.

Carl Yu tell mi she free it up fer yu?

Adrian Why not?

Carl What she si in a lickle bwoi . . . a fine looking young man such as yerself?

Adrian Ca mi nuh stop fer nuttin, when mi fling down a woman.

Carl Sweet bwoi, *eeh?*

Adrian Better believe. Mi fuck her good, mi fuck her plenty, her words!

Carl Mi believe yu.

Adrian Is why yu laugh?

Carl Nuttin, nuttin, yu a bad man. A Stulla lover.

Adrian Why yu stop, being a bad man?

Carl Why?

Adrian   Mi cousin always tink yu woulda bin a *Don* by now. Wid yer own garrison.

Carl   But I didn't.

Adrian   Mi know yu didn't

Carl   Calm yerself.

Adrian   So, why?

Carl   Ca mi si my brudda get shot, dead up in front of mi own eyes. Yu know why 'im dead? All him say he admire what de *JLP* have to say.

Adrian (*readies his gun*)   Yu *JLP*?

Carl   Mi is nuttin, so rest yerself. It was either diss or be in a gang.

Adrian   Wa wrong wid being in a gang?

Carl   Yu tell mi.

Adrian   No, yu tell mi.

Carl   Mi nuh like de idea of being owned, by anybody!

Adrian   So, yu joined de enemy?

Carl   Mi ran away from de enemy. As far as my legs could tek me. So could yu.

Adrian   What mek yu tink mi want to?

Carl   Yer eyes.

Adrian   And what yu si?

Carl   Someone scared, someone terrified. Someone who knows him well over him head and don't know to get out.

Adrian   Mi nuh know who yu looking at, but it can't be mi.

Carl   Tell mi yer name.

Adrian   Shut up.

Carl   Yer family name.

Adrian   Yu nuh hear mi say shut up?

Carl   Yer mudda name, anyting!

Adrian   Why?

Carl   Why not? What harm it go do?

Adrian   Yu want get inside my head? Like dem *CSI* people on de TV?

Carl   Mi just want know yer name.

Adrian   *Adrian.* Mi name Adrian.

Carl   Please to meet yu, *Adrian.*

Adrian   Wat yu want?

Carl   What yu tink?

Adrian   Mi can't do dat.

Carl   Him kidnap two policeman, Adrian. Diss only gonna end one-way, bad.

Adrian   Yu go protect mi?

Carl   Yes.

Adrian   From him?

Carl   Him only a man, Adrian,

Adrian   Lie bad yu nuh!

Carl   My people come looking fer mi.

Adrian   Bring dem come.

Boss Man *enters.*

Carl   And deh is as mad as de Joker! Dem have guns too, yu nuh. De si yu carry gun, in deh minds, yu is a man, and de will shoot yu dead, no word of a lie. Yu want dat fer yerself? Dis fuck ries gone on for too long Adrian, Joker playing de arse wid himself. Yu want die like him.

Boss Man   Joker playing what? Joker playing what? The arse wid himself, is dat what mi hear yu say? Or did mi hear yu call him Adrian? Which is it, which one mi hear, nuh tell mi I hear both, nuh tell mi dat, otherwise, we go have a serious problem, yu understand?

Adrian   Listen, yeah?

The **Boss Man** *slaps* **Adrian** *against the head.*

Boss Man (*snaps*)   Put on him fucking blindfold.

Adrian *does as he is told.*

Boss Man   Now bring yer backside here.

Adrian *is clearly frightened as he approaches the* **Boss Man**.

Boss Man   Yu have a sister?

Adrian   Mi have two sisters.

Boss Man   Mudda? Yes or no, yu have a mudda?

Adrian   Yes, mi have a mudda.

Boss Man   How would yu like mi to go pay a visit to yer mudda? How would yu like it, if mi fling her down, and fuck her till she bleed, mi nuh business if she scream. How yu like dat? How would yu like it, if mi tek yer sisters and dagger each one a dem? Mi go mek yu watch. De mi go a put a gun to yer head, and mek yu, yes yu, Adrian, mi go mek yu fuck both of yer sisters, and yer mudda. Mi go mek yu fuck dem from mornin' till night. Yu tink mi won't do it, try mi, fuck up some more, si if mi won't do it. I is de Joker's number one. Mi nuh have no time fe no bwoi! Yu tell him yer name, what else yu say?

Adrian   Nuttin.

Boss Man   It had better be nuttin, otherwise, mi tek yu to yer mudda right now.

Adrian   We were just talking.

Boss Man   Yu nuh talk. Yu do what mi tell yu, yu understand?

Adrian   Yes!

Boss Man   Nuh fuck up again. Do not!

Adrian   Yeah man!

Boss Man *leaves.*

Adrian *stands guard.*

Carl   Adrian? Adrian? Yu alright? Why yu nuh answer?

Adrian   Leave mi alone.

Carl   Come on bwoi, yu know yu can't.

Adrian *presses the gun against* **Carl**'s *head.*

Adrian   Yu deaf? Yu want us both dead.

Carl   Mi sorry.

Adrian   Just be quiet, nuh man

Carl   Adrian?

Adrian   Mi say shut up. Yu nuh hear him ay wat him go to my mudda?

Carl   Yu in over yer head yer nuh, bwoi.

Adrian   Mi say leave mi.

The Police Station

James *is in the middle of a heated row between himself,* **Sarge** *and* **Marcus**.

James   I want him questioned.

Sarge   Say what?

James   Right bloody now.

Sarge   Bwoi, nuh mek mi lick yu down, yeah?

James   Are you going to question him or not? I mean this is a police station, you are a policeman, that is correct?

Sarge   For what, exactly?

James   The Joker has implicated him somehow.

Sarge   Hey, just shut yer mout for a minute.

James   I will not shut up.

Sarge   Marcus?

Marcus   Marcus what? What, yu tink yu can help mi?

Sarge   Let me try nuh man? Talk to mi.

Marcus   Mi can't.

Sarge   Yes yu can. Is English bwoi chatting trut here? Does Joker have summin on yu? Tell us man, we can sort it out.

Marcus   Lawd help mi.

Sarge   Tell mi, tell us everything, yeah? Now, nuh man!

Marcus   One of Joker man call. De say he have two of our men.

Sarge   Dem dead?

Marcus   No man, deh not dead. Joker want make a trade. Him life fer dehs.

Sarge   Dis Joker man! What a bwoi, renk!

Marcus   Him say his men have Carl and Neil.

Sarge   Lawd, Jesus!

James   Right, that's it.

Sarge   Hey bwoi, where do yu think yu are going?

James   To tell your superintendents, then he can plan a course of action, where do you think I am going?

Sarge   No, yu don't.

James   Get out of my way, please.

Sarge   James, tink about it, yeah.

James   About what?

Sarge   If we tell de super, what do yu think will happen?

James   If, Sarge?

Sarge   Alright den *when* we tell him, what do yu think will happen?

James   We get our men back.

Sarge   My men!

James   Nothing else matters.

Sarge   Yes, what it matter 'bout a few *Jamaicans*, right? Are yu sure yu are nuh *Bajan*?

James   What?

Sarge   If tell de super about wa gwan, de Super go call de *JDF* like when try catch *Dudus*.

James   If that is what it takes, so be it.

Sarge   Say what yu want about de Joker, and mi have said plenty. But de people love him. Who would protect him, who would fight! Yu nuh been in a slum James, ware people have no water to wash demselves, and even when de do, it as dirty as hell. Where lickle pickne have to walk through a whole pile a shit on de streets, and mi mean *shit!* From people's houses mi a talk. A whole kinda disgusting nastiness goin on in de slum, nastiness! Our government, cha fart, deh nuh care. Joker care!

James   Come on.

Sarge   *Dudus* care! We send in de *JDF*, dat mean guns, dat mean tear gas, dat mean *Tivoli* all over again, a goddamn bloodbath, mi promise yu. Yu nuh si what happen James, not just man dat get shoot up in deh head, but gal and pickne too. Not again, yu understan', not here! Not in my yard. Mi won't let it. Marcus?

Marcus   Marcus, what?

Sarge   What else is deh?

Marcus   What else what, ah shit yu a talk.

Sarge   What else de Joker have on yu. Why he mek yu do diss? Deh has to be more. Come clean nuh man.

Marcus   Him, he, him . . .

Sarge   Spit it out.

Marcus   Him have my son, Dennis.

Sarge   What him have yer son too?

Marcus   No. Not dat kind of have.

Sarge   So what? Marcus man!

Marcus   My bwoi Dennis, him kill dat man.

Sarge   What man?

Marcus   Hotel, Hadleigh Hotel, cha rass.

James   Andrew Parker? Are you saying your son killed Andrew Parker?

Sarge   Marcus, mi nuh joke now. Yu better tell me, wa' gwan?

Marcus   Dis Celia, work at de hotel. She go school wid my bwoi. Been sweet fer my bwoi, him fer years, and she nice yu si. She lose count de amount of time she want free it up for him.

Sarge   So wat wrong wid him?

Marcus   Wat yu tink, him, him . . .

Sarge   Him what?

Marcus   Him love up, man!

Sarge   Oh Lawd. And? Marcus, nuh man?

Marcus   Parker pick up my bwoi in de bar, tek him to de hotel, him get fresh, too rough. Dennis lick him down wid a lamp. Stupid gal Celia call mi, mi tell her to fuck off, ever since he lie down wid man, mi nuh have no son.

Sarge   So why yu help him?

Marcus   Ca she is Joker's sister.

Sarge   Dis Celia? Backside!

Marcus   She hate him more dan we. She want tell mi about him hiding guns round her house and in him car and shit . . . But only if mi get my bwoi out of deh.

James   Just a minute, someone made a call saying that they saw the Joker there that night.

Marcus   Yes, Celia, dat dumb fucking bitch! Of all nights Joker pick to visit his sister, he have to go and pick dat one, cha rass! Joker know she into summin, he mek her tell him what happen. Den mi get a call from him, telling mi, him own mi now, and unless mi want everyone to know 'bout Dennis, mi go do wat him say! Mi tell Celia to keep her mout shut. She tink she go help by playing policewoman, calling the station, tellin yu ware Joker is. Now Joker vex wid mi, ca mi nuh warn him in time about de arrest.

Sarge   So he claim two of our men? Joker have jokes yu si! All dis foolishness fer him son, some nasty good fer nuttin.

Marcus   Nuh call him dat.

Sarge   Yu one call him dat!

Marcus   If anyting is nasty, it's this blasted island. All dat music and TV.

Sarge   Oh lawd, diss shit again.

Marcus   Feeding our pickne nuttin but shit. *America* dis, *America* dat, no *Jamaican*, not a trace.

Sarge   Alright, nuh man.

Marcus   And we have nuttin to say, I mean wa gwan wid dat?

Sarge   Wa gwan wid yu?

Marcus   *Bob* and him *Wailers* with *Catch a Fire*. Greatest reggae album ever recorded. *1962* when we get our independence, fling out de English! *George Headley*? Him de only Jamaican in test history to have more dan *twenty* innings average over *sixty*, the greatest cricket player dat we have. Dass wat gwan Paul, it all gone!

James   Listen to me, this is serious.

Sarge   Nuh shit?

James   You need to inform your superiors right away.

Sarge   Oh, shut yer damn mout! Listen up, ca mi am only ever going to say diss once. Ask him bwois where and when?

James   What?

Sarge   Tell him we can do de exchange, wherever de want meet.

James   You are not actually thinking of releasing the Joker, are you?

Sarge   Mi nuh thinking of doing it, mi go do it.

James   No, you are not.

Sarge   Mi nuh have time fer yu bwoi.

James   Well then I suggest you make the time, *Sergeant!*

Sarge   I don't know who yu tink yu are chatting to.

James   He's a suspect in an on-going murder investigation.

Sarge   No, Marcus's bwoi is yer suspect, gwan have him.

Marcus   Hey, Sarge nuh man.

Sarge   Yu can shut up too. (*To* **James**.) Yu are not involved, bwoi.

James   You are consorting with known criminals, you are making deals. I am a witness to that, sorry but I think I am involved.

Sarge   Well my heart right here is bleeding so bad fer yu. Yu si it? Yer fart.

James (*scorns*)   *Jamaica!*

Sarge   Dass right. *Jamaica!* Gwan home, yu nuh belong here.

James   Just try and explain to me why you are doing all of this?

Sarge   Mi tell yu already, *Christopher Dudus Coke*.

James   But it doesn't have to be like that.

Sarge   But it is. Marcus, call de Joker's friends.

James   No, no.

Sarge   Say what?

James   This is not happening to me again.

Marcus   Again?

James   I am not having this come back at me in any way! Don't make me go above you.

Sarge   Yu know what, gwan above mi. Gwan find de Super for all de good it will do, good luck finding him dough, by now him have him head in de biggest pair of titty dis side of *Kingston*. Diss is nuh *London*. Yu understand? Marcus's bwoi kill Parker, him all yours, job done, what more yu want?

James   You are letting the Joker go.

Sarge   Lad, mek dis bwoi shut up!

James   How the hell do you think you are going to be able to cover that up?

Sarge   Who say we go cover it up? We know wat dis mean.
But it a choice between dat and letting two of our bwois, and
probably a whole heap of innocent people die yu
understand?

James *storms out.*

Sarge   Mi tink 'im go cry.

Marcus *leaves to follow.*

Sarge   Lawd please, yu have to help mi, ca mi nuh know
where diss rass idiot tink him going?

Marcus *turns around to face* **Sarge**.

Sarge   Yes, it's yu, mi chat to.

Marcus   Mi go mek de call, like yu say.

Sarge   Mi nuh finish wid yu, sit down!

Marcus *does as he is told.*

Sarge   No, what exactly in de hell am I supposed to do
wid yu?

Marcus   Paul listen, before yu go on so, yu have to know, I
didn't know him were gonna tek two of our men, yu have to
believe mi.

Sarge   Alright, mi believe yu. Now, we got dat outta de way,
wat de hell mi supposed to do wid yu? Huh? Yu don't have
nuttin?

Marcus   Mi sorry.

Sarge   Mi nuh ask if yu were sorry, mi ask, what mi
supposed to do?

Marcus   Mi nuh know.

Sarge   Yu nuh know?

Marcus   Wat yu want from mi?

Sarge   Some kind of fucking explanation would be nice.

Marcus   If yu hadn't have come in early like you always do, none a diss would have happened.

Sarge   Yu blaming mi? Diss is my fault?

Marcus   It had to be yu dat tek Celia's call.

Sarge   Yeah it had to be mi, ca I am a policeman. I don't know wat yu are. No wurtless *Don* go own me! What de hell happen to yu, Marcus?

Marcus   Yu know what, mi bwoi, Dennis.

Sarge   Hey, fuck yer bwoi, mi nuh want to hear about yer bwoi, him mek mi sick!

Marcus   Yu know yu nuh mean dat.

Sarge   I mean it.

Marcus   Him yer godson

Sarge   Don't remind mi.

Marcus   I can't stop loving him, Paul. He's my son. And if yu ever had pickne of yer own, yu would understand.

Sarge   Him go against, God!

Marcus   Fuck God.

Sarge   Wat yu say?

Marcus   Mi say fuck God! Fuck yu, fuck anybody who tell mi I can't love my son. Him mek me mad, but 'im my son. I have to help him.

Sarge   Yu shame mi.

Marcus   Yu would rather mi carry on so like Neil, or Carl?

Sarge   Yeah, mi would.

Marcus   Who de hell is pure in dis station anymore, Paul? Or any other station in Kingston, or anywhere else in diss miserable fucking world for dat matter? We is all bad men.

Sarge   Why yu nuh come to mi?

Marcus   Ca mi ashamed. Yu think mi want any one to know my son come like dat? Mi never tek joker's money, on Denise's grave, mi swear to yu.

Sarge   Yu just tell him tings?

Marcus   Yes.

Sarge   Like what?

Marcus   Drug busts dat we go do. Tings like dat.

Sarge   *Tings like dat!* What de hell happen to yu? *Nuh fuck wid Marcus Blake, nuh budda! Dem say him have Maroon blood in him veins!* Yu remember dat? Ca mi do! De one man, de only man who can beat a confession outta anybody! Stories mi hear 'bout yu, mek me shit myself. Ware him deh?

Marcus   Not one penny, Paul, may de lawd strike mi down . . .

Sarge   Marcus, do mi a favour. Shut yer mout and keep it shut. Nuh bring de *lawd* into dis. We go way back and more for mi to hear any more of yer fuck ries today! We will get diss taken care of, yu have to get yer bwoi out, yer understand, far out, out of diss country, yu hear.

Marcus   But yu tell James.

Sarge   Mi tell him what he want hear. How long yu tink yer bwoi go last in jail? Wid him, *ways?* Get him out.

Marcus   Alright, mi work on it.

Sarge   Work fast. A lot fast. *Florida* or summin, just get him out. Mi putting yu out, early retirement, starting tomorrow. Yu hear mi?

Marcus   Mi hear yu.

Sarge   Gwan mek yer call.

Marcus   Paul . . . I . . .

Sarge   Get out!

Marcus *leaves.*

A Room

Carl *is still tied up and blinded.*

Carl   Bwoi? Bwoi? Yu there? Please? Please, please, bwoi?
Come on . . . talk to mi.

Adrian   Mi can't.

Carl   Mi knew, mi knew yu hadn't gone.

Adrian   Shush.

Carl   Thank yu.

Adrian   Fer what?

Carl   Fer staying.

Adrian   Man tell mi to. Nuh thank mi. But yu must shush.

Carl   Mi can help yu.

Adrian   Shut de fuck up, yu nuh hear mi?

Carl   Tink Adrian, think.

Adrian   You have a fudda?

Carl   Of course mi have a fudda.

Adrian   He still alive?

Carl   Yes.

Adrian   My fudda work all him life in a Bauxite mine. He
die two year ago cos of the whole heap a' dust he have in him
lungs. Me one had ti tek care of my mudda, ca she in a
wheelchair. Mi supposed to take her to *Hellshire* beach today,
so she can feel the water on her toes, once a week, every
Tuesday, then I go buy her a nice thick slice of Bammy fer
her to eat. I do dat fer her. De only time she ever smile fer
me. Mi nuh have a choice.

Carl   Yeah yu do.

Adrian   He go rape mi mudda yu know how it go. Yu know wat he go do to mi. Who go look after mi mudda? Who go tek her to the beach? Who go wash her feet? Buy her some Bammy?

Carl   I will.

Adrian   Yu?

Carl   I promise to look after she, yu have my word. I promise to look after yu.

Adrian   Yu promise to look after yerself, ca dass all yer about *Carl Mitchell!*

Carl   Come on, bwoi.

Adrian   Why yu so blind? Why yu nuh si? Once yer in . . .

Carl   . . . Yer in. Mi know.

Carl *manages to break free.*

Adrian   Hey!

Carl   Mi sorry.

Carl *knocks* **Adrian** *down and tries to escape, but the* **Adrian** *finds his gun, picks it up and aims it at* **Carl**.

Adrian   Carl!

Carl *turns around slowly to see the* **Adrian** *aiming his gun.*

Carl   Alright, easy, yeah.

Adrian   Yer fucker, yu!

Carl   Easy, bwoi.

Adrian   Bastard!

Carl   Mi had to.

Adrian   Yu know mi almost . . .

Carl   Almost what?

Adrian   Nuh mind.

Carl   Tell mi?

Adrian *tries to steady himself, he still aiming the gun at* **Carl** *but is shaking.*

Carl   Come on bwoi, let mi go. Mi go help yu, mi go help yer mudda, mi mek sure de Joker won't go anywhere near dem. But yu have to let mi go, yu know dat. Come on, bwoi!

Adrian *is about to lower his gun when the* **Boss Man** *bursts in, carrying a machine gun. He walks over to* **Adrian** *and slaps him down to the ground.*

Boss Man   Pussy 'ole!

Adrian   Mi sorry. . . .

Boss Man   Mi tell yu to speak? Outside!

Adrian *does as he is told and leaves. The* **Boss Man** *approaches* **Carl**.

Boss Man   Turn around.

Carl   Yu go kill mi?

Boss Man   Turn yer arse around.

Carl   Please, please mi beg yu, mi have a lickle girl.

Boss Man   Mi nuh give a shit what yu have, turn around. Nuh fucking mek mi tell yu again.

Carl *slowly turns himself around.*

Carl   Please man, please, I beg yu. Lawd, forgive mi, please.

The **Boss Man** *ties up* **Carl**'s *hands.*

Boss Man   What yu bawling fer? Eh? Yu be dead already if mi want dat. Your policeman friends, de want exchange yu. Too bad, ca mi never kill a policeman, if mi did, yu know what would happen? Mi get a rep dis big! It sent out a signal, yu nuh fuck wid de *joker*, in yer life! Tell mi summin, why yu people hate him so much? Eh? Him run a tight ship in him garrison. Him look after everybody. Food, clean water, whatever de need, Joker get it, for a price. A price deh can afford. Him look after dem, after us! Him just picking up from where *Dudus* left off. Dat is more dan be said fer dat fucking bitch *Simpson Miller*, yu know!

Carl   Mi thought Joker was *PNP*.

Boss Man   She a wurtless cunt. All a' dem . . . As soon as de get in power, deh ferget about deh own people. But Joker won't. Why yu can't leave him alone. Yu want slice of what we have? Is dat it? Mi know about yu, mi know how yu carry on so. De two a we, we steal, we deal, but Joker look after him people, who yu look after, apart from yu? Come wid us, if yu want. Deh is enuff bredren, enuff! Come nuh? Come, or bring yer fucking nose out of our business, yes? Tell yer people to keep deh noses out! Dat way, every one get along fine.

Carl   We de police.

Boss Man (*grabs his own crotch*)   Police dis! Yu call yerself *police?* Yu mek joke if yu tink yu a de police!

Boss Man*'s phone rings.*

Boss Man (*answers*)   Wat yu want? Say what? Alright, we move. Now, cha rass!

Boss Man *hangs up. He aims his gun gain at* **Carl***.*

Carl   Hey I thought yu say yu nuh kill mi.

Boss Man   De *JDF* are coming, now what the rass diss have to do wid dem? Is yu who call dem?

Carl   How the hell mi do that?

Boss Man   Yu tell the boy to call dem?

Carl   Mi nuh tell the de boy to do nuttin.

Boss Man   Move.

Carl   Please, just . . .

Boss Man   Move yer backside out.

Boss Man *leads* **Carl** *out.*

A Field

Sarge *and* **Marcus** *are waiting along with a handcuffed* **Joker** *in the park.*

Sarge   A *Bajan* man enters a restaurant and while sitting at him table him notices a gorgeous woman sitting at another table alone. He calls de waiter over and asks for a bottle of de most expensive champagne to be sent over to her knowing dat if she accepts it she will be his. De waiter gets de bottle and quickly takes it over to de young lady, saying dat it's from de gentleman. Woman look at de champagne and decides to send a note back to de him, she say, 'for mi to accept diss bottle yu need to have a Mercedes in your garage, a million in de bank and nine inches in your trousers.' De *Bajan* sends back a note of his own, it reads . . . 'jus so yuh know . . . mi av a bran new benz an mi av over ten million inna de bank but nuhbaddy go mek mi cut three inch off a wah mi av inna mi pants . . . suh yuh can jus send back di champagne!'

Marcus *struggles to laugh.*

Sarge   What? Yer, mi nuh want to laugh either.

Joker   Mi hear dat one.

Sarge   What was dat?

Joker   But it was a Jamaican not a *Bajan*. Why yu change it, yu nuh like *Bajan*s?

Sarge   What was dat, man?

Marcus   What was wat?

Sarge   Dat noise

Marcus   Mi nuh hear nuttin.

Sarge   I did. Yu know I had no idea.

Marcus   'Bout what?

Sarge   Dat a dog could talk.

Sarge *sucker-punches* **Joker** *hard in the stomach.*

Sarge   Utter one more fuckin' word to mi! Yu understand? Mi nuh wan trouble, but yu fuck wid us again, and trouble yu have.

Joker   Guns.

Sarge   Yer nuh hear mi say, not anudda word?

Joker   Mi want mi guns back. All a dem.

Sarge   And mi want fuck *Beyoncé*, but dat nuh go happen as well. Yer claart!

Boss Man *enters with one of his soldiers and* **Carl** *and* **Neil** *ahead of him.*

Boss Man   Ware dem deh?

Sarge   Ware who?

Boss Man   *JDF*, nuh fuck around!

Sarge   No one call the *JDF*, wa wrong wid yu?

Boss Man   Deh on deh way.

Sarge   Wat yu chat 'bout?

Boss Man   Deh are coming here now.

Sarge   How de hell deh know about this; we didn't say nuttin to no one.

Marcus   James.

Sarge   What?

Marcus   Dat damn fucking fool of a bwoi!

Joker   Him want kill all of us.

Sarge   Hey!

Boss Man   Before God mi go kill yu all first.

Sarge   Everyone just shut up and calm down. No one here yet, just us, alright? So, let's do dis and gone.

Boss Man   Yu have him fer mi?

Sarge   Move yerself.

Sarge *pushes* **Joker** *towards* **Boss Man** *who motions* **Neil** *and* **Carl** *to move with the tip of his gun.* **Neil** *walks on, but* **Carl** *stops. He grabs holds of* **Joker** *and holds him.*

Neil   Carl? Carl? Wa gwan man, come!

Sarge   Come bwoi, we have to go now.

Carl   Ware deh bwoi?

Sarge   What him say?

Carl   What happen to de bwoi?

Joker (*to* **Boss Man**)   Wat him chat 'bout?

Carl   Where deh bwoi?

Neil   Forget de bwoi, man.

Sarge   Move yer arse, bwoi.

Marcus   Let him go, Carl.

Carl   Mi want fer know.

Sarge   We don't have time fe dis.

Joker   Mi like yu bredren.

Carl   Mi nuh yer fucking bredren.

Sarge   Carl?

Marcus   Bring yer backside over here, nuh man.

Carl   Where is Adrian?

Boss Man   Nuh worry about him.

Carl   Tell mi where him deh.

Joker (*to* **Boss Man**)   Yu had better deal wid diss madness yu nuh!

Neil   Carl!

Boss Man   Yu wanna know where he is?

Carl   Tell mi.

Boss Man *walks towards a trashcan*

Neil   Carl, nuh, let's just go, man.

Sarge   The *JDF* are on deh way, they are going to shoot our rass! Come on.

Carl   Where is he?

Boss Man *flips over the lid from the trashcan. He gestures to* **Carl** *to look inside.* **Carl** *looks inside and shrieks.*

Sarge   What, what yu si?

Neil *looks inside the trashcan.*

Neil   Oh Lawd, Jesus Christ!

Sarge   What de hell?

Boss Man   Now yu know, cha rass.

Carl   Him only a bwoi.

Boss Man   Who want play man.

Carl   Him nuh do anything, he never breathed a word, he would rather die!

Boss Man   So, him die.

Carl *goes to attack* **Boss Man** *but is shielded by one of his soldiers.*

Carl   Lawd help mi, I go kill yu.

Neil (*holds him off*)   Carl!

Joker   Yu want keep a lease on diss one, fer mi?

Sarge   Yu nuh tell mi what to do. Carl come.

Carl   Bastard!

Joker   Silence yer dawg, nuh mek mi do it fer yu.

Carl *is in a rage.*

Sarge   Carl? Carl? Look at mi, listen to mi, look at mi. LOOK AT MI! It's over.

Carl   We de police man, de can't do dat!

Sarge   Yu want tell the *JDF* what de hell we were doing here? Yu want lose yer job? Yu want go jail? Think it through, nuh bwoi.

Carl   Nuh man, no, No!

Sarge   Him keep, mi promise yu, him keep!

Carl   Mi go kill yu, I swear.

Sarge   Carl? We need to go, right now.

Carl   We can't let dem get away wid diss.

Sarge   Yu nuh hear mi say him keep?

Carl   It's not right.

Sarge   Nuh tell mi what is nuh right. None a' diss is alright! Mi do de best wid what mi have. Listen to mi. Joker is a crook, but yu is crooked! Yu and Neil wid yer lickle schemes on dem street corners, how yu run tings, eh? Nuh tell mi what is right.

Carl   Sarge?

Sarge   It was you or him! Gwan clean yerself, ca yu stink. Mi say go.

Neil   Carl come on, deh is nothing we can do. Come on, man.

Neil *leads* **Carl** *away.* **Joker** *is greeted by his men with cheers of delight.*

Joker   Hey, policeman? Policeman, mi say! No hard feelings, right?

Sarge   Fuck off.

Joker (*laughs*)   Look pon dis way, better de devil yu know, dat de one yu don't.

Joker *leaves with his men, laughing and cheering.*

Sarge (*calls*)   Mi go find yu, before God, mi go find yu.

They quickly depart the area.

The Station

Marcus *comes storming into the station. He finds* **James** *at his desk.*

Marcus   Was it you?

James   Sorry?

Marcus   It was you, right?

James   Marcus, I do not understand.

Marcus   You one find the Super, don't ask me how, but you find him, you call him. And yu tell him. Yu tell him to gwan fetch the *JDF*, right? Right?

James   Marcus?

Marcus   Right?

James   I'm a police officer.

Marcus   Oh lord.

James   You're a police officer. We have a duty.

Marcus   Fuck duty! Yu and yer rass claart duty just kill a lickle bwoi.

James   What boy, what are you talking about?

Marcus   Nuttin but a pickne!

James   What happened, did the *JDF* open fire on you?

Marcus   The *JDF* didn't do shit ca we got our backsides outta deh quick time.

James   Then what are you talking about, who is this boy?

Marcus   The bwoi weren't nuttin. He woulda stayed nuttin, if yu kept yer mout shut. Wat de hell do yu tink is going on here? You really tink we nuh tell the Super nuttin ca he love going to de titty bar and nuh business 'bout wat we do? No, we nuh tell him nuttin, ca him will open his mout' to anybody fer the right price. Anybody! Yu hear mi?

James   Oh God.

Marcus   Yeah, yu hear mi. But if I were yu, yu had better get yer arse out, before Carl catch up wid yu.

James   Look, Marcus . . .

Marcus   Yu couldn't shut up, you couldn't keep yer blasted tail quiet.

James   You weren't going to do it. It was my a duty as a police officer . . .

Marcus   Say that word again, say duty one more fucking time, mi dare yu!

James   What happened out there? Just tell me.

Marcus   Yu care?

James   Is it done?

Marcus   Yeah, it done, no thanks to yu. Why the hell yu can't leave well enuff alone, eh? Don't yu know, don't yu understand, all yu do is mek shit worse, ca yu don't know, yu don't know nuttin, yu don't know nuttin 'bout nuttin.

James   Do you think you are any better?

Marcus   No, mi don't! Dass what's funny. Dass wat's wrong. Yer as lost as we are, yer nuh have nuttin.

James   Marcus?

Marcus   Gwan man, leave mi.

James   Look?

Marcus   Mi nuh joke, Carl go kill yu when he si yu.

James   What about your son? Is some one arresting him and bringing him here for questioning as we speak?

Marcus   No.

James   No?

Marcus   Mi say no.

James   That is no good to me, Marcus!

Marcus   Lawd dis bwoi love to talk!

James   Look?

Marcus   Him my son. Mi one know where he is. Mi go get him.

James   When will that be?

Marcus   When mi done! Cha rass! Yu still here?

James   What are yu going to do?

Marcus   Leave tings alone, nuh man.

James   Look, I know you probably think I don't have the right to ask this.

Marcus   Probably?

James   Whatever it is you are planning.

Marcus   Lawd, shut diss fool up fer mi.

James   Can you at least wait until I leave?

Marcus   What?

James What happens after I am gone is really none of my concern. All I care about is a result, so do London. A man has been arrested and charged for Parker's murder, and I assisted in some small way to his arrest. I've done my job. That is all I have ever wanted, to make it right. Whatever happens afterwards, happens. But the key word is afterwards, Marcus. Do you understand what I am telling you?

Marcus So, now yu want play?

James So it would seem.

Marcus How much yu tek, de money, truth now?

James Marcus, I didn't.

Marcus Gw'y!

James I didn't! But four of my colleagues did. I saw them do it. I said nothing. I lied for them.

Marcus Why yu nuh say nuttin?

James Because I was the only one who was black. Because I always have something to prove. Why make it even harder for myself by being a snitch?

Marcus Yu get fuck?

James Yeah, mi get fuck! Mi get well and truly fuck!

Marcus Black is black, bwoi. No matter where we go, we always get fuck!

James Do we have a deal?

Marcus Deal fer what? Wat yu chat 'bout?

James Your son, Marcus. You have to get him out. I told you, all we want is an arrest. Parker had friends in high places. But not high enough if you see what I mean. Don't you see? I'm the favour. I'm the *bangarang*.

Marcus I don't have time fer dis.

James   Yes, that's right, you don't have for time for this, you don't have time for me. You don't even have time for your son.

Marcus   Shut yer mout about him.

James   You don't have time for anyone. I should leave you to your bottle, ennit?

Marcus   Yu don't know mi. Yu don't know diss station, and yu sure as hell know nuttin about diss island.

James   I know enough.

Marcus   Did yu know dat when de sun rises over Kingston in de mornin', it's as pretty as heaven! Or when yu walk through de streets of Denham town, bullet holes in every single wall, everybody still manage to stop to smile at everybody. Ca de fight to live on. Ca de have spirit yu si? It's de spirit of de *Maroons* me a chat 'bout.

James   Oh what is that now?

Marcus (*sighs*)   Deh were African slaves left to fend fer demselves by de Spanish when the British tek over de island in 1655. Deh tek refuge in de mountains, deh stay deh fer years and swear blind deh go kill anyone who try put chains back on dem. So if yer strong, if yu have fight, yu have deh spirit of de *Maroons* in yu. Dass wat deh people on diss island have, James. Deh may not know it, deh may not believe it, but deh have it! Yu understand?

James   I can buy you some time. I can change my flight, leave tonight if it helps.

Marcus   It helps! James, jus gwan yeah. Go!

James *gets his things together.*

James   You know, I was a good copper once, a bloody good one. All I wanted was to feel that way again.

Marcus   Yu do diss ca' yu want to mek tings all good wid yerself.

James Yes.

Marcus Yu shoulda stayed in England fer dat, nuh bring yer shit here!

James *goes.* **Marcus** *finds the bottle of whiskey. He unscrews the cap but cannot bring himself to drink it anymore. He pours the remainder into the trash can.*

A Bar

Carl *is drinking alone. He has no emotion whatsoever on his face.* **Neil** *enters, still looking quite shaken by his ordeal.*

Neil Hey.

Carl Mi thought summin had happened to yu.

Neil Nuttin go happen to mi, not anymore. Mi go find Manny and mi go kill him, before God mi go dead him. Twice over. Yu know?

Carl *refuses to speak. He continues to show no emotion.*

Neil Yeah, yu know. Yu know more dan mi. Wa him do, to yu, dat man?

Carl Nuttin much. Yu?

Neil Apart from pressing a gun to my face, pulling de trigger ever time, and every time mi thought mi dead, nuttin much. Mi tired Carl, yu tired?

Carl Yeah Neil, mi tired.

Neil Those fucker dem. Manny, Joker, all a dem. I'm sick of diss shit, so fucking tired of diss shit, tired, tired, fucking tired!

Neil *stands up. He lets rip.* **Carl** *watches but says and does nothing.*

Neil Fuck diss shit, fuck diss shit, fuck it! All a yu, yu hear mi, mi say, fuck it! Fuck all a yu, fuck all of yu! Mi go kill a yu, come on, mi say come on, mi want kill yu, all of yu, yu mudda fuckers, mudda fuckers, come bring yerself, bring dem come. Come on. Come on, mi say come on, come on, go kill yu, mudda fuckers, mi go kill yu, mi go kill yu . . .

Neil *breaks down in tears.* **Carl** *remains silent. He barely moves an inch.*

Neil   Jamaica dead, man. Yu know? Carl? Say summin nuh man?

Carl   De lickle bwoi couldn't have been older dan eighteen, if dat.

Neil   Carl?

Carl   Mi de same age when my brudda get kill.

Neil   Carl?

Carl *goes to leave.*

Carl   Yu say Jamaica dead? Well, I'm not. Not yet.

Neil   Ware yu go?

Carl   I'm going to *Hellshire beach*.

Neil   *Hellshire?*

Carl   I have to go tek a lady in a wheelchair.

Neil   Yu go wat?

Carl   Let her feel de water on her toes. Buy her a nice thick slice of *Bammy*.

Neil   Nuh sound like yu.

Carl   A promise me a mek. And dis is one promise I want keep. Diss is one promise, I'm going to keep! Gwan home Neil. Yu tired.

Neil   Yeah.

Neil *watches* **Carl** *go as the sun outside begins to set.*

Blackout.

The Firm

The Firm premiered at Hampstead Theatre on 27 October 2017, with the following cast and creative team:

Trent	**Delroy Atkinson**
Gus	**Clinton Blake**
Fraser	**Simon Coombs**
Leslie	**Jay Simpson**
Selwyn	**Clarence Smith**

Director	Denis Lawson
Designer	Alex Marker
Lighting	Neill Brinkworth
Sound	John Leonard

My deepest thanks to the Barnfield boys: Godwin Nwaokobia, Julius Francis, Michael Hearn and Steve Macaulay, for your friendship, your trust and for telling me so many brilliant stories.

The Firm

For Lincoln Hudson, my brother

The Firm was first presented at Hampstead Theatre on 27 October 2017, with the following cast and creative team:

Trent	Delroy Atkinson
Gus	Clinton Blake
Fraser	Simon Coombs
Leslie	Jay Simpson
Selwyn	Clarence Smith

Director   Denis Lawson
Designer   Alex Marker
Lighting   Neill Brinkworth
Sound   John Leonard

My deepest thanks to the Barnfield boys: Godwin Nwaokobia, Julius Francis, Michael Hearn and Steve Macaulay, for your friendship, your trust and for telling me so many brilliant stories.

Characters

Leslie, *white, late forties / early fifties*
Gus, *black, late forties / early fifties*
Trent, *black, late forties / early fifties*
Selwyn, *black, late forties / early fifties*
Fraser, *mixed race, twenties*

Setting

A renovated pub in South London. Present day.

The play opens in an expensive-looking refurbished pub. Comfy-looking leather seats. The bar would look at home in a fifties American diner. Clean tile floors. Cream-coloured walls. There are several bottles of expensive champagne and champagne glasses on the bar.

An old-fashioned fifties-style Wurlitzer jukebox, looking quite pristine and brand new rests in the corner.

Leslie *and* **Gus** *are onstage.* **Leslie** *is standing on a chair, putting up a 'Welcome home Sean' decoration on the wall.*

Leslie   . . . Anyhow two, twos, as soon as me and Selwyn got nicked yeah, on remand we was, no messing, no question. After they are done processing us in the nick, they are marching us through reception on our way to the wings, when they have to stop and deal with some incident that's been going on. They sit us down in an office, warning us not to move an inch or even breathe. Have I not told you this?

Gus   Well, you're telling me now.

Leslie   For only about thirty seconds yeah, they have their backs to us, can't see us or what we are about. Selwyn is going all telepathic, telling me with his face to have a gander to my right, over by the desk. As I live, Gus, there is an open safe and straight off my eyeballs were going all Roger Rabbit. No one knows about the sight of corn better than me, right or wrong?

Gus   Oh, I know, you thieving little cunt.

Leslie   I could tell, within seconds, there was about five hundred quid in there. Must of have been petty cash or summin. Without skipping a beat, I swear to you, I leap over the desk, swipe the notes out from that safe, stuff them down my pants, and back in my seat, like the Flash!

Gus   Fuck off!

Leslie   Three seconds to spare –

Gus   Move!

Leslie   – before the screws turned around again, without a clue to what happened, not a whiff! If I lie, I die. Am I good?

Gus   You're a legend, Leslie. It's always been said.

Leslie   Selwyn as well.

Gus   How come they didn't search you?

Leslie   Search for what? They already had us stripped bare, we were on our way to the wings with our bags, weren't you listening? Two days later, we're ghosted out. Case dismissed. According to my brief, the CPS fucked it right up for themselves, crucial evidence gone missing or summin. So, on my way out, this screw grabs my neck, holds me up against the door, going, 'It was you, yer cunt, weren't it, weren't it?' 'Weren't what?' I ask. He goes, 'I don't know for the life of me how, but it was you who swiped that money, weren't it, in less than twenty seconds? Who the fuck are you, Houdini's long lost boy?' I goes, 'Nuh, nuh, don't be silly.'

Gus   You had that money all that time you were inside?

Leslie   I fucking walked out of the nick with it. As soon as we were on the out, I treated me and Sel to a proper full English.

Gus   I'm scared to ask this, where'd you hide it, the money?

Leslie   Kept it on me, down my pants.

Gus   You had a monkey up yer arse?

Leslie   No, not up my arse, down my pants.

Gus   24/7?

Leslie   Who's ever gonna think I have five hundred boys on me in there?

Gus   Yer a legend, mate.

Leslie   Gotta give it up for Sel, though.

Gus   Why? You did the graft. It's your tickle.

Leslie   Cos he eyeballed it in the first place, he put me on it. Him and his eagle eyes are legendary all over South, Gus, for a paper shout, you know that.

Gus   Is this your way of saying, you are not going to have a word with him for me?

Leslie   I did have a word.

Gus   Well, what was it that you said to him?

Leslie   What it was you told me to say to him.

Gus   Which was what, Les?

Leslie   That your answer is no.

Gus   Well that does not seem to be working.

Leslie   Well, I'm sorry about that.

Gus   I can't be dealing with his shit, Les.

Leslie   What do you want me to do, what do you want me to say?

Gus   Higher.

Leslie *moves the sign higher.*

Leslie   I don't know why you are getting so wet about it. You know Selwyn already, man.

Gus   That is why I asked you to talk to him. One phone call, mi mek, just one, to bring the boys back together, and he's on my arse wid it, non-stop.

Leslie   You should let him roll with it, like I do. Let him chat his shit, get it out of his system and that. So he thinks he is still the big man. Then you blow him off. Did he tell you who it was?

Gus   Some younger. I mean, who robs a supermarket nowadays? Answer me that, it doesn't mek sense.

It's dropping down.

Leslie *adjusts the sign.*

Gus   Higher, mate, come on.

Leslie   It's fine as it is.

Gus   Alright, but you know how Shaun feels about his name?

Leslie   By the time them gals we got for him are done, the last thing he will be worrying about is his name.

Gus   Just as long as they ain't some ugly-ass bitches.

Leslie   Trust me, blud.

Gus   *Blud?* Did you just say *blud* to me? Where did that come from?

Leslie   Nowhere.

Gus   Just do me a favour. At some point tonight just take Selwyn aside. Tell him I said no, and that he needs to have a word with himself. And while yer at it, make sure that he takes his pills.

Leslie   I was planning on having a good time tonight, I'm not Selwyn's babysitter. Leave him alone if he wants to carry on wid his hype.

Gus   I don't want him giving me the arsehole and go flaring up like he does.

Leslie   He just wants to feel we are still the firm.

Gus   We are still the firm.

Leslie   Of course we are.

Gus   But?

Leslie   There is no but.

Gus   Bollocks.

Leslie   Bollocks yourself. We ain't had a session in years.

Gus   And whose fault is that?

Leslie   How's Naomi doing?

Gus　Naomi?

Leslie　Her new school and that.

Gus　Oh, Leslie, that was a classy segue.

Leslie　Step off.

Gus　Just praising yer, cha rass. Full of subtext and shit.

Leslie　Call it what you like, am just asking after my goddaughter, that is all.

Gus　She's sweet, least she will be.

Leslie　Will be?

Gus　I had Andrea giving me the arsehole the other night. Turns out, Naomi has been calling her every day, crying about how she hates her new school and that she wants come home.

Leslie　She's thirteen, mate.

Gus　She's a thirteen-year-old with a forty grand a year education who needs to sort her shit out. I gave her a bell myself, I goes, 'Naomi, run away if you feel but don't even think about bringing yourself home, I don't business at all if yer thirteen. You'll be a thirteen-year-old uneducated bitch gal wid no home, so tek yer arse back to that school and hit the books.'

Leslie　You really said that, you said 'bitch' to yer own daughter?

Gus　Damn right, I said that. Except the bitch part. Forty grand a year though, Les, I mean, have a word!

Leslie　That's a lot of cheddar.

Gus　My cheddar. I do what I want with it.

Leslie　Yes, you most certainly do, mate.

Gus　I saw Sam Hardy's little sister the other day. Sharon.

Leslie   And?

Gus   She was saying Sam took another turn. They can't cope with him any more, they're gonna put him in a nursing home. Shame that.

Leslie   Now, *that's* a segue. Little bit over the top, but a segue nonetheless, eh, Gus?

Gus   Anyhow, I funded Sharon a couple of grand, on behalf of us, the boys and that. The guy's a cabbage now. I thought it was the least we could do.

Leslie   You're a proper hero, Gus.

Gus   She seemed happy.

Still don't look straight enough.

Leslie   Well, I'm done with it.

Gus *pours* **Leslie** *a glass of champagne.*

Gus   Salut!

Leslie   Salut!

They clink their glasses.

Gus   Twelve years, Les.

Leslie   Long time.

Gus   Motherfuck! Now we gotta be sure?

Leslie   About?

Gus   We don't go all emotional and that. We don't cuddle up to him, none of that shit.

Leslie   Did you say cuddle?

Gus   No huggy-kissy from anyone. Let's be men about it.

Leslie   I ain't kissing Shaun. I never thought about kissing him.

Gus   I know you ain't.

Leslie   Right.

Gus   Am just saying, let's rein it in.

Leslie   Is there a reason why you are telling me this?

Gus   I don't want anyone getting carried away.

Leslie   You mean you don't want me getting carried away, don't yer? What the fuck, Gus?

Gus   Ease up, yeah?

Leslie   You ease up, cunt.

Gus   Down, boy, calm.

Leslie   I am calm. I am calm as I can be with calm. It's about her, isn't it?

Gus   No, it isn't. Claire is a sort, a raving, lawd knows what she sees in you, but there you go. Them's the breaks. I look forward to meeting her one day.

Leslie   Who's Claire?

Gus   You don't know the name of your own woman, Les?

Leslie   Her name is Jan.

Gus   It's what I said.

Leslie   You said Claire.

Gus   Never again Jan! Got it.

Leslie   Never mind yourself about me. You want to find yourself a woman, quick time. You and Andrea broke up how long, three years?

Gus   Two years.

Leslie   She's moved on, time you did.

Gus   Point taken.

Leslie   Giving me shit.

Gus   Are you done? Seriously? I rank you, Les, you know that.

Leslie   I didn't plan to move in on it. She's my probation officer, Gus. Two twos, when I met her, I took one look, and say, Jesuuuss, wat de rah! What I wouldn't give to fling dat down sometime! Just my type an all. Kim Wilde lookalike, before the flab.

Gus   Kim Wilde?

Leslie   The singer, Gus.

Gus   This trout of yours is a white chick?

Leslie   Yeah.

Gus   You change sides?

Leslie   I never changed sides.

Gus   Nobody love de black pum more than you, Leslie.

Leslie   I love all pum. I'm the United Nations on all things to do wid de pum. Point is, grinding your probation officer, regardless of the colour of de pum my friend is a big no-no!

Gus   Don't do it then.

Leslie   You mad or what? Jan had it all going on for herself, tight blue jeans and a blouse that hug de body. You know what she did for me on our first date?

Gus (*excited*)   Oh, yes?

Leslie   Made me a cup of tea.

Gus   What?

Leslie   Not your regular PG Tips and that, herbal or something, and it was proper nice! Take out the teabag, a teaspoon of honey, and that'll work! *You get me?* Then she stroked my face all good, rubbed my shoulders, proper nice.

Oh lawd! She knows right where to go, every time! What? Why are you looking at me like that?

Gus   'You get me?'

Leslie   What you want now?

Gus   First it was blud, now, it's *you get me*?

Leslie (*holds his crotch*)   See it deh? Jan's good for me that's all.

Gus   You know me, Les, as long as you are happy, I got your back.

Leslie   When Jonny Parsons chased me up Woolwich High Street with a Stanley, you and Trent standing there, pissing yourselves, that kind of having my back?

Gus   More like when I funded your rent for six months when you were on remand, that kind of having yer back.

Leslie   OK. Fair do's. (*Sips more champagne.*) This shit is proper nice.

Gus   Twelve motherfucking years, Les! Cha-rass!

Leslie   I predict a good night ahead.

Gus   As long as Selwyn reins it in.

Leslie (*looks around the pub*)   Respect, Gus, you are doing well. Looks nice.

Gus   It will be if we ever get it finished. Toilets need looking at. A few more tiles to lay, English bwois too lazy, man. Eastern Europeans, however, know all about it. They know what a hard day work is. And Somalians. They don't know what a tea break is.

Leslie   Yeah, fuck minimum wage.

Gus   And I found another pub. Up in Blackheath. Right shit-hole from all accounts. Gonna do my magic there as well. From morning till night. Not one word of complaint from my workforce. Not one. Brexitards can kiss my arse.

Leslie   Yep, very well indeed.

Gus   She's good for you, this Mary.

Leslie Jan!

Gus It's what I said.

Leslie You said Mary, yer cunt.

Gus Well I meant Claire.

Leslie Jan! Her name is Jan. *Dayz!*

Gus 'Dayz'? You saying *dayz* now?

Leslie You want get merked?

Gus That's it.

Leslie Power down, big man.

Gus *Blud! Dayz! Merked!* Why are you talking to me like a *younger?*

Leslie I don't mean nothing by it, it ain't me.

Gus Bloody sounds like you.

Leslie It's this kid who I was sharing my room with at the hostel. He was coming out with all of it, *you get me, you low dat,* its infectious, what could I do?

Gus You could have stopped.

Leslie You know, I thought I had my feet well under the table there, my own room, telly, I felt like a lawd of my own creation. Well sweet. Then this cheeky little rass neck, straight out of some young offenders, shows up.

Gus Oh yes, cheeky how?

Leslie He kept moving my shoes around, you know what I am like with my shoes, Gus, with my things in fact, all of my things, I like them where I left them. I tell him to leave well enough alone, but all he does is grin, like it's meant to mean something.

He is about to turn on his e-cigarette.

Gus By the door.

Leslie   It's a vape!

Gus   I don't business.

Leslie   Fuck's sake.

He stands by the door to have his smoke.

Gus   What was his play?

Leslie   Fucked if I know. I fronted him up a few times, respect your elders and that, but he denied all knowledge. He reckons it was the mice.

Gus   What a renk!

Leslie   Him and his grin. It was everything in me not to grab him by the throat and show him summin.

Gus   But you didn't though, Les?

Leslie   Do I look like I want to go back inside? Besides, he was big.

Gus   Big?

Leslie   Yeah, big. Not big as in fat, like Trent. I mean, he's stacked, can handle himself.

Gus   So what you are saying is, you were scared?

Leslie   I didn't say I was scared of the yout. I'm saying the yout was big.

Gus   So what if he was big?

Leslie   He could have a knife or summin.

Gus   I thought weapons weren't allowed in there?

Leslie   They're not allowed. But you could sneak one in, dead easy. The security in that place is a joke. The geezer at the front desk don't speak English, not a word of it.

Gus   So, you were scared of this yout?

Leslie   Not of him, but he might have had a knife.

Gus   Were you scared, Les, yes or no?

Leslie   I was scared of the knife, Gus, is that not allowed?

Gus   But he didn't have one.

Leslie   What are you now, Old Bill? He might have. But you know what the kids are like around here. They don't think they are summin, unless they are carrying summin.

Gus   'S right, just don't be telling me you were scared, Les. That you are getting soft in your old age.

Leslie   A minute ago, you said I shouldn't touch him. And less of the 'old', please?

Gus   You shouldn't touch him. But don't be scared to touch him, there's a difference.

Leslie   I was this much away from parking a chair into the side of his head. Good enough for yer? It took Claire two hours to calm me down one night.

Gus   You mean Jan!

Leslie   My bwoi.

Gus   Fuck off! If this kid's giving you bollocks, jog on out of there.

Leslie   No need, the kid's gone.

Gus   You can do better.

Leslie   I can't afford better. And go where exact? I can't move in with Jan, she'll lose her job.

Gus   You know where.

Leslie   I said no.

Gus   'Kin 'ell, Leslie. Not only do you choose to wine and dine yourself at the local food bank and not let me fund yer. You'd also rather sleep in some shite-hole hostel than one of my flats?

Leslie   Where our *wall* used to be?

Gus   Here we go.

Leslie   Remember the wall, Gus?

Gus   You been thick?

Leslie   We can't all be rich privileged wankers like you, can we? We're not allowed.

Gus   Yes, thank you, *Jeremy Corbyn*.

Leslie   Also, Jan's words were 'No associating with known criminals'.

Gus   Is that what she sees me as? A 'known criminal'? Facety gal. Have I ever seen the inside of a courtroom? I don't think so! If thass she feel, what you doing here then?

Leslie   A long overdue session with my bruvvers is one thing. Crashing at your poncy gaff where our beloved wall used to be –

Gus   Shut up about the wall.

Leslie   – is extracting the Michael a touch.

Gus   Well, I am funding everything this evening, *everything*! So just for tonight, for the love of Shaun, put yer pride away.

Leslie   Yes, Dad!

Sound of knocking on the door.

Three knocks. We're on.

Gus   Finally. Now, remember.

Leslie   Yeah, yeah, no feely-feely, touchy-kissy, 'kin 'ell!

Gus   Hold up a sec, I got it all set up to do this, watch me now, see it deh.

He turns on the jukebox. With merely the touch of a button, he presses it to play 'Glad All Over', sung by the Crystal Palace football team of 1990. He and **Leslie** *sing along.*

The door swings opens. It is **Trent**. *They stop singing.*

Gus   Fuck's sake, Trent.

He turns off the jukebox.

Trent   Fuck's sake what?

Leslie   You lead him in first, we said.

Trent   I know what we said, but about that –

Leslie   Gwan then.

Gus   Where is he, parking?

Leslie   You got him parking your car, Trent?

Trent   Hold up.

Gus (*calls*)   Shaun? Shaun? Batty bwoi, ware yu deh?

Trent   Gus?

Gus   You had better not have been smoking skunk in your car again, what if you got pulled over, you woulda got him sent right back.

Trent   Gus?

Gus   Think it through, Trent.

Trent (*trying to get a word in*)   Gus, man –

Gus (*calls*)   Shaun? Where him deh?

Trent   I dunno.

Gus   Yer dunno.

Trent (*looks around*)   Nice yard, Jesusss!

Gus   Trent, where is Shaun?

Trent   Well, let me give it to you straight, Gus. *Mi. Nuh. Know!*

Gus   But you said you were bringing him.

Trent   I know what I said. I went to his muddda's yard as agreed, hardly my fault if he isn't there now.

Leslie   He had to be there.

Trent   Well, he ain't there.

Leslie   You call him?

Trent   Yeah, I *call* him. I had it all arranged and shit. He would head for his mum's after his release. I drive up there, bring his no-good, skinny white Irish arse back here.

Gus   So?

Trent   So, he wasn't there, Gus.

Gus   So where then?

Trent   I'm getting bored saying this, mi nuh rhatid know! Joke is, his mum ain't seen him neither.

Gus   What time did he go out?

Trent   You don't get what I am meaning, Gus.

Gus   Well, hurry up and mean then.

Trent   His mum ain't seen him at all, not since he got out.

Leslie   Bollocks.

Trent   Ask her. Go see her.

Gus   Well, that ain't right, that don't make any sense.

Trent   Believe it don't. His mum says the last time she see him was a week and a half ago, when she last visited him in the nick.

Leslie (*chuckles*)   You don't think they kept him in, do yer? That he done summin.

Gus   You mean hit a screw?

Leslie   It wouldn't be the first time, would it?

Gus   Only explanation.

Leslie   Stupid motha!

Gus   He can't hold it in.

Trent   Excuse?

Gus   I wonder what the screw say to get him all flared up?

Trent   Excuse?

Gus   Something about Palace, has to be.

Leslie   If that screw was Millwall.

Gus   No, don't. Cos that's just carnage, we are talking.

He and **Leslie** *chuckle at the thought.*

Trent   I said excuse?

Leslie   Giving it all that, like a lobster. Can you imagine?

Gus   Game over, cha rass.

Leslie   You know it.

Trent   Yo. Excuse me?

Gus   What, what you want?

Trent   A word if I may?

Gus   Gwan nuh!

Leslie   Keeping us hanging. Spit it out.

Gus   Rass!

Leslie   Innit!

Trent   Shaun was released. They bring his arse out yesterday, Just as they planned. No bother. No mention of PaIace or Millwall. Happy? Two twos, the purest kind.

Leslie   You sure about this?

Trent   I checked with dem. He should have been there at his mum's, waiting for me, as per the plan.

Gus   This is a weird one. We had this planned, cha rass. You pick him up, soften him up with a couple of whiskeys. Plenty more here. A couple of sorts all paid for, ready and waiting to give him a proper PSE, right or wrong, Leslie?

Leslie   Pepsi and Shirlie! They've only got a website, can you believe?

Gus   Him gonna bruc some serious ass tonight. A few hours' sleep at a five-star if he is lucky, finally, the grand finale, a three p.m. kick-off at the Park. No way on planet Earth is Shaun missing any of that. He should be here, he wanted to be here, it mek no sense.

Leslie   You know him, he loves to piss about too much. He'll come charging through that door any moment, glad all over, asking, where Pepsi and Shirlie at?

Trent   Exactly. So, what you have for me, gents, cos I is gasping?

Gus (*points to the champagne*)   Gwan.

Trent *pours himself a glass.* **Leslie** *examines his waistline.*

Leslie   That's a fair bit of timber you got going on there, Trent. Diet not working for you again?

Trent (*holds his crotch*)   See it deh, suck it nuh. Lawd, mi need this. This is mate's rates, yeah?

Salut!

Gus/Leslie   Salut!

Trent *downs it in one.*

Trent   Ooh! This is the tits!

He has another.

Gus   Booze ain't going anywhere you know, Trent.

Trent   Blud, just let me drink yeah?

Gus   You as well?

Trent   Me as well, what?

Gus   Wid this *blud*?

Trent   Fuck is this?

Leslie   Leave it.

Trent   Trying to.

Gus   You alright there, Trent?

Trent   Yeah, man. I'm fine.

Gus   From the time you come in here, you look all out of breath.

Trent   It was nothing, I'm sweet.

Gus   What was nothing?

Trent   I said I was fine.

Gus   But you said it was nothing.

Trent   What was?

Gus   What de rass is wrong with everyone tonight? Straight answer to a straight question, two twos, Trent, what is up?

Trent   Nothing is up, nothing much.

Gus   Which is what? Tell me now before you get a slap so hard, your Zulu ancestors are going to feel it.

Trent   Just a little encounter I had on the way here.

Gus   An encounter?

Trent   Nothing for you to get the arsehole about. It was a couple of youngers.

Gus   Youngers?

Trent   Them ones from the estate, with their jeans down to their arses.

Leslie   Saggers.

Trent   Prancing around the manor like they own it.

Leslie   And they don't say manor, it's all postcodes now.

Trent   I know that, 'kin 'ell!

Gus   I don't give a rass what they call the manor.

Leslie   Endz. That's what they call it.

Gus   Did you not hear me say?

Leslie   Gus, it's all around man, it can't be helped. Like it or no, this is their turf.

Trent   Come on, you know this.

Leslie   Bit hard to Trent, him living in West Norwood and all.

Gus   West Dulwich, actually, if you must envy me all your life, get it right, Les.

Leslie   My bad.

Gus   Do they work? Do any of these jokers pay tax? A single penny of it? Talk to me, Trent, and don't say to me nuttin happened.

Trent   I was scoping the manor, looking for Shaun.

Gus   Yes?

Trent   I was stepping to my car, and these youngers were all hanging around the corner, like they were into summin. I almost walked into them, I caught eyes with one of dem, must be the big man, he gets in uptight saying he didn't like the way I was looking at him, that I was eyeballing him. I wasn't.

Gus   You weren't.

Trent   No.

Gus   But you said that, you said you weren't?

Trent   Yeah.

Gus   Why?

Trent   Why?

Gus   Why, Trent?

Trent   Gus, I don't know, I just did.

Leslie   Because he wasn't, Gus.

Gus   Weren't what?

Leslie   Eyeballing him for fuck!

Gus   Did you lay him out, Trent?

Trent   Gus, there was about eight of them.

Gus   So that would be a 'no' then?

Leslie   What did you expect him to do?

Gus   Go tell the yout summin about himself and his mum, at least.

Trent   I did do summin!

Gus   Yes, Trent, my boy, more like!

Trent   I asked him . . .

Gus   Say that again?

Trent   Told! I told him to step off.

Gus   You didn't ask?

Trent   What do you take?

Gus   What did you say?

Trent   You know.

Gus   No, I don't know.

Trent   'Mind yourself, young one. Grown-up walking, going about his business, so make a path for me, yeah?' Respect and that, the whole package, complete verbal.

Gus   And did they make a way for you?

Trent   Oh, why can't you just leave it, Gus?

Gus   Just look at me and answer the question. Did they make a way for you?

Trent   No, they didn't.

Gus   Fuck!

Trent   But I handled it, Gus. Hear me, fer trut.

Gus   Handle it how? How did you handle it?

Trent   Like I said, man!

Gus   They rough you up?

Trent   More of a jostle.

Gus   A jostle?

Trent   I didn't think it was worth the agg.

Leslie   You think right, Trent, you done good. It was not worth the agg. Hear him, Gus, now drink up. (*Toasts.*) To Shaun.

Trent   Gus?

Gus   That's my name.

Trent   We cool?

Gus   We cool. It's alright, Trent.

Leslie   Excellent, 'bout time. Now drink!

Gus   As long as you are sure, Trent.

Trent   You think I am lying to you now?

Leslie   Trent, he's fucking with yer.

Gus   You do not have a thing to worry about.

Sound of someone approaching the door.

Hear that?

Leslie   Told you, what did I say, he's fucking about.

Gus   Here we go.

He turns on the jukebox again to play 'Glad All Over'. They all sing along.

Doors open.

Leslie   Yes, Shaun!

Trent   You bastard, yu . . .

It is **Selwyn** *and* **Fraser.** **Selwyn** *hobbles in on one foot.*

Selwyn   I don't know how you arse bandits are mistaking me for Shaun.

Gus   Is this some fucking joke?

He turns off the jukebox.

Leslie   Where the rass is this guy?

Selwyn   Shaun ain't here?

Gus   Does it look? (*Recognises* **Fraser** *immediately.*) Well, ain't dis a bitch.

Wa gwan, Selwyn?

Selwyn   My nephew. He's alright. Innit, bwoi?

Fraser   Yeah, I am fine, thank you very much.

Gus   This is a big man party we have going here, Selwyn, tonight! I got my place all set up for everyone.

Selwyn   Real nice by the way.

Gus   But you bring some lickle yout to it?

Fraser   I'm twenty.

Selwyn   Whoa there, yungsta, cool yer jets. No mind him, Gus.

Fraser   I'm old enough to drink, I am a big boy, I can tek care of myself.

Gus   True say you can, cos I didn't hear anybody say you have permission to talk.

Selwyn   Mouth shut, younger. What did I tell you?

Gus   Is this you being fresh, young one?

Fraser   Nuh man.

Selwyn   Leave the yout, Gus. Please?

Fraser   I didn't mean no offence.

Selwyn   How about you just wait in the car for me, yeah? Like I suggested to you in the first place?

Gus   You want him to stay in the car all night, Selwyn?

Selwyn   Well, it's kinda clear you do not want him here.

Gus   Did I say that? Trent, help me out here, did I say that?

Trent   Nuh man, you didn't.

Selwyn   Alright then.

Gus   You should really let the boy speak for himself yu nuh, Selwyn.

Fraser   Look, I mean no disrespect. I would really like to stay and hang with you guys, but I will go if you want me to.

Gus   What you tink, Les? Les? Earth calling Leslie?

Leslie   What, what you want?

Gus   Your attention on this if you don't mind.

Leslie   Fuck me, already.

Gus   What you have to say?

Leslie   I got nuttin to say.

Selwyn   His mind must be on the latest bit of ebony has home waiting for him. That's what it is.

Gus   Ain't you heard, Sel? He is getting it on with his probation officer.

Selwyn (*laughs out loud*)   Lawd Jesus!

Gus   He's a naughty boy, our Les.

Selwyn   A suit as well as an ebony. Gwan, Leslie!

Gus   She ain't no ebony.

Selwyn   Move yerself!

Leslie   You move!

Selwyn   No one love de black pum as well as you man, gw'y!

Leslie   I don't just like black, I don't know where the life of this is coming from, I really don't . . . Fucking hell and Jesus wept . . . she's a snowball.

Selwyn   White chick?

Leslie   Yes, Sel, white! So white, it mek you sick.

Selwyn   White don't mek me sick. Pum is pum mate, I ain't no racist.

Leslie   Well, I am happy to hear that, Sel, that makes me feel so much better about myself!

Selwyn   I don't know where you hear that from, that white makes me sick. No idea, at all.

Leslie   I happen to love her, alright?

Selwyn   Love?

Leslie   End of discussion, at least I hope it is. I really hope it is.

Gus   I know it's love, Les. Better believe it is love. You going off in a daydream like that. Gotta be love shit, the purest kind. Strongest kind, Celine Dion and all that.

Leslie   Oh, fuck off. See it deh.

Gus   (*to* **Fraser**) You want hang, hang, as long as you don't mind big man talk.

Fraser   The best kind.

Gus   So, which are you? Which one of Selwyn's sisters are you?

Selwyn   He don't come from that side, Gus. Two, twos, my dad's side he raise up in. That is where he come from. One of my dad's brother's kids or summin.

Gus   And does your dad brother's kid have a name?

Selwyn   Oh shame, only just realised. I didn't even say.

Gus   Well, you can say it now, can't you?

Fraser   Fraser.

Selwyn   Yes, yes, boys meet Fraser, Fraser, meet de man dem.

Fraser   Pleased to meet, honoured to be here.

Gus   Honoured?

Fraser   Well, yeah. It's ca it is you, I mean it is you, all of you in fact. It is, innit?

Gus   Innit what, what is?

Fraser   You're the firm right?

Gus   And what you think you know about our firm?

Fraser   Legends! Each and every one a' you.

Gus   So what bring you here?

Fraser   Just helping Selwyn here out, my uncle.

Gus   Out?

Selwyn (*holding up cans of beer*)   Wid these for one. This is a party, yes?

Gus   This is also a pub, as you can see.

Fraser   Yeah. I can see, nice.

Gus   Why you bringing a crate of beer to my yard, Sel?

Selwyn   I dunno, I just thought.

Gus   You didn't think.

Selwyn   We're having a session; we always have beer for a session.

Gus   Look at my bar, look around. I got the grand opening tomorrow night. But I wanted you here, I wanted my boys to be here. We had it all planned. Why don't you listen to me, why don't you ever listen to me?

Selwyn   Alright, man, sorry. Calm it down.

Fraser   Still a party though, yeah?

Leslie   With no guest of honour.

Fraser   Unlucky.

Selwyn   Come, Fraser. Back in a sec. We got more beers in the car. Well, we might as well bring them in. Dat alright, Gus?

Gus   Gwan den.

Selwyn   Come, Fraser.

Fraser *follows* **Selwyn** *out.*

Gus   I got enough drink flowing, and he brings beer!

Leslie   Take your tampon out, Gus, listen.

Gus   What?

Leslie   That's him.

Gus   Who, what, when, who?

Leslie   This kid Selwyn just bring in. Large as life. It's him.

Gus   Gonna need more than that, bruv.

Leslie   The kid I shared the room with. At the hostel! The yout!

Gus   Who him?

Leslie   I couldn't believe it at first.

Gus   For real?

Leslie   Breezing himself right in here, like he doesn't know me.

Gus   The same little fucker that was taking your shoes?

Leslie   Hiding my shoes.

Gus   But him that?

Leslie   Yes.

Gus   Him?

Leslie   Him, Gus, him!

Gus   Well, this is interesting.

Leslie   He must have a game going on.

Gus   Well, obviously. Breezing himself in here like he's summin. And him see you too. And he must know that. What kind of nonsense is this? We go find out what it is. His game.

Leslie   Well, whatever it is, just leave me out of it.

Gus   Leave you out of it?

Leslie   Whatever it is.

Gus   What the fuck are you going on about, whatever it is, Leslie? I haven't even done nothing yet, I ain't made a move or nuttin, am just merely speaking out loud and shit.

Leslie   Come on, Gus, we know how it go.

Gus   Oh really, Leslie, and what might that be? You tell me how it go?

Leslie   I don't want no trouble.

Gus   What trouble? Why do you think I want to do summin? I tell you, Leslie, you really are on a one-way ticket train ride to being a fully paid-up prime-time pussy, innit? This Claire . . .

Leslie   Jan!

Gus   It's what I said.

Leslie   You said Claire.

Gus   Oh fuck what her name is. Point is, you are well under manners!

Leslie   Yes, Gus, and I am loving it.

Gus   A shit yu a talk!

Leslie   Mind yer own.

Gus   You want focus here? Yes, or no? This kid has me curious. Him show up here. You know him. With all that, you are not in the slightest?

Leslie   Nope.

Gus   Pussy den.

Leslie   I'm sorry I opened my mouth.

Gus   Just answer me these two things, Les. Just two things. Why don't you wanna know what this little boy's game is?

Leslie   I don't want trouble. I'm done with that life. I promised Jan.

Gus   I don't see her here.

Leslie   A promise is a promise. You taught me that.

Gus *sucks his teeth.*

Leslie   Right. Second question?

Gus   For as long as we have both known Trent, coming on forty years if you can believe that, for as long as we can remember, I never known him to keep his mouth shut about anything. This is one brer who has made a religion of putting his nose in other people's business.

Leslie   What's the question, Gus?

Gus   Here's the question. Don't you think it's a little peculiar he has kept his mouth shut for so long, he ain't stepped in or anything like that, even now, when we are chatting his name?

Leslie   Alright, I give you that, that is strange.

They both look towards **Trent**.

Gus   Trent?

Trent   Lawd, Jesus.

Gus   He speaks! You have something to say to me, Trent? Do I want to hear it?

Trent   Yes, and no. But mostly, no.

Gus   I'm intrigued already. Come then.

Trent   The youngers I was having trouble with, earlier today, he was one of them.

Gus   Come again?

Trent   He was one of them boys, he had the biggest mouth as well.

Gus   How can you be so sure?

Trent   He got into my face, Gus.

Gus   The one who accuse you of eyeballing him? Him dat?

Trent   The very same, Gus, the one and only, without a doubt. The slightest!

Gus   Yes, alright, Trent.

Trent   You asked, you wanted to know, why I was all quiet.

Gus   Yes, now I can't get you to shut up. Let me think, nuh? Les?

Leslie   What now?

Gus   Are you just going to stand there, and go all silent again?

Leslie   Alright, then, it's ripe. What else you want me to say?

Gus   Some lickle yout is having his way with two of my boys? He has some jokes!

Selwyn *comes back in, carrying more beers.*

Selwyn   No, you are alright, boys. Don't even worry about giving the cripple a hand, you all just stand there like you case is about to come up. Trent, you've been putting on a bit of timber there, bro.

Trent (*sighs*)   And here it come.

Selwyn   Is it that hard to take the skin off the chicken? Hungry fer trut.

Trent   Why don't you go away and grow yourself a foot?

Selwyn (*grabs his own crotch*)   See mi foot deh?

Gus   Tell me about this kid of yours.

Selwyn   Not my kid, I know we all look alike.

Leslie (*chants*)   Oh, racist!

Gus   Alright then, this younger. Tell me about him.

Selwyn   I have told you.

Gus   I don't think you have, man.

Selwyn   Yes, I did. He's from my dad's side.

Gus   That's my point, Sel. I don't think he is a relation of yours.

Selwyn   Of course he is.

Gus   You sure about, no offence?

Selwyn   None taken, he's my blood, Gus, why would he lie about that?

Leslie   Yes, Sel, why would he lie?

Gus   You have officially got me and my head going, Selwyn.

Selwyn   Look, our paths crossed a few weeks back, at work of all places!

Trent   He work with you at the supermarket, Selwyn?

Selwyn   You don't have to say like that you know, Trent.

Trent   Like what, you fool?

Selwyn   'The supermarket'!

Trent   Oh cha!

Selwyn   Like I should be ashamed.

Trent   Well, are you?

Selwyn   It's a motherfucking job, so step.

Gus   Hey!

Trent   One question is all I ask.

Gus   Trent!

Trent   And he gets the arsehole like always.

Selwyn   Yer fat fucker, yu.

Trent (*holds his crotch*)   See it deh?

Gus   Are the two of you done? Selwyn, tell me about this yout?

Leslie   Two twos, Sel.

Selwyn   Alright. Like I was saying, we met at work. He was shopping and shit, saw me, then stepped towards. Telling me he thinks we are related and shit I ask how, he explains he is my Uncle Carl's middle son, from his first marriage. He gimme dates and stats, all seem pucker, above board and that.

Leslie   You never gave a fart about your dad's lot.

Selwyn   I still don't.

Gus   So, why you reach for him?

Selwyn   Business of course, what else?

Leslie   Business?

Selwyn   The best kind, the kind of business we do, or at least we used to.

Leslie   Did it ever occur to you, Selwyn, he may have found out all that shit about yer family?

Selwyn   Yes, thank you, Leslie, it did.

Leslie   A lie you a' tell, man.

Selwyn (*holds his crotch*)   See it deh, suck it nuh!

Gus   What is this, are we fucking infants now?

Selwyn   It did occur, but why lie? What is there to be gained from that, someone, tell me?

Gus   You said business?

Selwyn   Yeah, man, big business.

Gus   Not the same business that you have been going on and on about, Selwyn?

Selwyn   I brought him here because I thought you need persuading.

Gus   Are you telling me this is the boys' ting?

Leslie   He don't look a day over eighteen, Sel. And him tink he bright already?

Selwyn   I know; I couldn't believe it first when I hear him chat. We are talking some serious wedge here, Gus.

Trent   How much?

Gus   Oh, he speaks again! You want in now, Trent?

Trent   I want to hear first, is that not allowed?

Gus   You should want in to buss this kid's head in.

Selwyn   For what?

Gus   Tell him.

Trent   Me and this kid of yours we had a run-in, earlier today.

Leslie   Him and some youngers were troubling him.

Trent   They weren't troubling me!

Leslie   It's what you said.

Trent   He didn't like the way I eyeballed him. That's it. End of.

Selwyn   Why are you surprised?

Gus   Surprised?

Selwyn   Well, they are all like that these days

Gus   Is this you defending them, Selwyn?

Selwyn   I am only stating a fact, Gus.

Gus   A fact, is it now?

Selwyn   Alright then not a fact merely an observation. An observation about what these youts like to go on wid.

Gus   The kind of youths who do supermarkets, Selwyn?

Selwyn   Yes.

Gus   The kind of youts round that know nothing apart burn up shop in Charlton and teif shoe, cha rass!

Selwyn   That nonsense was six years ago, Gus, it was nothing worse than what we done. Brixton '85, anyone?

Trent   Now, that was a session.

Leslie   Yeah, an entire fleet of Maggie's boys chasing us up Brixton Hill.

Trent   We gave them a spanking.

Leslie   They gave us a spanking.

Selwyn   About the boy, I say he is alright. He rolls with the BMC.

Gus   The what? Who?

Selwyn   Bare Money Crew. They're the top firm around here.

Gus   Oh, are they now?

Selwyn   He's their top boy.

Gus   What, him? Oh, do me one, will yer?

Selwyn   I asked around, he checks out.

Gus   Stop before you cream yourself. (*To* **Leslie** *and* **Trent**.) Any of this mek sense to you?

Trent   BMC are hardcore, Gus.

Gus   So, what do the BMC want wid us, ca' they deh fucking up my night here.

Trent (*calls*)   Come on, Shaun, anytime now, mate!

Leslie   You sure he's on the level, Sel?

Selwyn   Word is, yeah.

Leslie   Word is? Don't you know for sure?

Selwyn   How am I supposed to know for sure?

Leslie   Ask around nuh?

Selwyn   What do you think I did?

Leslie   You said 'word is'. Sounds like you were playing Chinese whispers or summin.

Selwyn   I was told, by those on the in, he's a top boy. What more you want? Gus, all I am saying to you is hear him out?

Gus   Saying? Sounds like you begging to me, Selwyn.

Trent   True dat.

Selwyn   Trent, could you spend one day without kissing Gus's arse? Do you think that it's possible? Just one?

Trent   Tek yer pills, yu nuthead.

Selwyn   Gus? You go hear him out, man?

Gus   Oh, I will, backwards and forwards, cover to cover, will I hear him out. I'm gonna weigh him in. Ware him deh?

Selwyn   He's still outside. He had to take a call.

Gus   Well, unless it's Rihanna him chat to, it's time he wrapped it up, bring his arse in for me. Like right now, Sel.

Selwyn   Yeah, on it, man.

He goes.

Gus   Gonna get to the bottom of this fun and games, that's for sure.

Leslie   Careful now, Gus, you might start enjoying this shit again.

Gus   Livvy got ghosted out from the Scrubs, right?

Leslie   Six months ago.

Gus   You think he might know where Shaun is at?

Leslie   Shaun weren't in Scrubs wid him that long.

Gus   Call him anyway. See if he knows anything.

Fraser *follows* **Selwyn** *in carrying more beer.*

Fraser   Dayz, bruv, you have enough here for a week, let alone a night.

He can feel all eyes on him.

Summin I can help you wid?

Gus   Is there a problem you have, Fraser?

Fraser   A problem?

Gus   Yes, you yungsta, do you have a problem here?

Fraser   Do you think I have a problem, Gus?

Gus   Sorry, I forget. You don't like being eyeballed, do you, Fraser?

Fraser   Say? Sorry?

Gus   Nuh, man, it is I who should be sorry. Seeing as you are Selwyn's family and that. We ain't had a proper intro and shit.

I'm Gus. This is Trent, who you met earlier today, and of
course you know Leslie, seeing as the two were room buddies.

Selwyn   Say what?

Fraser   Oh, didn't I say?

Selwyn   No you rhatid well didn't.

Fraser   Did you ever find your shoe yet, Leslie?

Selwyn   Alright, what is this, wa gwan, younger?

Fraser   Nothing much.

Gus   Nothing much, he says.

Leslie   I don't like people touching my shoes.

Gus   And Trent. Tell him about Trent.

Selwyn   Yes, tell me about Trent.

Fraser   Just a couple of my brers trying it on.

Trent   You all bloody were.

Fraser   Just messing bredren, nothing personal, I swear.
I could see how upset you were.

Trent   Now hold up.

Fraser   I told them all to dial it down, didn't you hear?

Gus   You never said that, Trent.

Trent (*panicking*)   I know!

Fraser   None of them meant to make you feel afraid, Trent.

Trent   Afraid?

Gus   You said.

Trent   Yes, Gus, I know.

Gus   So yes or fucking no then, Trent? Were you scared?

Trent   No.

Gus   So, how come he?

Trent   I can't help what this younger is going wid.

Fraser   Maybe I should go?

Gus   Maybe you should stay right where you are, younger. And I mean, right there.

Fraser   If you insist.

Leslie   Oh he does. Best not forget.

Fraser   I didn't, I wasn't, I mean look at you, Durnfield boys, every one of you. Top-notch firm in all of South.

Gus   I know it can't be just me, but I can't help but feel you are tekin the piss a little.

Fraser   What do you think?

Gus   I am thinking that you have a game here.

Fraser   Good one, is there more?

Gus   You make a move on Leslie, then you start on Trent, now Selwyn. What is it about us you find so fascinating? What up wid that?

Fraser   I don't mean no disrespect. I just wanted to know what you lot were all about, that's all.

Selwyn   Tell me summin, are we fam or not?

Fraser   Do we even look like fam?

Selwyn   I thought so, especially around the eyes.

Fraser   Give it up, Selwyn, I played you.

Gus   So, why?

Fraser   Why do you think, Gus?

Selwyn   Yer lucky I don't hand you yer own arse.

Fraser *laughs.*

Gus   Boy thinks it joke!

Fraser Well, it was, wasn't it? I mean no offence, Selwyn, but I don't fight cripples.

Trent True say you don't know Selwyn, innit Gus? They don't call Sel crunch fer nuttin.

Gus You know why they call him Sel crunch, boy?

Fraser I think I am about to.

Gus Whenever we tooled up for an encounter, a session –

Leslie And there was many.

Gus Selwyn here would have the guy down, and he would crunch, not bite, but crunch the brer's ear. Do you know what an ear looks like when it gets crunched by Selwyn? Like a cornflake.

Fraser That's some nastiness, right there.

Gus Is that all you can say?

Fraser I needed to get close, meeting Leslie was coincidental. I couldn't believe it at first. It was like God's way of saying, I should do this ting.

Gus What *ting*?

Fraser I chose to make it personal with you, Selwyn, sorry. Look, I know we can do some business together.

Gus The job?

Leslie The same job you have been talking Gus's ear off about, Sel? No one does supermarkets any more. If you knew us all as well as you claim, you would know we never did. That shit wasn't for us.

Fraser You never took things that didn't belong to yer? You were a bunch of fucking teifs.

Gus You wanna watch yer mout for me?

Fraser Are you telling or asking?

Gus True talk now, supermarket is a joke, yes? It has to be.

Fraser   I never said supermarket. Selwyn, what you bin saying, man?

Selwyn   Move yourself from me now.

Fraser   Not a problem.

Selwyn (*warns*)   Hear me.

Trent   I beg you. younger, hear him.

Fraser   Hard not to.

Gus   If it's not a supermarket, then what? What is it?

Fraser   It's a woman.

Gus   A woman?

Fraser   Let me explain.

Gus   I think you had better.

Fraser   She works in the supermarket, same one as Sel.

Selwyn   Selwyn to you.

Fraser   Every Friday, Selwyn says he sees her, putting all the takings together. It should be two of them working in the office, but it's run by a couple of Sikhs, too tight-fisted to have someone working with her, leaving her on her own, a woman. By the time she gets around to it, there must be about ten grand in there at least. Woman is one dem you know . . .

Gus   No, I don't know.

Fraser   Scared ones, innit, Sel? Selwyn. You said.

Gus   Never mind Sel, carry on.

Fraser   One a' dem, who clutch their handbags like their life depended on it whenever they see us. So you know?

Gus   Know what?

Fraser   We go in and we reach her. One look from us and she will give it up, quick smart.

Gus   And what if she doesn't?

Fraser   She will.

Gus   But what if she doesn't, Fraser?

Fraser   She will.

Gus   I am getting so arse-bored with people not answering my questions tonight, what if she doesn't? What would you expect us to do then?

Fraser   What do you think?

Gus   Tell me.

Fraser   Come on, you know.

Gus   No, I don't know.

Fraser   Well, you shut her up, innit?

Leslie   Shut her up?

Fraser   Yes.

Gus   You mean hurt her? You want us to hurt this woman, is that right, Fraser?

Fraser   It won't come to that.

Gus   Yes or no, my young friend, if she, this woman, can't keep her tail quiet, do you expect us to hurt her?

Fraser   Well yeah. Alright then, yeah. I expect you to handle the bitch.

Gus   Mind yerself.

Fraser   I expect you to hurt her. I expect you to shut her mouth and keep it shut for her. Is that clear enough for you?

Gus   Tell me summin. What exactly do you think should be happening to you, right now?

Fraser   I am not here to make a fool of you. We all know how much of a legend you are in these parts. Before you went legit. How many businesses you own now?

Leslie   Six, that we know of.

Gus   Never mind me, young one. It's the brers behind me.

Fraser   OK then, you all have reps this big.

Trent   Believe that.

Fraser   I have to say though, I ain't impressed.

Gus *delivers a hard blow in* **Fraser***'s stomach.* **Fraser** *drops like a heap.*

Leslie   Jesus, Gus!

Gus   You impressed yet? You didn't see that coming right, not a whiff.

Trent   Yes! How you feel now, bitch?

Fraser*, completely winded by that punch, struggles to breathe.*

Gus   Get up, bwoi, carrying on like it hurt. Don't make a big ting about this yeah?

Leslie   You'll be alright, yungsta, just tek a breather, yeah?

Fraser   Fuck off, man.

Leslie   Hey mind yerself.

Fraser   You mind yerself! We brers or summin?

Trent   Listen, like he's the dogs.

Gus   Coming in here, of all nights, to my place, a special night for us, insulting our ears with some dumb-arse plan! You ain't no top boy! BMC, don't mek me laugh. If yer so hard core, how come you ain't reached for me yet? I just put you down, bwoi, but instead of flinging yerself at me, yu stand there like yer about to cry or something, gw'y!

Fraser   That's gonna cost you, nigga.

The air in the room freezes

Gus   Bwoi, you have any idea how many tear-ups we've had over the years, with mouthy skinheads with gobs this big, that we introduced to the business end of a piece of two-by-four timber, who couldn't shut up from calling us that? And don't even get me started on Maggie's boys.

Selwyn So who are you then? (*Rages.*) From which blood claart you creep down from?

Trent Sel?

Gus On yer way bwoi, now.

Fraser That's not very nice, Gus.

Gus Move.

Selwyn I wanna know first.

Gus No, you don't.

Leslie I thought you wanted to know what his play is.

Gus Bwoi nuttin but a joke, man.

Fraser Is that why, Gus? Is that why, ca I was a joke. Or was it cos I was a mistake? That's what yu said to her, innit?

Leslie Her?

Gus Bwoi, don't mek me tell yu again.

Selwyn Who's yer mudda?

Fraser Tell him, Gus.

Gus Will you just forget dis fool.

Selwyn Who, fer fuck . . . ?

Leslie Come, bwoi, show us some brief.

Fraser Tina Hardy. Ring a bell to any of you?

Trent Tina Hardy?

Leslie Sam's sister? You were on it wid her, Gus?

Gus I was on it wid a whole heap, how am I supposed to remember?

Leslie   Are you winding me up? Sam Hardy's lickle sister, Gus?

Gus   What about her?

Leslie   The one who got herself up the spout when she was still at school, that was you? Gus, answer me nuh, was that you?

Trent   Dis yer yout, Gus? Him yer bwoi?

Gus   He ain't nuttin to me.

Fraser   That I do know.

Leslie   Why didn't you tell us straight up?

Selwyn (*to* **Fraser**)   Why didn't you tell me?

Gus   More to the point, Selwyn, you didn't tek one look at this bwoi and realise this was jokes? Did they amputate your brain as well as your foot?

Trent   Soff!

Gus   Soff? I don't know what the H you are coming out wid big man?

Trent   Gus, what?

Gus (*mocks*)   Gus, what? Getting all scared and shit ca some lickle yout's face you off!

Trent   I wasn't afraid.

Gus   So you say, so you lie. And Leslie?

Leslie   Yes, my turn.

Gus   Like you know it all.

Leslie   What's your question now, Gus?

Gus   You don't have summin to say, come on, white boy, speak to me.

Leslie   Leave me the fuck alone.

Gus   You is soff!

Leslie   She was fifteen.

Gus   She was sixteen, nearly.

Leslie   You were twenty-eight.

Gus   We did nothing wrong.

Leslie   You sure?

Gus   What's yer beef, man? I had time for Tina.

Trent   True say you did.

Gus   She was bright.

Leslie   You mean she was fit.

Gus   We're done talking about her, understood?

Fraser (*mocks*)   The Durnfield boys!

Gus   You feel like getting hurt again?

Trent   Must be.

Fraser   You are such a tough man, Trent, especially when you are standing near Gus, you fat bastard. Is that why you let yourself go, cos you couldn't compete?

Trent (*snaps*)   One more jibe about my weight, yeah?

Gus   Trent?

Trent   From anybody! One more!

Gus   Selwyn, while this lickle fassyhole is still breathing and able to walk, take his rass neck back to wherever you find him and keep him deh. Leslie, hello, you call Livvy yet?

Leslie   I got a text, he ain't seen him.

Gus   Find Gerry then. Call Gerry. Gerry Cleary, Les.

Leslie   Yeah, I know who Gerry is, Gus, thank you. (*Points to* **Fraser**.) But aren't you forgetting summin?

Gus   Sel, did I not say throw this boy's arse out?

Leslie   Is he yours or not?

Gus   I don't blasted know. Maybe.

Leslie   I don't see what the problem is.

Gus   You never do, mate.

Leslie   If he's yer bwoi, claim him for fuck

Fraser   Yeah, come on, Gus, claim me.

Gus   This bwoi!

Selwyn   Him an eeeedyat!

Fraser   Yes, well this eeeedyat have your attention now, innit?

Gus *goes for* **Fraser** *again.*

Fraser   Come then, finish me off, I promise you, the biggest mistake you will make, nigga!

Selwyn   Enough wid that word.

Fraser   What, 'nigga'?

Gus   Bitch mout like yer mudda.

Leslie   Him yer bwoi? Yes or no? Just say it, Gus.

Gus   Alright, him mine, so what?

Trent   You is Sam Hardy's nephew? Lawd Jesus!

Gus   I thought you went over the river, live by Chiswick way?

Fraser   Mum move back six months ago to care for Sam. I grew up hearing stories about you, how he rolled with you lot, the firm! Long before he had Aunty Sharon and Mum wiping his arse for him, that is.

Leslie   So, why didn't you tell us straight up who you were?

Fraser   Well, seeing the way you all left things with Sam when you last see him, I thought that was obvious. One minute the lot of you are tight as a drum, the next he gets mashed up in the head, and none of you go visit him in hospital, or at home. I mean, what is that?

Gus   Grown-up tings.

Selwyn   So about this supermarket?

Gus   Lawd Jesus, Sel, there is no supermarket.

Selwyn   I work there.

Gus   We ain't no harming no woman.

Selwyn   Who said anything about harming her, you heard what the boy said.

Gus   Are you sure? You want to up your dosage, Sel.

Fraser   I say it can work.

Gus   Who tell you to speak, you have a say?

Fraser   Sel is in, who else? Les?

Leslie   I am more curious that you did not tell us about Tina. Not a whiff, Gus.

Gus   Him my bwoi, we have the same blood, what more you want?

Fraser   Thanks for that.

Leslie   Schoolgirl or no, when she started to grow a pair, nearly every bro in the manner had half a mind to get it on wid that.

Fraser   You know I am standing right here.

Gus   She was a kid, Les.

Leslie   That didn't seem to stop you. In fact, I seem to recall you warning the entire firm that no one goes near, no one even thinks. Yet you slide on in without saying a word?

Gus   Yes, Les, summin like that.

Fraser   So, we go do dis ting?

Gus   Some one tek this bwoi out before I do summin.

Leslie   We don't hurt civilians, Fraser, we never did.

Selwyn   Not exactly true is it, though, Les?

Gus   Selwyn, shut up, man.

Fraser   Say?

Selwyn   It's ca' of what happened, innit?

Leslie   Sel!

Selwyn   It's why you want me to shut up?

Fraser   What happened?

Gus   Nuttin.

Trent   Leave it, boy.

Fraser   I want know.

Selwyn   I don't see a boy here, I see man, and he want know.

Gus   Sel, tek yer arse and sit down. (*To* **Fraser**.) And you, I'm gonna give you ten seconds to jog on.

Fraser   Bit late in the day for you to be barking orders.

Gus   Five seconds.

Selwyn   This is about the betting shop.

Leslie   Shut yer mout, Sel!

Selwyn   I thought we were done with that shit. I thought we were past that.

Fraser   You chatting about Sam's betting shop? The time he got robbed? Oh my . . . Was that you lot?

Gus   No, it wasn't us lot, it was this lot.

Leslie   Here it comes. Again!

Gus   Nuttin but a bunch of damn stupid eddyatts.

Leslie   Sam wasn't supposed to be there, what do you want? (*To* **Fraser**.) He wasn't supposed to be there, yungsta.

Trent   It was proper madness; we were going on wid back then.

Fraser   You know, Aunty Sharon always had a feeling you lot had summin to do with that.

Gus   So, what you want, we say sorry, summin like that?

Fraser   I couldn't give two licks about that place, or Sam for that matter. I barely know him. He'd come in and out of my life like a cold. I only had time for him was when he would tell me about rolling with you lot. Happiest days of his life, so I could never understand, for the life, how he gave up everything wid you, to open blasted bookies! You shoulda slapped him hard when he was coming out with that noise. How could he give you up? Shoulda slapped him. Hard!

Leslie   He's paying for it now, don't you think?

Fraser   I don't give a fuck.

Leslie   You didn't rate him?

Fraser   How could I rate a man like that?

Gus   But you rate us?

Fraser   Remains to be seen.

Gus   Do the job yerself if yu tink yer so bright.

Fraser   I need summin.

Gus   What that, a hug?

Fraser   A rep.

Gus   You want a rep?

Fraser   Wid the BMC fer fuck.

Leslie   We thought you rolled with them?

Gus   That you lead dem?

Fraser　Can be and will be. If we do dis ting, they are bound to recruit me, they will have to.

Gus　Well. I have heard all shit now.

Fraser　You owe me, bredren.

Gus　Don't call me bredren. I don't owe you jack.

Fraser　Come on, Sel, I know yer game.

Gus　You don't speak to him.

Selwyn　You don't speak for me, Gus.

Gus　You want do this shit? For real?

Selwyn　Maybe I need to

Gus　You don't need to, no one needs to, not that bad.

Selwyn　I do, Gus.

Gus　When have I ever not funded you, Sel. When have I ever not sorted you out large, for anyting?

Selwyn　Fuck yer funds, Gus.

Leslie　Power down, nuh.

Selwyn　Leave me alone, Les. This ain't about you, Gus.

Gus　So what then? Wa' gwan.

Selwyn　That blood-claart supermarket, and everyone in it. It's graft man, fer trut. 'Excuse me, I said excuse? Tell me which way it is to the deli counter.' They don't even bother asking, they don't even say please? 'Do you have fromage frais, light fromage frais I should say?' 'Would you mind going into your store room to see if you have any fennel left.' 'I went to the aisle as you said, but I still cannot find a can of pulses, only butter beans and chickpeas. I asked for pulses, do you even know what they are?' Listen yeah, I don't give a fucking blue-arsed rass about yer can of pulses, fuck yer can of pulses! Fuck it! Fuck off out of my face wid yer pulses. Tek yer pulses and ram dem up yer hole, bitch! You know how much dough me and my firm earned on a good day, bitch, enough to buy us a shop full of pulses, each! So step now before you know what is fucking good. Gus, it is everything in me not to tell them about themselves, every rhatid day! Tha, my friend, is *what gwan*.

Trent   Sel, come on, think this shit through.

Selwyn   You know, you ain't so bright these days yu nuh, Trent?

Trent   What?

Selwyn   When was the last time you grafted, and I mean serious grafting?

Trent   I'm doing alright.

Selwyn (*mocks*)   Doing alright! When was the last time you had some proper corn in the palm of your hand, Trent?

Fraser   We're talking ten large here, Trent.

Trent   We don't hurt people, Sel.

Fraser   You hurt Sam. Corn is corn, right? That's all there is, that what it's all about. You want it, you know you want it, you are sweating all over for it.

Leslie   Listen to him chat so, Gus's bwoi.

Gus   He ain't my bwoi.

Fraser   Gotta be worth a try, Leslie?

Leslie   My turn now?

Fraser   What do you have so bright, that you pass up this?

Gus   A woman.

Fraser   She must be some woman for you to look yer nose down on ten large.

Leslie   There are a hundred other ways to earn yourself a rep, Fraser.

Fraser (*defensive*)   Yeah, I know.

Leslie   Yet you choose this one.

Fraser   One wid less risks, no one gets hurt.

Gus   Where have I heard that before?

Leslie *goes behind the bar, pours out a couple of whiskey shots.*

Gus   Pardon fucking me, Les, but Les, what you doing?

Leslie   Pouring your boy a drink, man. And don't tell me you don't drink, you want play wid man, right here so. Step up. Show me summin.

Fraser *downs his shot in one. Then another.*

Fraser   Bring it.

Leslie *pours another.* **Fraser** *downs it again.* **Fraser** *wants another.*

Leslie   You sure?

Fraser   Are you lame or summin?

Leslie *pours one more.* **Fraser** *downs it again.*

Gus   Well that's OK then. Boy turn man now. He get a bit of hair on his chest. So, let's all go out and do this ting. Yeah! Never mind the fact it's a dumb-arse plan, and we find ourselves back inside again.

Leslie   Again?

Gus   Doing at least ten years' bird.

Leslie   You've never done time, Gus.

Gus   So, what you telling me, Les, you want this to go tits up, so it will be a first for me?

Leslie   Who said I was going along? I'm with you, bruv, it's a shirt-arse plan. Two grand a man? That won't even keep you in cufflinks. I'm just getting to know yer boy here. I just want to know, why you never told us about you and Tina?

Gus   I don't know why.

Leslie   A lie yu a' tell.

Trent   The only time you keep shit to yourself is when it's too important to you.

Gus   Oh, is that right, Trent, thank you for making that so clear to me.

Leslie   Is that what it was, Gus, Tina was important to you?

Fraser   So important, I ain't seen his arse for fifteen years.

Leslie   'Seen'?

Gus   The fun's over, boy.

Leslie   Hold up. (*To* **Fraser**.) How old are you?

Fraser   I'm old enough, yeah,

Leslie   How old?

Fraser   Twenty.

Leslie   So, the last time you see him, you were five?

Gus   Is there a point coming this year, Les?

Leslie   You didn't tell us.

Gus   I think we have established that.

Leslie   Not only did you fool around wid Tina –

Gus   It wasn't like that.

Leslie   – but you had a yout wid her, a yout you knew about.

Fraser   He took me out sometimes.

Gus   Who tell you to speak?

Fraser   The park, I remember the park.

Trent   Durnfield Park?

Leslie   You never told us.

Gus   Get off it, Les.

Fraser   We would play football, one on one. I remember, he got me a football top. It must have been my birthday or summin.

Leslie   Your birthday?

Gus (*warns*)   Les?

Trent   What football top was it?

Selwyn   The next two words that leave your lips had better be Crystal Palace.

Fraser   What you take me for, Sel?

Selwyn   Hear him call me Sel now!

Fraser   I'm an Eagle through and through.

Selwyn   'S right then, as long as we are clear. On the same page.

Gus   We are nowhere near on the same page here.

Leslie   That is no way to talk your yout, Gus, now is it?

Fraser   Am used to it.

Gus   What him say? Used to it?

Fraser   Used to you not being around.

Gus   Oh man, fuck off with that please?

Fraser   You told her you were bored, you had yer fun, didn't want to know, yes or no?

Gus   Oh well, then it must be true then.

Leslie   You said it weren't like that.

Gus   Why don't you find out where Shaun is instead of digging your nose in my business?

Trent   At least you made him a Palace boy. You got that right.

Gus   As opposed to what, Trent?

Trent   I dunno, Gus, sometimes I feel –

Gus   Feel what?

Trent   That you're Millwall in disguise.

Gus (*holds his crotch*)   See it deh, suck it nuh.

Fraser   Oh man, this is it, innit?

Trent   This is what?

Gus   What you want now?

Fraser   The banter. Sam said you were all full of it, you could go at it all night long. On the *wall*.

Selwyn   The *wall*!

Trent (*reminisces*)   Our fucking *wall*, man.

Leslie   They knocked it down

Trent   I know they knock it down, I got eyes, Les.

Leslie (*grabs his crotch*)   See it deh!

Fraser   Tell me about it, tell me about the *wall*? While we are waiting for Shaun.

Gus   We? Four shots of Rémy, don't mek yu a man yu nuh, it doesn't mek you one of us.

Fraser   Aright, whilst *yer* waiting for Shaun, better fer you?

Gus   Don't let me tump yu again, yungsta.

Fraser   No way will I let you.

Gus   Leave now, whilst you can.

Leslie   He ain't going anywhere.

Gus   I don't want to hear one more sound of pussy talk coming from you, Leslie, you hear me?

Leslie   He's yer bwoi, I want to know him, even if you don't. How's that for pussy talk?

Gus   Well, Leslie has some jokes tonight.

Leslie   Tell Fraser about the *wall*, Trent.

Trent   Why me?

Leslie   Ca' you were there first, tell him.

Fraser   Oh yes, come on, gimme a tale.

Trent   The *wall* was our life; you understand? From the top of Albert Street Park till where the old church is. That four-foot high, forty-feet long, beautiful fucking *wall*, man. I'm eleven years old, first day of my new school, as I stepped in, I see Shaun. And he wants to fight me. I don't know why, I never clapped eyes on him before but he wants to fight me.

Selwyn   He just didn't like the look of yer.

Trent   He was the school crazy. Every school had one, and he was ours. It was my first day, I didn't want to fight, get my uniform all torn up, fucking hell. But I'm on his radar, he's got me in his sights, how do I get out of this, I thought, then my big sister steps in.

The guys laugh as they remember this.

Donna, God rest her soul. As big as me, my family, we are all built. We're stacked. She gives him one tump and he goes flying. Now, it was the first day at school, like I said.

Gus   Two twos, Trent.

Trent   I'm going as fast. As I say, first day at school. Not many people around. Shaun is not recovering at all from getting knocked out by my sister, he could barely stand up, crying like a bitch gal, begging me not to tell anyone what happened. That sister of mine could tump though, like a man, Jesus! Her and her iron fist. She'd size you up, then boosh! And I am talking about a first-class arse-whopping deluxe-combo meal, Mike Tyson style wid a side of fries – boosh, I promise you!

Gus (*losing patience*)   Trent?

Trent   Alright. Anyway, as a sign of appreciation for keeping quiet about him getting turned over by a gal, Shaun offers to take me to the *wall*, where his big brother Tommy liked to hang wid his boys, his crew. Shaun was their dogsbody, he would get their fags from the Paki shop, hold their coats, send messages, get people on the phone for them from the phone box, see that kid at the beginning of *Goodfellas*, just like him. And for all that, he would get funded. Fiver here, tenner there. Shaun told his brother, I was with him, so I would get funded as well while they worked.

Fraser   So, what did they do for work?

Trent   Everyting! Daily, nightly, cars would pull up, all kinds of trading was happening, bit of burn, pirate videos, credit cards, bottles of booze, stereos, rings, watches, name it, bruv. The best oysters and creepers from all over the manor would congregate to the *wall* most days, they'd buy, trade and feast, all night long. You'd juggle with whatever came your way. When Tommy got sent down for a ten, his crew started to scatter. Shaun and me were growing, we got to know these three (*Points to* **Gus**, **Leslie** *and* **Selwyn**.) from the children's home, soon we spent more time on the *wall* than at the home. Before we know it, this van pulls up, belonging to the Barton youth club, these boys jump out, sit on the *wall*, our *wall*, trying to move us along saying it's theirs now. Shaun weren't having it, as far as he could see, Tommy gave him that *wall* to look after till he got out. He be fucked if he was giving it up to a bunch of wannabe rugby-playing poofs! One of those Barton boys looked useful, though, really fucking. I go to Shaun, maybe we could share it, it's a long enough *wall*. Truth is, my rear end is puckering.

The guys laugh at the thought.

This Barton boy was glaring. Shaun was glaring. I'm standing in the middle of them with my arse this much away from a full evacuation. Before I know it, Shaun whips out this monkey wrench and pummels this Barton boy's face in. 'Have summa that,' he goes. No one knew what day it was, especially them

Barton boys. They just took their man and drove off, they never bothered us again. Shaun had earned his first rep, he was the talk of the manor for weeks! To this day, I have no idea where he was hiding that wrench on his person and how he whipped it out so fast. It was like it was attached to his arm or summin.

Leslie   Robo–Shaun!

Selwyn   I had both of my feet then.

Trent   That's it, Sel, bring it down for me.

Selwyn   I'm not bringing it down – fuck off, man, I'm agreeing wid yer. We was top.

Gus   I hate that word *was*, enough of it.

Selwyn   From the time.

Leslie   It was a good memory, Gus, don't spoil it, yeah?

Gus   How am I spoiling it, Les?

Leslie   You weren't even there, you were off somewhere, tapping Andrea weren't it? Or Tina, as it now appears.

Gus   I wish I was there, I should have been there. Sorted you total bell-ends out.

Leslie   Sorted out what? The Barton boys got a hiding.

Gus   It should never have got that far.

Leslie   There is no pleasing you, is there Gus? Gotta make us feel we can't do nuttin without you.

Gus   You want to ease up on the booze for me, Les?

Leslie (*to* **Trent** *and* **Selwyn**)   Why don't you two speak up for once?

Trent   You have been knocking them back, Les.

Leslie   Not me, Gus! Tell him how it go.

Gus   Well come on then, Trent? Sel? Tell me how it go? What you have fer me?

Leslie   They won't.

Selwyn   I can speak for myself, Leslie.

Leslie   So speak! Gwan nuh.

He gets a message on his phone. He reads it.

That's from Gerry, he ain't seen Shaun either. I wish Shaun was here right now. He should be here.

Gus   Why? What's Shaun going to do, what's he going to say?

Leslie   Go tell you about you about yourself for one thing. Give it to you straight, like always, both barrels, in yer face, right deh so!

Gus   You give it to me, whatever this is, come!

Leslie (*points to* **Fraser**)   Why did you not tell us about him, Gus? Sam's sister, of all the gals you could have had. Why her?

Fraser   Yes, Gus, why her?

Gus   Don't mek me hurt you again, younger.

Fraser   I wouldn't try that.

Gus   Like you have a say in any of this.

Trent   Look, why don't I do a drive around again, find Shaun? (*To* **Fraser**.) Easy, puppy.

Fraser   Puppy? You had an absolute mare with my boys today innit, Trent? Since I come in here, you can barely look at me.

Trent   Fuck off, young one, right now. No offence, Gus.

Gus   For what, he ain't nuttin to me, yer deaf?

Leslie   Your *boys*, Fraser?

Fraser   For real.

Leslie   But you are not *their* boy.

Gus   More like yer their bitch.

Fraser (*rages*)   What yu say!

Gus   I say bitch! B-I-T-C-H.

Fraser   Fuckin –

Gus   Don't rise up, unless yer put up!

Leslie   Hate to say, Fraser, but yer old man has a point. What were you inside for?

Fraser   Breaking and entering, assault with an offensive weapon.

Leslie   First time? Don't lie.

Fraser   Who's lying? First time, what of it?

The guys laugh.

What, what of it?

Leslie   No one ever gets caught doing summin for the first time.

Gus   Unless yer schupid!

Leslie   I can't get out of bed without groaning or feel summin inside of me is creaking, he wants to lead us out on a job. We're too old for this shit.

Fraser   You're still the firm!

Leslie   Firm of what? We got cameras everywhere now, CCTV and shit. The days of a good honest creep are gone. It's in the past, young one.

Selwyn   Why can't it be now?

Trent   Sel. Sit down.

Selwyn   Why can't it be again?

Gus (*to* **Selwyn**)   You go sit down, tek yer pills, and forget about this rhatid supermarket. (*Points to* **Fraser**.) As soon as this boy jogs on, like right fucking now. We go find Shaun, then we go do what we said we'd do, have a mighty session, drinks all round, *capice*?

Selwyn *loses it, grabs a stool and throws it across the room, then smashes some bottles along the bar.*

Gus   What the fuck is dis huh!

Selwyn   I said, why can't it be now, why can't it be again?

Gus   Lawd, help me put this fucker down!

Trent   It's alright, Gus.

Gus   I ain't alright, look what him do to my yard.

Trent   Let me handle him.

Selwyn *grabs a chair leg and begins waving it around in a frenzy.*

Selwyn   You don't speak me for me, Trent. We go do this ting, we go show everyone, who we are, Durnfield, yer understand?

Leslie   Sel?

Selwyn   No fucker go leave here till we do.

Trent   Sel, look at me, look at me, man.

Gus   Yer gonna clean this shit up.

Trent   Gus, I got this.

Selwyn   No one.

Trent   Sel! Look at me. Look at me, mate.

Selwyn *looks at him.*

Trent   Come on, bruv, you know what's next, do it for me. Do it, Sel.

Selwyn *shuts his eyes.*

Trent   This space right here, this is yours . . . This belongs to you, yeah?

Selwyn   Yeah.

Trent   Yer safe in your space, no one can trouble you in your space.

Selwyn   I won't let anyone trouble me in my space.

Trent   Is your space, yer safe, Sel, safe.

Selwyn   Safe, safe!

Trent *slowly takes the chair leg away from* **Selwyn**. *He sits him down and cradles him, almost like a child.*

Selwyn   I am safe in my space.

Trent   Yer safe. Let's do the chant. Come on. (*Ever so softly.*) *Everywhere we go.*

Selwyn   *Everywhere we go.*

Trent   *People wanna know.*

Selwyn   *People wanna know.*

Trent   *Who we are.*

Selwyn   *Who we are.*

Trent   *Shall we tell them?*

Selwyn   *Shall we tell them?*

Trent   *We know our manners.*

Selwyn   *We know our manners.*

Trent   *We fight with spanners.*

Selwyn   *We fight with spanners . . .*

Trent/Selwyn   *We are respected, wherever we go. Doors and windows open wide, open wide! We are the Durnfield boys, once again, we are the Durnfield boys!*

Trent   Peace.

Selwyn's *eyes remain closed.* **Trent** *leaves him to rest and turns round to face the others.*

Leslie   Nice.

Trent   He shouldn't drink so much. It messes up his medication.

Gus   It tek him to trash my yard for you to say that?

Trent   I'll fund you for the damage, Gus.

Gus   With what? My corn? So basically I am funding myself.

Trent   I'll find you the corn yeah? I'll graft 24/7 if I have to.

Leslie   No one grafts any more, Trent. It's over!

Trent   I ain't over.

Leslie   You are a fifty-year-old white-van man, deal wid it.

Trent   I'm forty-nine.

Leslie   Sorry, my mistake.

Trent   I had a six-pack once.

Leslie   Oh!

Trent   You remember my six-pack?

Leslie   Lawd Jesus!

Trent   Tell me I didn't look criss back then? Tell me, Les! That when it comes to getting wid gal, any gal, I could leave you all behind. Tell me I didn't lay my pipe all over South, yer cunt. Tell me, if you lie, you die. I want that shit back, brudda.

Gus   Join a rhatid gym then.

Leslie   Or come swimming with me.

Trent   Say what?

Leslie   Come swimming with me, and Jan.

Trent   I can't swim, Les.

Leslie   She can teach you.

Trent   Teach me?

Leslie   It's all about believing you're not going to drown, Trent, just float. That's what she did for me, she held me up in the pool, I just lied back in her arms, and I trusted her.

Trent   I ain't lying down in no pool for your woman, fuck off, Les.

Gus   Gym it is then. I bought one, you know. I'll let you join for a discount, Trent.

Leslie   Gus with the jokes now.

Gus   I ain't laughing, Les, I am crying. I am welling up in here, fer trut. All night, I can't believe what I have been hearing. Trent sweating bacon cos of some youts, Selwyn close to tears. You panting for the love of some uppity white bitch.

Leslie   Leave it, Gus.

Gus   You'll be baking biscuits next. We're the Durnfield boys, what de rass happened to that?

Trent (*points to* **Fraser**)   Him is what happened for a start. Maybe you should focus on straightening him out.

Gus   Damn right, I go straighten him out right now.

Enough of this fuck ries.

He grabs **Fraser** *and drags him to the door.*

Fraser   Yes, Gus, do what she said you would do.

Gus   Yes, know-it-all Tina, knows it all right?

Fraser   I didn't mean Mum.

Gus   Who then?

Fraser   Did you even ask her if she even wanted to go to that school? Did you not check her face when you told her?

Gus   Say that to me again?

Fraser   That she was happy where she was?

Gus   Naomi?

Fraser   That she doesn't want to be where you want her to be?

Gus   What the fuck you doing wid her?

Fraser   We found each other on Facebook.

Gus   I don't give a rass lick where you find her.

Fraser   She my sister.

Gus   You ain't nuttin to her. You stay away from her.

Fraser   Joke is, she is only trying to help you.

Gus   Shut yer mout.

Fraser   She heard you on the phone, dread.

Gus   Don't call me *dread*.

Fraser   To the bank.

Leslie   Oh, yes?

Fraser   Business tight, can't afford the fees.

Gus   Shut yer damn mout!

Leslie   Yer empire starting to crumble, Gus?

Gus   It ain't gonna happen.

Leslie   Sounds like it already is, mate.

Gus   Ca' I don't pussy out on tings, I see shit through.

Leslie   Unlike the rest of us, that's what you mean, right?

Trent   Lawd please, mek Shaun walk through this door right now, so we can end this foolishness.

Selwyn   Shaun?

Trent   Space, Selwyn, yer personal space.

Fraser   Why do you hate me so much?

Gus   I don't know you.

Fraser   You used to know me. Or maybe it's Mum you hate?

Gus   She don't mean nuttin to me. She still want me to say I'm sorry about Sam, you want me to say I'm sorry. I'm done wid saying sorry.

Fraser   Bwoi, she really got to you, innit?

Gus   Fraser, I'm going to give you ten seconds, yeah.

Fraser   That's the first time you said my name all night.

Gus   Five seconds.

Fraser   Fuck yer then. Fuck him! Who's wid me? Who's wid me? Come on, man, it's a sweet job, the woman will give it up, I know it.

Leslie   Like Sam did?

Fraser   Forget Sam, you lot have.

Leslie   I wish I could bwoi, believe me.

Fraser   I told you I ain't bothered by that.

Leslie   Robbing his bookies was supposed to be a sweet job. Sam was the best Oyster I ever knew, a top earner, he covered the whole of South, he would graft like no other, just don't ask him to fight, he couldn't fight his way out of nuttin, innit boys? So, what made him think he could tek the three of us on, I have no idea.

Trent   Me neither.

Leslie   It was like he was in a rage about summin.

Trent   Let's move on.

Leslie   Like he knew it was us.

Trent   You done?

Leslie   It was Selwyn who hit him first. When he saw Sam
go for me. You wanna know what it's like being hit on the back
of the head by Selwyn? It's like having an anvil dropped on
yer nut. That should have been the end of it, we shoulda just
dashed right out of there, I don't know what it was, maybe we
were too coked up or summin, it was the sight of Sam trying
to get back up, like he was ready for round two. Trent started
us off, we kicked him back down, and we kept on kicking him
and kicking him, and kicking him, until it looks like his nut was
gonna explode or summin.

Fraser   Alright!

Leslie   Alright what? I thought you said you weren't bothered
by that? That's yer uncle, our friend. We are the reason why
he can't wipe his own arse any more 'bout. Alright? That does
not bother you, not even a touch? Bwoi, I have known some
proper bastards in my time, who have done some hardcore shit
that you wouldn't believe. But every single one of them had
the touch, even they. A touch of conscience that makes us all
human. You telling me you are badder than them, that you
have no touch, that you can see us stamping on yer uncle's
head and you don't want to fling yourself at us right now, wa'
wrong wid yu? Tell me about the supermarket, tell me about
this woman who will give it up for us, like that? Tell me, Fraser,
fucking tell me how high up you are in the BMC? Tell me you
want this, tell me nuh? Do what yer old man tells yu, tek yer
arse out of here and don't ever come back. Fuck off out of it,
go. I said, jog on!

Fraser *leaves.*

Gus   You he listens to?

Leslie   Not bad for a mug, hey, Gus? But then we are all
mugs to you, right? We all done bird, except you.

Gus   Cos I used my noodle. None of you listened, none
a' yer!

Trent   So, it's our fault?

Gus   Don't even think about bringing yerself to me, Trent. Stay which part yu deh, from the time that younger come in here you bin pissing yer pants.

Trent   You would have been afraid as well, Gus.

Gus   Pussy-hole!

Trent   More scared than I have been in my life, yes, alright! Dat don't shame me.

Gus   I don't know you.

Leslie   Why did you ask him if you should say sorry?

Gus   What you on wid now?

Leslie   You asked the boy if you should say yer sorry about Sam.

Gus   Yeah, ca you idiots caved his skull in.

Leslie   Yes, us, not you.

Gus   Right?

Leslie   So why are you saying sorry?

Gus   I didn't say sorry.

Leslie   I know you didn't. But Gus, why would yer, why? It was us, not you. Why? Gus? Why? Earth calling Augustus!

Gus   Watch yourself, Leslie!

Leslie   What did you do man?

Gus   Fucking hell, Shaun. (*Calls.*) Where you at?

Selwyn   Shaun not coming.

Leslie   Sam shouldn't have been at the bookies that night. We had it planned. He wasn't supposed to be there.

Gus   Fuck is this?

Leslie   He wasn't supposed to be there, Gus. Not unless someone told him about it. Not unless he was warned.

Trent   What dis?

Leslie   Was it you, Gus? Did you warn him? Did you warn Sam, Gus? Did you tell him we were coming? Gus?

Sound of a car window being smashed outside. Car alarm goes off.

Gus   Motherfuck . . . what that?

Leslie   I'll go. Trent, keep him here.

Gus   What that? Yer gonna keep me here, Les, did I hear you right? You telling Trent to keep me here?

Leslie   Don't let him leave.

He goes outside. **Trent** *blocks* **Gus**'s *path.*

Gus   Don't fuck around, Trent, not tonight.

Trent *blocks* **Gus**'s *path again.*

Gus   Trent? Behave yourself now.

Trent   Come on, Gus.

Gus   'Come on, Gus'? Come on, Gus, what?

Trent   Don't do this.

Gus   You really tink you are gonna stop me? Do you want to make one with me now?

Trent   Gus?

Gus   You and yer fat arse.

Trent   Don't.

Gus   Mister Waga Waga, gonna put me down at last? Feel free to slap yourself hard for even thinking that.

Trent   Just calm down, please?

Gus (*laughs*)   You have never lifted your hand to me in all yer entire life. Don't be an eddyatt and tink you can start now.

Trent   I'm just doing what Les say.

Gus   'What Les say'? Am I a prick? Since when you start taking orders from the *white boy*?

Trent   Come on, Gus, we're not eleven no more.

Gus   Since when, Trent?

Trent   Les ain't no *white boy*.

Gus   Then what is he?

Trent   What you mean . . . he's Durnfield. He's one of the firm, he's us!

Gus   He can fuck off, him and his ho!

Trent   Oh, that is scathing.

Gus   You go move?

Trent   Ever since you went all suit and tie on us, it's like yer soul just left. I can't deal, Gus.

Gus   You go cry in front of me again?

Trent   I wasn't crying.

Gus   Pussy-ole, you dat!

Trent   You didn't tell Sam about us, did yer? Did yer?

Gus   Move.

Trent   Fer trut, Gus? Did you put him on us?

Gus   Mi say move!

Leslie *comes back inside, dragging* **Fraser** *along with him.*

Gus   Tell me it ain't what I think it is?

Leslie   I can't help you there.

Gus   My car?

Leslie   He went all medieval on it. Glass everywhere.

Gus (*looks outside*)   Oh, dis bwoi. Dis fucking bwoi!

He goes for **Fraser**. **Leslie** *blocks him.*

Gus   You as well, Les?

Leslie   Tell me first.

Gus   Mind out of my way, Les –

Leslie   Tell me about Sam first

Gus   So I can dead him right now.

Leslie   You told him, you told Sam, you told him we were coming. Didn't you? Fucking didn't you? I know it, you flapped your gums to him. You told him we were going to rob him. I know you did it.

Trent   Tell him he is talking shit, Gus. For me, man, please, tell him!

Leslie   Yes, Gus, you tell me, you tell me now. Tell me, I am talking shit. Tell them too, tell them!

Gus   So, what was I supposed to do, Leslie?

Leslie   You did?

Gus   What was I supposed to do?

Leslie   You did. Oh God.

Gus   Was I really supposed to stand by, and watch you lot fuck yourselves in the arse?

Trent   Oh, Jesus, man! This is rass!

Leslie   Fuck what, Gus? Fuck what? It was a sweet plan, sweeter still if Sam weren't there.

Gus   That give you the right to teif him?

Leslie   Fuck's sake, it's what we do.

Gus (*points to* **Fraser**)   No, it's what they do! He was one of us.

Leslie   He left us. He walked away. He wanted to be a taxpayer. That gave us the right to fleece him, like any other mark.

Gus   Shit don't mek it right.

Leslie   This coming from you who was poking Sam's little sister behind his back? Yes, you are a proper gent aren't you, Gus?! Fifteen years old.

Gus   Fuck off from me.

Leslie   We were bruc. We were grafting 24/7, but no one was trading on the *wall*, no dough was coming in. You know how it was.

Gus   So, why you nuh come to me?

Leslie   We just wanted to do something different, anything, make links of our own.

Gus   I would have funded you all, till death, you know that.

Leslie   That didn't involve you, because all you do is bark orders, tell us we can't make moves. Going on about the good old days of the firm, all of us, all on the *wall*, rubbing our faces in it with your success, wid your money. Only showing up when you are fucking rolling around in it.

Gus   Oh come outta my range if yer gonna cry about it.

Leslie   They tore down our *wall*, Gus. They bloody tore it down, and for what? To build some fucking flats that no one I know can afford? And you bought one of them.

Gus   I bought three actually.

Leslie   Oh, you fuck.

Trent   Gus man?

Gus   Shut yer noise, Trent, just for once. You think I didn't know things were on the slide for us, Les? That everyone out there had deh tings on a lock-down? I saw it coming. Why didn't you? That I didn't know you muppets were gonna do summin stupid? As soon as you started sniffing the white, I knew. And you fucked it up like I knew you would.

Leslie   You fucked it for us.

Trent   You break my heart man, Gus. See it deh!

Gus   You break mine! Wid yer rass claart tears.

Leslie   Fuck is this anyhow? What the fuck is this?

Gus   This is your family, Les. We cater for each other.

Leslie   Fuck this family. Fuck all of it, you hear me, fuck it! Jan's my family now, and she's at home waiting for me.

Gus   We wait for Shaun.

Selwyn   Shaun's not coming

Trent (*losing patience*)   Sel?

Leslie   I got a woman waiting for me, Gus. A woman who loves me, finally. She's got a nice cup of herbal tea ready for me, I bet.

Gus   You must be getting deaf in yer old age, Leslie, we wait for Shaun.

Leslie   You wait for Shaun, I'm gone.

Gus   Yer been a total pussy about this, I hope you know that.

Leslie   I'm gone, Gus, I'm done. Don't make stay.

Gus   Why?

Leslie (*snaps*)   Cos I will fucking dead you, as God is mine.

Gus   Come nuh.

Leslie (*composes himself*)   No.

Gus   Come nuh!

Leslie   She wouldn't want me to.

Gus   Oh this fucking Jan.

Leslie   Get off it, Gus.

Gus   She tamed you good.

Leslie   Don't!

Gus   You wouldn't be crying this much if she was an ebony now would yer?

Leslie   Oh what de fuck?

Gus   Would yer? Would yer?

Leslie   It's my heart that is breaking now as well, Gus.

Gus   Would yer, Les? While I'm on it, how long do you think you can keep her, you with no pot to piss in, Mister Jobseeker Allowance? How long before she gets bored, dumps like you like a cold, marries some rich white fuck, then one Easter Sunday she can brag to her herbal-tea-drinking dykes about how she went slumming for a bit of rough down South.

Leslie   Jan is good for me.

Gus   Jan's a cunt.

Leslie   She saved my life. She's God's gift.

Gus   Does she make you leave your balls at the front door, Les?

Leslie   Not working, Gus.

Gus   Does she have to show you where to put it now?

Trent   Oh over the line, mate.

Gus   I bet she does.

Leslie   Jan made me know I am better than this. That I don't want this. That I am too bloody old for it. Shaun would dead you right now, if he was here, Gus, he would dead you.

Selwyn (*getting louder*)   Shaun not coming.

Leslie   Trent, shut him up, nuh!

Trent   Shaun not coming, what you mean Sel?

Selwyn   Him not coming is what I mean.

Trent   How you know that?

Selwyn   He told me.

Trent   He told you?

Selwyn   You deaf?

Trent   When did he tell you?

Selwyn   Today. On the *wall.*

Trent   The *wall*?

Gus   The *wall* is gone, Sel.

Selwyn   Where there used to be the wall I mean! Outside the flats. Walking up and down like he did not know what day it was. I don't know what happen, but doing bird this time messed him up good.

Leslie   What has that to do wid him not coming, Sel?

Selwyn   He said that he couldn't deal with us any more, that he knows things had changed, that he can't go back inside not ever. He's done with grafting, he is done with us.

Gus   You didn't think you should have told us that before?

Selwyn   I thought he would change his mind

Gus   You thought?

Selwyn   I dared him to do it, to walk away from us, I said he couldn't. That me, him, all of us too tight to let that happen. I didn't think he would have the front, I knew he'd come, ca' we're solid, I just knew.

Gus   Do you see him here, Sel? Do you? Is he standing right here with us? For fuck's sake!

Leslie   Sel. You really should have told us.

Selwyn   I am telling you now.

Leslie   Before, man, before, oh what is the rhatid use? You last see him on the bridge you say, yes or no, Sel?

Selwyn   Yes!

Leslie   I gotta find him.

Gus   Is he alright now?

Trent   Yeah, he's all calm now.

Gus   Good, cos I want to tell him summin.

Trent   Gus, don't, man.

Gus   Tell him about himself, it's due. You know what, Sel, you really know what? Go back to yer supermarket, yeah, go back to your can of beans and pulses, yeah, cos that is all you are good for, and I ain't just saying that, cos you ain't no grafter, you never were, you never knew how to graft without one of us being there for you. Yu understand? Tell me you understand, you fucking waste of carbon, yer using up my oxygen, tell me, nuh!

Leslie   Gus!

Gus   Lay a hand on me again, Leslie, and it's you next, before God mi swear to you!

Leslie *removes his hand from* **Gus**'s *arm.*

Leslie   I'm going to find my friend.

Gus   Him my friend too.

Leslie   I don't want you anywhere near.

Gus   You think you can stop me, Les?

Leslie   I'll stop yer.

Gus   Are you high?

Leslie   We're done. We're done.

Gus *faces* **Trent** *and* **Selwyn.**

Gus   What? What you have to say, what?

Trent   What time on Saturday, Les, for the swimming?

Gus   Are you fucking joking, Trent?

Leslie   Half-nine, Greenwich Pools.

Gus   This for real?

Trent   Deal me in.

Gus   Yes, Les, you deal him in. Gwan, Trent, go on, get your swimming cossie out, let the whole of South see yer wurtless fat-arse self. Well, go after him, like you always do, like you keep doing, you and Sel, nuttin but a dawg, the two a' yer in fact, I'll throw you a bone each, yeah, go! You still here, fucking go, will yer, jog the fuck on! Go.

Trent   Come, Sel.

Selwyn *slowly follows* **Trent** *and* **Leslie** *towards the door.*

Gus (*mocks*)   Shaun not coming, Shaun not coming, yer crazy mad up in the head one-footed fuck! (*Calls.*) Pussy dem! All a' yu! Nuttin but a wurtless fucking white boy, nuttin but a stupid fat bastard, yer waga-waga. A one-foot mad-up fool. You ain't no firm, Durnfield my arse, I was Durnfield born and true, true and born, I was the firm, me one! Me! All my life I have looked out for you, every single one of you.

Leslie (*points to* **Fraser**)   You want to look after somebody now, Gus, look after him!

Leslie *leaves followed by* **Trent** *and* **Selwyn.**

Gus *sees* **Fraser** *is still there.*

Gus   What do you want from me now? What? Fucking what?

Fraser   You owe me.

Gus   You can't still be giving it about joining the BMC? Did you hear nuttin of what Leslie said to you? Well? Big-time gangster! If you're so bad, where's yer blade? Where's yer tool?

Fraser *reveals a kitchen knife from his coat pocket.*

Gus (*laughs*)   Wat dat? What does that prove?

Fraser   You owe me.

Gus   Have you ever had a session, Fraser? An encounter? A right royal punch-up? Where you get so close you can smell the other guy's breath? When you can feel the bones in your fist cracking in half as it lands against the side of another brer's face? Have you ever in your life had one of those?

Fraser   You owe me.

Gus   Trent's right, that little fat bastard is actually right for once. You youngers scare us. You know why? Ca' yer selfish, ca' you don't give a shit about anyone but yourselves.

Fraser   This from the brer who fucked his friends over?

Gus   You would rather die than learn, innit? You know nuttin about creeping. You don't graft, you don't earn, you don't think, you just tek. Young, old. Rich, poor. It don't matter, does it? It's your world now, as fucked as it is. Slash and grab, innit?

Fraser   Well, come then, big man, school us.

Gus   Move.

Fraser   School me.

Gus   Go cry somewhere else.

Fraser   So, if I ain't got them, what else have I got?

Gus   Yer mum?

Fraser   She don't want to know, bitch dashed me out.

Gus   You speak that way about yer mudda?

Fraser   What about you? Boy, she really hurt you. She really did, some lickle yat in school uniform who couldn't keep her legs closed . . .

Gus   Hey!

Fraser   How did you know who I was? When did you realise?

Gus   From the second you breezed yourself in here. I know dem eyes from anywhere.

Fraser   Is that why you never claimed me? Were you ashamed or summin? Was I a mistake?

Gus   Ask her.

Fraser   I done nuttin but ask her. All she does is lie and hold out.

Gus   Damn right she lies. Telling you I was bored wid her, and decided to step? That fucking lying bitch.

Fraser   Yer holding out as well, that must mek you a bitch as well, yeah?

Gus   Careful, bwoi.

Fraser   Just tell me why, man.

Gus *starts pouring several shots of whiskey.*

Fraser   You go tell me?

Gus   Let me see you do this again.

Fraser   You go tell me, Gus?

Gus   Man up, show we what you have.

Fraser *downs in one a shot of whiskey. Then another. Then another.*

Fraser   I can do this all day. Why you never tell them about me?

Gus   You are never going to go away, are you? Fuck up my night for me.

Fraser   Tell me why.

Gus   Lose the only family I have ever had. Ever wanted, ever cared about.

Fraser   Tell me.

Gus   Fucking you.

Fraser   Gus?

Gus   I ain't no perv.

Fraser   I never said.

Gus   It wasn't like that.

Fraser   So, how was it then?

Gus   I didn't want them to fuck it up for me. When the council tore our *wall* down to build flats, yeah, I cried.

Fraser *scoffs.*

Gus   I was welling up! It was the end of an era. What the rass we're going to do now, all that shit. Yer mudda walked by on her way to school, put her arm around me, she look like a gal, but she come like a woman. The way she smiled and shit. That was beautiful. She was beautiful, I wanted summin beautiful, who doesn't? You have a problem wid that? You have a problem, Fraser? Answer me, nuh!

Fraser   No, I don't have a problem with that.

Gus   One thing I wanted to keep to myself, one thing from their eyes and deh jokes, one ting!

Fraser   So what happen?

Gus   That's all yer getting.

Fraser   Come on, what happened?

Gus   Come near Naomi again, I'll bruc you in half.

Fraser   She's my sister.

Gus   She is nothing to you, you're staying away.

Fraser   She hates that school.

Gus   I don't care what she hates.

Fraser   The fess are bleeding you dry anyway.

Gus   That's my problem, not hers, not yours. You tell her from me, her arse is staying in that school, make sure that is the last thing you say to her, capice?

Fraser   Big man, Gus.

Gus   Believe that.

Fraser   Your boys have gone.

Gus   Last warning, bwoi.

Fraser   The *wall* has gone.

Gus   Hear me.

Fraser   This place, as good as gone. Gone, all gone.

Gus   Cos of you.

Fraser   Cos of you! Tell me what happened wid Mum.

Gus   Was this your plan all along?

Fraser   Tell me.

Gus   I bet it was.

Fraser   Tell me, man.

Gus (*snaps*)   Bitch gave me a choice, her or dem.

Fraser   That why you told Sam?

Gus   For all the good. As soon as you come outta her, shit started to change. Like she a full grown-up now, telling me she don't love me no more, we ain't going anywhere. I mean, what kind of bitch do that, a lying bitch is what, a no-good lying free-it-up-for-anyone skank bitch who mek me feel I is nuttin but a dirty old man instead of someone who would lie down in traffic for her. Happy now?

Fraser   Happy?

Gus   Tek yer arse out.

Fraser   You dash me, ca' Mum dash you? I'm supposed to be happy? No, you knew messing around with a fifteen-year-old was a big no-no, that is why you couldn't tell yer brers, ca' you knew it was wrong.

Gus   You need to step.

Fraser   You could at least man up about that.

Gus   You tink yer bright?

Fraser   Brighter than you.

Gus   Crying like a gal cos the BMC don't want you till you prove yerself, that kind of bright? Why do you want to join a gang for? Why is that so important to you? You can't even say, can you?

Fraser   Yeah I can.

Gus   I'm listening.

Fraser   Ca' without a gang, you're an orphan. With a gang, you walk in twos, you walk in threes and you walk in fours. When your crew is the best, you're out in the sun, you're home free home.

Gus   Are you quoting *West Side Story* to me?

Fraser   No!

Gus   Yeah you are, that is from *West Side Story*.

Fraser (*lying*)   No it ain't.

Gus   It is from *West Side* motherfucking *Story*! It's at the beginning of the film, Riff is with Tony asking him to join him at the dance to help take on the Sharks. You don't feel shame?

Fraser   Me shame? Well how do you know it's from that?

Gus   How you think?

Fraser (*realises*)   Yeah. I swear, Mum used to watch that film on DVD every blasted week.

Gus (*agrees*)   Who do you think bought her the DVD?

Fraser   Best part of the film for me when the guy says that. You walk in twos, threes, fours. When your crew is the best . . . It's how I feel.

Gus   But you are not part of their crew.

Fraser   It's still how I feel; you have a problem with that?

Gus   No, I don't have a problem with that.

Fraser   Cos you can jog on if you don't like it.

Gus   I got no more time for you, I got this place to open tomorrow night.

Fraser   You fucked it all up for yerself, Gus.

Gus   If by that you mean I used my head, that I made money, proper money, more corn than those fools and the whole of South put together, yeah, Fraser, I fucked it right up. I would have given her everyting but that still weren't enough for the bitch.

Fraser   You can't mek someone love you.

Gus   And you can't mek me claim you.

Fraser   She went off you, she dashed you, man up about it.

Gus   Then hold you in my arms as my own? I claim you for all of the world to see? I bet you can see it, right now you are seeing pictures. Innit? You and me, with my arm over you? Father and son! Never heard such stupidness in my life. You think I going to forget what you done to my car? You know how much corn I shelled out for that? Let this be the last time I tell you this. You got ten seconds to step, and I mean ten seconds. You here a second longer, and you are cleaning this shit up, all a' it.

Fraser   Why wait?

He starts picking up pieces of glass on the floor.

Gus   Lawd Jesus, wat dis bwoi doing now? What you doing?

Fraser   Cleaning this shit up, you have a problem with that?

Gus   You want cut yourself? All that glass, think it through nuh, bwoi? There's a dustpan and brush behind the bar.

Fraser *finds the dustpan and brush from behind the bar. He begins sweeping.*

Gus *picks up and tries reassembling the broken chairs and stools. After a brief moment of silence* **Gus** *looks over at* **Fraser**.

Fraser   What?

Gus   A supermarket?

Fraser   It got me here with you, didn't it?

Gus   So you did plan all this.

Fraser   She still woulda given up it, though, telling you. And you ain't got nothing for me on that, not after what you did to Sam.

Gus   What they did to Sam.

Fraser   You sent him there. Your own friend!

Gus   You tink I'm proud of how it went down?

Fraser   I don't give a fuck how you feel, Gus.

Gus   Yet here you are.

Fraser   Yep. Right here, so.

They continue to clear up in silence.

Gus   When you done in here, deal wid the shit outside.

Fraser   What shit?

Gus   My car! All eighty grand of it.

Fraser   Right.

Gus   Better believe, right!

Fraser   You ain't all that.

Gus   Bored now.

Fraser   None of yer. I should have went for Les, when he told me to, I'll show him I have bloody truth.

Gus   You already did

Fraser   What you say?

Gus   By not going for him you already did show you had truth. More truth than the rest of us could ever put together, you understand? You didn't go low by not going for him, you went high, if you are half as smart as you think you are, you'd understand what that means. Don't be like me. Don't be like us, or anything like yer so-called brers. For fuck's sake just be you, yeah? That is all you've got. That is all I have for yer, young one, now you go sort my car out or what?

Fraser (*sincere*)   Dad . . .

Gus   . . . My car, gwan.

Fraser *leaves.*

Gus *gives up trying to repair the stools. He paces around the room.*

He is lost in so many thoughts and feelings.

He eyes the jukebox. He knows what to do with himself now. He turns it on. It plays 'Glad All Over'. He continues to be lost in his thoughts. He watches **Fraser** *from the door. He goes out to join his son.*

Blackout.

Advice for the Young at Heart

Advice for the Young at Heart premiered at Heart Redbridge Drama Centre, London, on 12 September 2013, with the following cast and creative team:

Candice	**Alix Ross**
Sam	**Matt Bradley-Robinson**
Clint	**Adrian Richards**
Kenny	**Joe Stamp**

Director	Natalie Wilson
Designer	Emma Wee
Sound Designer/Composer	Helen Skiera
Lighting Designer	Charlie Lucas
Movement Director	Lucy Cullingford
Fight Directors	Rachel Bown-Williams and Ruth Cooper-Brown of RC-Annie Ltd
Dramaturg	Lin Coghlan

Advice for the Young at Heart

Characters

Candice, *mixed race, seventeen years old*
Sam, *white, eighteen years old. Kenny's brother*
Kenny, *white, twenty-one years old*
Clint, *mixed race, seventeen years old*

Setting

Outside a lock-up, 1958 and 2011

Candice *enters. She is on the phone.*

Candice   Right, I am here. I said I am here, Ryan, by the lock-up, so what do want? You never told me that. You never told me that, Ryan. Oh come on man, look I know you hate the guy, but that's no reason, so you don't think busting him up is a little excessive? So he likes Manchester City? Yeah, I know, I said I know! You don't have to keep repeating . . . Don't tell me to shut up, don't tell me . . .

She hangs up. She puts the phone down.

Bastard man, who does he think?

She paces up and down. Her phone rings.

No. No.

She does not answer. It stops. Then rings again. She continues to wait until it stops again.

Go away. Leave me.

The phone rings again. And again. She decides to wait again.

I can do this all day, you know. I can. True say, you don't know me.

She eventually caves in and answers the phone.

Alright, I am sorry; I said I am sorry, what do you want? So, what you want me to do? I'm here; alright I will wait for him here. I'll keep him here until you come. Speak up, I can't hear. Alright. I said alright, Ryan; I will do it, happy? Just do me a favour though, don't hurt him up too bad. Just a couple of slaps, that's it. Alright, thanks. (*Smiles.*) Yeah, love you too.

She hangs up.

Sam *enters, dressed as a Teddy boy.*

Sam   Hey, *pudding*!

Candice (*cringes*)   Will you please stop calling me that.

Sam   You used to like it.

Candice   When I was eight!

Sam   Alright, just as you like, Candice!

Candice   You look *flush*!

Sam   I thank you!

Candice   That was a joke, by the way.

Sam   A joke?

Candice   Yes, Sam, a joke. 'Something said or done for amusement.'

Sam   You have a problem with what I'm wearing?

Candice   If I did, you wouldn't be here. How old were you?

Sam   What, now? Seventeen. And I thought I knew it all. I suppose we all do, when we're young.

Candice   And you used to go out, looking like that?

Sam (*mimics*)   'Looking like that?'

Candice   Yes, 'looking like that'!

Sam   Oi, less of it.

Candice   You can't tell me what to do any more Sam, you're dead, remember?

Sam   Don't call me Sam, its *Grandad*.

Candice   Is it?

Sam   Back in the day . . .

Candice   Your day!

Sam   Alright, back in *my day*. This was proper.

Candice (*mimics*)   'Proper'?

Sam   A couple of bob, this all nearly cost me.

Candice   And it shows.

Sam   You've got no idea what a couple of bob is, do yer?

Candice   Cos I ain't as old as you.

Sam   Ah, what do you lot know?

Candice   I know more about clothes than you.

Sam   I refuse to let you spoil my fun, Candice.

Candice   Fun?

Sam   Cos I tell yer, I was grinning like a Cheshire cat when I first bought this whistle.

Candice   Whistle?

Sam   Whistle and flute. Suit.

Candice   Well, say that.

Sam   I just did. Months of saving it took me, at one point I thought it was going to take me years. Have a word with my blue suede shoes, go on, have a look. Have a feel. Have you washed your hands?

Candice   So funny that I forgot to laugh.

Sam *sings part of the chorus of 'Blue Suede Shoes' like Elvis.*

Sam   Elvis Presley. Famous singer. Hello?

Candice *looks at him blankly.*

Sam (*sighs*)   Just be gentle.

Candice   Like a gal, you.

Sam   And my suit. Don't crease it.

Candice *feels the suit.*

Sam   Well, waiting?

Candice   Yeah man, it's nice.

Sam (*mimics*)   'Yeah man, it's nice'? Months of saving it took me.

Candice   Yes.

Sam   I can't be a proper Ted without my suedes, can I?

Candice   No, I suppose not.

Sam   Thank you. I'm off to the flicks tonight. I'm taking your gran to see *South Pacific.*

Candice *scoffs.*

Sam   She wants to see it, not me. I wanted to go and see the Kirk Douglas film, *The Vikings*!

Candice   Saddo!

Sam   Oi, less of the saddo, you. At least I am doing something with my life.

Candice   And here it comes.

Sam   What are you doing with your life then, Candice?

Candice   Nuttin.

Sam   Exactly. There is more to you than this.

Candice   Yer telling me that?

Sam   Yeah, problem?

Kenny, *also dressed as a Ted, enters.*

Kenny   You ready then?

Sam (*to* **Candice**)   Watcha do that for?

Kenny   You had better not have forgotten, Sammy boy.

Sam   Why are you remembering him again, you didn't even know him?

Candice   No, but you did.

Kenny   You had better not bottle out.

Sam   Get rid of him, will yer?

Candice   No.

Sam   There are things we need to say, darling.

Kenny   Sammy? Oi!

Candice   He's talking to you.

Sam   Alright, have it your way.

Kenny   Are you bottling out?

Sam   When have I ever bottled out?

Kenny   Good man, that is what I like to hear.

Sam   That is all you are ever going to hear.

Kenny   Nice threads.

Sam   I thank you!

Kenny   I'm glad to see you have taken it to heart, I really am. But there's more than a suit that will make you a Ted.

Sam   What else then?

Kenny *hands his brother a flick-knife.*

Kenny   Take this.

Sam   Since when are we using blades?

Kenny   Just shut up and take it.

Sam *takes the knife.*

Sam   Can you hear it, the noise?

Kenny   I hear it, hard not to.

Sam   Wass 'appening?

Kenny   That is the sound of our lot giving the blacks a right good hiding, that is what is happening. Teddy boys unite! We are going to smash them all to pieces, Sammy. Oh yes! For as long as it takes. That will teach them for coming to our country, nicking our jobs, taking our homes. The streets of Notting Hill are ours, and we are having them back. You alright?

Sam   Don't worry about me.

Kenny   You're my little brother; of course I worry.

Sam   I'm alright.

Kenny   Okay then, so listen up. Here is the plan. We wander round till we see a black. Preferably on his own. We corner him; we slap him around, followed by a good kicking. Just like before. You ready?

Sam   You said we'd stop this after the last time.

Kenny   I know what I said.

Sam   You promised.

Kenny   That was before a whole bunch of them blacks jumped our cousin Dennis the other week. He's still in hospital. It's one for one Sammy, that is the way the game is played. Ask Dad, if you don't believe me. He'll tell yer.

Sam   Yeah, about another bleeding black taking another one of his mate's jobs at the factory. How he didn't fight against Hitler during the war just so a bunch of blacks can come and take over our country. I don't need him to tell me, Kenny, I know it off by heart. (*Feels* **Kenny**'s *glare.*) Sorry.

Kenny   Would you like a backhander for a nightcap?

Sam   No, I wouldn't.

Kenny   You are well out of order.

Sam   I know.

Kenny   Our dad risked his life in the war.

Sam   I know that too.

Kenny   Well, show some respect then.

Sam   I will. Sorry.

Kenny   If they didn't want trouble, they shouldn't have bleeding well come here, this is our manor, our country; we have to fight for it. Right?

Sam   Right, right, yes, you're right, Kenny.

Candice *grunts.*

Kenny   Well, let's get on with it then.

Sam *turns to face* **Candice**.

Sam   Are you satisfied?

Candice   You are such a dog, do what he tells you.

Sam   He's my brother.

Candice   So, you're not a dog?

Sam   Gloria is expecting me; I'm going to be late.

Kenny   Are you coming?

Sam   Don't you care?

Kenny   Sammy?

Candice   Yer masa's waiting.

Sam   You're the one who keeps bringing me back, Candice. You want this.

Sam *and* **Kenny** *go. They walk by* **Clint**, *who does not see them.*

Clint   Yes, Candice, I got your texts. Wass 'appening?

Candice   Nuttin.

Clint   Come on girl, wass 'appening? Just tell me what are you up to?

Clint   You hear the sirens?

Candice   We're always hearing sirens.

Clint   It's kicking off in town, a whole heap of madness going on.

Candice   Yeah, I just got a tweet from Sharon.

Clint   Brers, piling into shops, taking what they want. And Five-O are just standing there, not doing a ting. No lie! It's all over Twitter and BB.

Candice   Well, good for them.

Clint   You had better believe! A whole heap of madness going on. You remember the stories your grandad used to tell us about when he was younger?

Candice   What stories?

Clint   About how peeps the same age as us were fighting in the streets as well, in Notting Hill, 1959, same as it is now.

Candice   It's not the same.

Clint   They were still rioting.

Candice   And, and it wasn't 1959, it was 1958! White boys banging up black kids.

Clint   Yeah, but yer grandad was safe.

Candice   Safe?

Clint   Yeah, safe.

Candice   And you believed all that?

Clint   Yeah I did, wass yer problem?

Candice   My grandad was nuttin but a coward.

Clint   Coward?

Candice   Can you please just shut about him.

Clint   You coming? Into town? (*Reads a text.*) Nathan says they are raiding Carphone Warehouse as we speak. Candice? Hello? You know, this ain't you.

Candice   And what exactly do you know about me?

Clint   It's like yer waiting for someone.

Candice   Fer trut, Clint. I don't think I have ever met a brer who sticks his nose into people's business as much as you.

Clint   Come on, just for a bit. Well, I'm going.

Candice   Bring me back something.

Clint   Like what?

Candice   Anything.

Clint   Alright.

Candice   You really think yer summin.

Clint   I know I'm summin. No one can do a supermarket sweep as well as *I*!

Candice   Prove it.

Clint   Time me.

Candice   Ten minutes.

Clint   Yer on!

He goes.

Candice *sees* **Sam** *enter. He glares at her.*

Candice   Yeah, what?

Sam   Please stop making me do this.

Candice   You still think you can boss me.

Sam   It was fifty years ago.

Candice   Fifty-three actually.

Sam   I made a mistake. I was nothing but a kid.

Candice   So?

Sam   Candice?

Candice   Waiting?

Sam   Alright, have it your way.

Kenny *enters. He joins* **Sam**. *They both see something across the street.*

Kenny   Nice, they are all coming outta the pub now.

Sam   Yeah, but they're all coming out in groups or couples. Look at those two, like they are courting or summink.

Kenny   Courting?

Sam   Well, they're holding hands and that. I don't think we are going to get one on his own around here.

Kenny   Let's just wait, be patient. There is always one.

Sam   It's going to rain again. I wanna go home.

Candice   Don't you move.

Kenny   What were you going on about, just then? Couples and groups?

Sam   I was just telling what I saw.

Kenny   I don't want to hear about them in couples or groups, Sammy – you make them sound like normal people.

Sam   Maybe they are.

Kenny   You what?

Sam   Not all of them, I grant yer, but some.

Kenny   They are not normal, they are blacks. Don't you forget it.

Sam   I got it.

Kenny   We are normal, they ain't.

Sam   Alright, you love to go on and on, dontcha?

Kenny (*sees something*)   Here we go, I told you to be patient.

Sam   What, what is it?

Kenny   We got one of them, one little black. All on his lonesome. He's heading for the alley, nice and dark. Right then, just as before, we follow him, you jump him, I butt him in the head. No messing, he's down like a heap. Then we kick the black off him. Does that sound like a plan to you?

Sam   It does, but . . .

Kenny   Oh, what is it now?

Sam   He looks alright.

Kenny Alright?

Sam He just don't look like one of the typical trouble-making blacks. He looks alright to me, Kenny?

Kenny How can you tell? What does he expect?

Sam Look, he's got a lot of books with him. He's probably a student or summink?

Kenny Sammy, in case you ain't noticed, but this is a war. Now, whose side are you on?

Sam Yours, of course, I am always on your side.

Candice Dog!

Kenny Music to my ears that.

Sam I'm just saying, that's all.

Candice Well, don't!

Kenny Course you are, but I'm the eldest, so what I say goes, alright?

Sam Yes, Kenny.

Candice Woof, woof!

Sam Let's go.

Kenny Let's have him more like.

Sam *and* **Kenny** *run off after the black man.* **Kenny** *is screaming obscenities towards the black man.* **Sam** *is hesitant. He gives serious thought to running away in the opposite direction. He chooses to follow his brother.* **Sam** *catches up with* **Kenny** *but looks in horror at the sight of* **Kenny** *kicking the black man.*

Candice (*scorns*) Mister Big Man!

Sam *turns around to face* **Candice**.

Sam Why can't you listen?

He goes to join his brother offstage.

Candice's *phone rings; she answers it..*

Candice   Yes, Mum, what you want?

Clint *enters.*

Candice   I ain't nowhere near town, Mum. Say what? Look, I will come home when I feel like it, yeah? (*Hangs up. To* **Clint**.) Right, you are my witness, if Mum asks, we didn't go anywhere near town. You were with me, all the time.

Clint   But I am wid you.

Candice   She's saying it is all over the news now, people looting and that. So what you get for me?

Clint   Okay, like I said yeah, a whole heap of madness going on.

Candice   Right, so what you get?

Clint   It was smash-and-grab, whatever you could lay your hands on.

Candice   What you get?

Clint   Carphone Warehouse was rammed.

Candice   Clint, don't make me slap you.

Clint *hands her a bag.* **Candice** *has a look. She takes it out.*

Candice   What is this?

Clint   It's an iGrill.

Candice   A what?

Clint   An iGrill.

Candice   Yeah, I heard that bit, what is it?

Clint   It's quite smart as it goes.

Candice   Oh really?

Clint   Yeah, you see you connect it via Bluetooth –

Candice   Right.

Clint   You download the app –

Candice   Yeah.

Clint   And it checks for you how hot your food is.

Candice   Is it?

Clint   Yes! That way you know your food is cooked exactly, the way you want it, and that . . .

Candice   Stop talking, right now – can you do that for me, please?

Clint   Sorry.

Candice   An iGrill!

Clint   It's all I could get.

Candice   You had better get back out there and bring me summin else.

Clint   Alright, but I ain't hanging round here all night.

Candice   You my friend or what?

Clint   Friend?

Candice   Yeah. Stop looking at me like that.

Clint   Like what?

Candice   Like that.

Clint   How else am I supposed to look, Candice?

Candice   Yer my friend, that's it.

Clint   I know, you said.

Candice   I ain't getting off wid yer. You ain't getting none.

Clint   Did I say?

Candice   You don't have to. Both of your eyes are doing all the work.

Clint   Do I look like I have a death wish? Everyone knows you are Ryan's property.

Candice   'Property'?

Clint   Well, why else would you . . .

Candice   Would I what, Clint?

Clint   Nuttin, just summin I heard.

Candice   Go on.

Clint   Lauren's eighteenth birthday party a few weeks back.

Candice   What about it?

Clint   I heard that something went down. You were upstairs, in one of the bedrooms, him and his brers . . .

Candice   Nuttin went down.

Clint   You don't even know what –

Candice   Are we clear on that?

Clint   Clear and loud. If you're saying nothing happened.

Candice   That is what I am saying.

Clint   Alright, but he's got you chirpsing some brer again, hasn't he?

Candice   I ain't no ho!

Clint   You chirps them, he shanks them.

Candice   So what? Too many brers round here with too much to say for themselves. Ryan is just putting them under manners, that's all.

Clint   Who is it?

Candice   And he ain't getting me to do anything. Ryan's my man, and I love him.

Clint   Who is it, Candice?

Candice   None of yer business. (*Sighs.*) Alex.

Clint   Alex?

Candice   It's what I said.

Clint   From school?

Candice   You know any other Alex?

Clint   What's he done?

Candice   I don't know, I don't care. I just –

Clint   – do what you're told.

Candice   Will you just close your mouth, please?

Clint   Yer grandad has only been dead a week.

Candice   Is this you closing your mouth?

Clint   He couldn't wait?

Candice   What has that got to do with this?

Clint   When's his funeral?

Candice   I don't know, next week or summin?

Clint   Well, you must be upset?

Candice   True say, you didn't know him.

Clint   I knew him as long as you.

Candice   He was a drunken old git, did nothing but smell of piss.

Clint   Easy, girl.

Candice   I'll say what I want. You didn't live wid him.

Clint   You used to love that old man

Candice   When I was little.

Clint   He used to take us to the seaside, every bank holiday, you and me would run around in the train. Then he would buy us big ice creams each on the pier.

Candice   Yes, so what?

Clint   So, he weren't all bad, that's what.

A text message is heard on **Clint**'s *phone.*

Clint (*reads*)   From Nathan. They are living it up in Phones 4U now. And the feds are still doing nuttin about it. He says he can get me an iPhone. You want one?

Candice   No ta, I'll stick with the BB.

Clint   A BB? Candice? I don't know what planet you are on. It's an iPhone or nuttin. Catch up, wass Ryan got?

Candice   Why are you asking me, cos I'm his property? A Galaxy.

Clint   If I get him the latest model, you think he will let me join his crew?

Candice   Clint, I reckon you will do anything to join his crew. I think you would kiss his arse for him.

Clint   Alright, so what are you doing for him? Leading Alex into a trap?

Candice   I'm gonna tell you one last time, mind your business about that.

Clint   Fine, I go mind my business elsewhere.

Candice   Just bring summin back for me.

Clint   So, now you want me to come back?

Candice   And it had better not be bruc!

Clint   I will see what Nathan is doing.

He goes.

Sam *enters.*

Candice   So, you did it then, yeah? You did it?

Sam   You happy now?

Candice   Do I look?

Sam (*mimics*)   'Do I look' . . . Talk English, will yer?

Candice   I think you will find it's 'speak English', not 'talk English', Sam!

Sam   Stop calling me Sam.

Candice   I'll call you what I like.

Sam   It's *Grandad*.

Candice   You think you earned the right?

Sam   I'm going to be late for the flicks at this rate.

Candice   You and *Uncle* Kenny.

Sam   Yer gran is gonna kill me.

Candice   Going out.

Sam   Yes!

Candice   Playing bad men.

Sam   Just let me go, Candice.

Candice   Make me laugh.

Sam   Where's Clint?

Candice   Not here.

Sam   But he'll come back, he always does for you.

Candice   Why don't you just shut up about him?

Sam   What, you can preach to me, but I can't preach to you?

Candice   You ain't got the first.

Sam   Do what Ryan wants.

Candice   Yer nuttin but a chief!

Kenny (*offstage*)   Sammy? Sammy?

Sam (*points at* **Kenny**)   You can bring him back as much as you like you know. Keep playing us around in your head.

Kenny *enters.*

Kenny   Sammy?

Sam   You'll have to face what they did to you.

Candice   They didn't do anything to me.

Kenny   What is up with you?

Sam   Candice?

Kenny   Why did you run away like that?

Candice *turns her back.*

Kenny   Why did you run?

Sam   I dunno.

Kenny   We are still in the blacks' neighbourhood.

Sam   I know where I am, Kenny.

Kenny   You don't go running off by yourself. You wanna get killed?

Sam   Stop worrying.

Kenny   You're my little brother; of course I worry. Next time you wait for me.

Sam   Next time?

Kenny   Come on.

Sam   What do you mean by next time?

Kenny   We gotta go.

Sam   There won't be a next time. Just leave me alone for a minute, will yer?

Kenny   What have you done to your shirt?

Sam   I got blood on it.

Kenny   So take it home, you lump. Mum will wash it.

Sam   It's the geezer's blood, Kenny!

Kenny   What you yelling at me for?

Sam   I don't know. I ain't got the faintest idea why I am yelling at yer.

Kenny   Are you trying to be funny with me, Sammy, are yer? We've done this before, we'll be alright.

Sam   He ain't dead, is he?

Kenny   Course not.

Sam   Don't lie to me.

Candice   Ooh, Sammy playing big man now!

Kenny   He ain't dead. He was breathing when we left.

Sam   We left him lying there in the street.

Kenny   So?

Sam   First time that has happened. A few kicks, a couple of slaps, that's all we are supposed to give them.

Kenny   And that is exactly what he got.

Candice   Yeah, exactly!

Sam   You kicked him in the head.

Candice   Act like a fool, get slap like a fool.

Sam (*to* **Candice**)   You know you don't mean that.

Kenny   Don't tell me what I don't mean. He shouldn't have gone for me.

Sam   What did you expect? If he's dead.

Kenny   I am telling yer, for the last time, he was alive.

Sam   Was?

Kenny   Alright, *is*, he *is* alive!

Sam   I'm going back.

Kenny   You what?

Sam   We can't just leave him lying there.

Kenny   You watch us.

Candice   Yer so brave!

Sam   Let me call an ambulance at least then. There's a phone box at the end of the road.

Kenny   We ain't calling anybody, Sammy.

Sam   I said me, Kenny!

Kenny   Sammy, will you shut up for one minute and think it through. What if someone sees yer? I don't know what's gotten into you lately.

Candice   Bricking it now, ennit, Sam?

Sam   I'm just getting tired of this.

Candice   Liar!

Kenny   It will be over soon. As soon as they get the message, get back on their boats, and sail back to wherever it is they come from.

Sam   That's not what I mean.

Kenny   It's what I mean. And what I say –

Sam   – goes!

Kenny   Have you got a problem with that?

Sam   No, Kenny.

Candice (*mimics*)   'No, Kenny'!

Sam   Let's just go.

Kenny   Since when do you tell me what to do?

Sam   Alright, I am asking yer, can we go?

Kenny   Okay then, we'll go.

Sam   Where are you going?

Kenny   Jesus H, I thought we was going.

Sam The phone box is this way.

Kenny Forget about calling the ambulance, will yer!

Sam Kenny, I'm doing it.

Candice Enough!

Sam *and* **Kenny** *freeze.*

Candice Bored now, just go. Both of you!

They leave.

Candice*'s phone rings.*

Candice Now what? Yes, Ryan? It's alright, take your time, I ain't going anywhere. Nor is he? No, but he'll be back any sec. Cos I know him. Look, he'll be here so stop worrying. You don't have to bark orders at me. Cos he can't keep his eyes off me, he never could. Just like you. Except he don't stuff his face all day wid Nandos! Joke! Unwind yerself, man! I said I'll keep him here, that means I will. Yeah, bye!

Candice *hangs up.*

Clint *enters.*

Clint Look at what I got you now. I got an iPad, iPhone. Digital camera, what you want, give me a price? Candice? Hello?

Candice Yeah, nice, thanks.

Clint So is Alex coming right now?

Candice What of it?

Clint Just asking.

Candice Yes, he's coming.

Clint Ryan is well out of order on this one. You should tell Alex what's going to happen to him.

Candice Good one, Clint, that is almost funny, coming from you. I need time.

Clint   For what?

Candice   Prepare, ennit? Psych myself up for it. This ain't easy, you know. I have to keep Alex here until he comes.

Clint   How you gonna do that?

Candice   Would you like me to draw you a picture?

Clint   Ryan's property.

Candice   Yes, alright, I am Ryan's property, are you happy now?

Clint   Do I look happy?

He reads a text.

Now he's raiding Foot Locker.

Candice   Who?

Clint   Nathan!

Candice   Get me a pair of trainers.

Clint   Get them yerself, come with me.

Candice   Size five.

Clint   Dayz man, what do you think this is?

He goes, passing **Kenny** *and* **Sam**.

Kenny   The Old Bill just came knocking.

Sam   Are they on to us?

Kenny   Calm down, they are knocking on everyone's doors. They came with nothing, they got nothing. But they want to come back and speak to you, so just tell them you were with me all night, got it?

Sam   Yes.

Kenny   We are in the clear, Sammy!

Sam   Yeah.

Candice   Shoulda got locked up.

Kenny   That calls for a celebration. I thought we'd go out again tonight, bit of hunting?

Sam   Don't you think you've done enough?

Kenny   No, I don't.

Sam   Well I have.

Kenny   Have you forgotten what we are trying to do?

Sam   Oh leave it out, will yer?

Kenny   What do you mean, 'leave it out'? These are our streets, Sammy, this is our country.

Sam   I don't care any more.

Kenny   Alright Sammy; come on, what is it?

Sam   Stop calling me that, it's Sam.

Kenny   Is someone picking on yer?

Candice   Yeah, you.

Sam   Course not.

Kenny   I wanna know.

Sam   No one is picking on me, it's nothing.

Kenny   Well, let's go home then. Mum is cooking corned beef.

Candice   Eurrgh!

Kenny   Your favourite.

Sam   I can't.

Kenny   What you mean, you can't?

Sam   I'm waiting.

Kenny   Waiting?

Sam   For someone.

Kenny   Someone?

Sam   A girl, alright?

Kenny   A girl.

Sam   Yes.

Kenny   You with a girl?

Sam   Will you just buzz off please?

Kenny   No way, I wanna see this girl.

Sam   Kenny!

Kenny   See if she's real, or inside your head, like the others.

Sam   She's real. She just started working in the chemist, across the road. She's knocking off in a minute, and I'm waiting for her.

Kenny   Alright, alright, don't throw your toys outta yer pram. You only had to say.

Sam   I have been saying it.

Kenny   My little brother with a girl!

Sam   Yeah, go on, laugh yer head off.

Kenny   How long has this been going on?

Sam   Three months.

Kenny   Three months!

Sam   Kenny, just go, will yer.

Kenny   You've kept it quiet, all this time?

Sam   Yer cramping my style, mate.

Kenny   You never used to keep secrets from me.

Sam   Kenny?

Kenny   You used to tell me everything.

Sam   And no more hunting. I mean it.

Kenny   It's like you are a stranger these days.

Sam   I know the feeling.

Kenny   Oi!

Sam   Come on, please.

Kenny   Alright, I'm going.

He goes.

Candice   Corned beef?

Sam   What's wrong with it?

Candice   I don't know how you could eat it.

Sam   That and two veg, lovely!

Candice   Errggh!

Sam   What about you, then, stuffing your face with chicken and chips. Errggh! (*Sees* **Candice** *smile.*) I saw that.

Candice   Saw what?

Sam   You smiling.

Candice   I'm not smiling.

Sam   You were a second ago.

Candice   Didn't I tell you to go?

Sam   Then why am I still here then? Where'd you get all that?

Candice   From the shop.

Sam   Candice Gloria Mullings?

Candice   Here it comes.

Sam   How many more times –

Candice   Mister nag!

Sam   – no more nicking.

Candice   No one says *nicking* any more, Sam.

Sam   Alright, no more *teifing*!

Candice *chuckles at the sight of her grandfather trying to talk street.*

Sam   Well, at least you are smiling again.

Candice   That wasn't a smile, that was a smirk.

Sam   I tell yer. When you were a baby your smile could light up a room, did you know that?

Candice   Stop it.

Sam   Stop what, worrying about you? I can't do that, darling.

Candice   I didn't see you telling your brother about Gran, Sam.

Sam   I'm building up to it. You know that.

Candice *scoffs.*

Sam   Just answer me this. What is the point in me going through this over and over again when you don't even listen, you don't even bother to listen?

Candice   It ain't about me listening.

Sam   It bleeding well should be.

Candice   It's about you learning not to bark yer hype at me. So jam it.

Sam   It don't work like that.

Candice   It does for me.

Sam   It's you making this happen, not me.

Candice   Come next week, when we bury you, when you are six feet under, you and me, we are done, finally. I will never have to see your face again.

Sam   You think so?

Candice   Bloody know so.

Sam   You'll miss me.

Candice   No I won't.

Sam   Yer lying, I could always tell.

Candice   You wanna bet? How much money you have?

Sam   Well, if that's how you feel, why wait till next week? Why don't I just hop it, right now?

Candice   I don't business, do what you feel.

Sam   Alright, I'm going. If I'm lucky yer gran will still be waiting for me.

Candice   Bye!

Sam   You know I never raised you to be so selfish.

Candice   You never raised me at all.

Sam   I was the closest thing you ever had to a dad.

Candice   But you're not my dad.

Sam   I was always there.

Candice   Yes, getting wasted on beer, shitting your pants every morning, that is when you weren't wetting yourself twenty-four/seven. Wandering off all the time, scaring us half to death! It was always me that had to go out looking for yer! You couldn't even remember your own name half the time. And that smell. You stank, man. No word of a lie, Sam, you stank all the time. Why did you have to smell so bad, what was that about, tell me?

Sam   It's about getting old. It's about your body winding down, just giving up, and there is nothing you can do about it. It happens to us all, Candice; it will happen to you one day, and to all of your mates. But I didn't mean . . .

Candice   Yeah, you didn't mean. Dad didn't mean to run out and leave us. Mum don't mean to sit on her arse all day, watching telly, one roll-up after another. No one means to do anything, but they still do it. Answer me summin, Sam, did you mean to hurt that boy, that black kid, did you mean to kick his head in so bad, to buss him up to within an inch of his life? Did you? Waiting? You can't even answer me, can you?

Sam   Why don't I just go?

Candice   So go.

Sam *goes to leave.*

Candice   Why did you always let him push you around, Uncle Kenny?

Sam   Like Ryan does to you?

Candice   Ryan don't push me around.

Sam   Come off it.

Candice   Just answer my question, how did you do it, how did you say no to him?

Sam   Cos I couldn't bear the thought of losing her.

Candice   You mean Gran?

Sam   From the moment I saw her, I loved her. Do you see?

Candice   Nuh!

Sam   Cos you don't want to.

Candice   You did it cos you love her?

Sam   Yeah.

Candice   Do you have any idea how bruc that is?

Sam   You wanted the truth. I've told you this before.

Candice   You dashed yer brother and yer whole family, for *lurve*?

Sam   You never listened.

Candice   Is that what you are saying?

Sam   Yes, Candice, that is what I am saying. Things were different back then.

Candice   What good is that to me?

Sam   It might be if you listened, if you tried to understand.

Candice   Kids were fighting then, kids are fighting now, what's changed?

Sam   I changed, so can you.

Candice   Will you please just get out of my head.

Sam   You think I want to upset you?

Candice   Why should I change? I don't love anybody, nobody loves me.

Sam   I love you.

Candice   You're dead.

Sam   I'll always love you.

Candice   Look, go if you're going.

Sam   Candice?

Candice   Is this you going?

Sam   I'll go, if you really want me to go, you know that, but do you? Do you really want me to go? *Pudding?*

Candice   Don't call me that. Not unless you want to die, again!

Sam   You used to like me calling you that.

Candice   I've grown up, can't you see?

Sam   You will always be my little *pudding.*

Candice   Oh man, it's like nails on a chalkboard when I hear you say that.

Sam   You know it's true.

Candice   Listen to you, like you and me used to be tight or summin.

Sam   Who was it that bought you your first bike, your mum? Who stayed up all night with you in the hospital when you had that nasty ear infection? Your dad? And who was still there when you woke up in the morning? Who did you fling your arms around, smiling from ear to ear, when you finally learnt how to swim? If that's not being *tight*, I don't know what is.

Candice   Alright then, we were. Until Mum told me the truth about you and Uncle Kenny!

Sam   But what was it that I told you?

Candice   Did you really love Gran, or are you just chatting more noise here?

Sam   With all my heart.

Candice   Lie bad!

Sam   *Pudding* . . .

Candice   One more time, say it one more time, I dare you!

Sam   Why are you doing this?

Candice   Ca' you mek me sick. Carrying on like the two of yer were sweetness and life itself.

Sam   We were.

Candice   Mum says, she says the two of you couldn't stop arguing.

Sam   Of course we fought. We were man and wife.

Candice   Cos you didn't like being married to a black woman any more. Cos Mum was a half-caste.

Sam   Don't say that. Don't you say those words.

Candice   You have.

Sam   How many more times, it was different back then, like it is different now. Things should always be different, they should always change, otherwise we'd all be still living in caves.

Candice   Don't chat rubbish to me. You hated my mum cos she half-caste.

Sam   That's not true.

Candice   It is true.

Sam   You are only saying all this because you are avoiding –

Candice   Avoiding what?

Sam   The truth about what that lowlife made you do.

Candice   Ryan didn't make me do anything.

Sam   Did I say Ryan?

Candice *gets a text, she reads.*

Sam   That's him, isn't it, Ryan?

Candice   Yeah, he's on his way now. And there is nothing you can do.

Sam   But there is something you can do. Candice? I'm here to help you, my darling, but you have to listen, you have to remember. Everything I told you, everything about me.

Candice   I do remember, Sam. That's the problem.

There is fighting on the streets. **Kenny** *comes onstage, fighting off a gang of black boys.*

Kenny   Well, come on then! Come on then, darkie, you want me, here I am.

Sam   Get rid of him.

Candice   No.

Sam   Get rid of him, Candice.

Candice   You said remember, so I'm remembering, what you told me.

Sam   But you have to listen.

Candice   Make me then.

Kenny   Come on, you blacks!

Candice   Make me!

Kenny   These are our streets!

Sam   Our bloody streets!

Kenny (*chants*)   Keep Britain white.

Sam (*also chants*)   Keep Britain white.

Kenny *shoves him away.*

Sam   Oi!

Kenny   Get away from me.

Sam   Ken?

Kenny   I don't know you any more.

Sam   What have I done?

Kenny   I said get away from me!

Sam   Watch the suedes, mate.

Kenny   Take it off.

Sam   Kenny?

Kenny   Take it all off, cos you ain't fit to wear them.

Sam   What have I done?

Kenny   You've got a girl have you, Sammy?

Sam   Yeah.

Kenny   She just started work at the chemist?

Sam   It's what I said.

Kenny   You didn't say what colour she was though, you didn't tell me that.

Candice   That's right, you didn't.

Sam   Wait, please?

Candice   Mum was right.

Sam   Alright!

Kenny   Alright, he says!

Sam   So now you know.

Kenny   I wish I didn't.

Sam   You didn't speak to her, did you? You didn't say anything to her?

Kenny   I didn't even want to look at her. Mum and Dad will have a stroke each if they knew.

Sam   I'm surprised they ain't already, all the grief that you have put them through.

Kenny   You break it off with her right now, do you understand me?

Sam   No.

Kenny   Sammy?

Sam   I said no.

Kenny   We don't mix with the likes of them, you know that.

Sam   Gloria.

Kenny   You what?

Sam   Her name is Gloria. Gloria Rosene Kiffin.

Kenny   Have you completely flipped?

Sam   If yer gonna talk about her, if yer gonna hate her, at least know her name.

Kenny   What do I want to know her name for?

Sam   Cos she's a nice girl, Kenny. She's lovely.

Kenny   Let her crawl back to her own country.

Sam   This is her country!

Kenny   This is our country!

Sam   That's Mum and Dad talking.

Kenny   Too bleeding right.

Sam   Will you just stop!

Candice   Why don't you stop?

Kenny   I'll stop when every single one of them is gone.

Sam   Here we go.

Kenny   When our dad has his job back at the factory.

Sam   Every time.

Kenny   Have you told her what you do? What you get up to with me?

Candice   Yeah, we're on it now, ennit?

Sam   Don't.

Kenny   What would she think of you, if she saw you a few seconds ago, chanting 'Keep Britain white'?

Sam   Alright, I'm stupid.

Kenny   Brain-dead more like.

Candice   For real.

Sam   Yeah, I'm brain-dead. Brain-dead cos I always do what you say. Cos what you think of me matters.

Kenny   Get on your knees.

Sam   She'd hate me, she wouldn't want to speak to me, she'd spit in my face if you tell her – are you happy now?

Kenny   Yeah, cos it's the way it should be.

Sam   Why? Why should it be like that?

Kenny Cos they're black.

Sam Why is it cos they're black? Why do we have to hate them cos they're black?

Kenny Cos Dad can't work cos of them.

Sam If you gave them a chance –

Kenny I don't want to.

Sam Cos that's you.

Kenny Bang on.

Sam And Mum, and Dad, and everyone else round here – well, not me.

Candice Lie bad!

Sam Not any more.

Kenny All this cos you fancy some coloured bird?

Sam I don't fancy her. I love her!

Candice Lie! You lie bad!

Kenny You can't.

Sam I do, mate. I'm gonna ask her to marry me.

Kenny (*in a rage*) Sammy!

Sam My name is Sam. She likes to call me Sam.

Kenny Alright, *Sam*! I'm gonna put a stop to this, right now.

Candice Sorry, man, but I like him.

Sam What you doing?

Kenny I'm gonna tell her what you and I have been getting up to these last few weeks. Our little hunting trips.

Sam No.

Kenny Watch me.

Candice No, let him!

Sam   Kenny!

Sam *attacks his brother. They wrestle each other to the ground.* **Kenny** *is the stronger and manages to pin* **Sam** *down to the ground and keep him there.*

Candice   Yer hurting him.

Kenny   Have you had enough?

Candice   Get off.

Kenny   Sammy, have you had enough?

Candice   Get off him, man.

Kenny   Tell me you've had enough, Sammy.

Candice   Sam, just tell him.

Sam (*in pain*)   Enough, enough.

Kenny *releases him.*

Candice   Now go, go away.

Kenny *leaves.*

Candice (*to* **Sam**)   Are you alright?

Sam   I'm not proud of what I did.

Candice   Beating up black kids?

Sam   Yes!

Candice   So you kept telling me. On and on wid it.

Sam   After that day, I never saw him again.

Candice   And that.

Sam   I never saw any of them again, ever! My whole family. Mum died soon after, then Dad, and Kenny wouldn't let me go to their funerals. He said he'd kill me if I came anywhere near. He wouldn't even let me go to his – he told his wife and kids to keep me away.

Candice   Boring, Sam! I know all this.

Sam   No, you don't know! You're hearing, but you are not listening.

Candice   You know what? Gran shoulda dashed you the minute she found out what you did. I can't believe she married you.

Sam   Cos she loved me.

Candice   You ain't got nuttin to say to me. I love Ryan.

Sam   Do you?

Candice   Move now, before I hurt you.

Sam   Make me go then, come on.

Clint *enters.*

Clint   I can hear you shouting from the other side of town. Who you chatting to?

Candice   No one. What you get from Foot Locker?

Sam   So, that's it?

Clint   Try these.

Sam   You'd rather be a common thief than talk to me?

Candice *inspects the shoes.*

Candice   Won't fit.

Clint   You said size five.

Candice   These are seven.

Clint   There's madness out there, what you expect? Yet you want me to go all the way out and come back again. If yer so desperate for shoes, come with me. There is still JD Sports. Come on, we'll fleece it together?

Candice   No, I wanna stay.

Clint   Alex will text you when he gets here, come on.

Candice   He'll be here any sec though.

Clint   Back in a bit then.

Candice   Why don't you stay?

Clint   What do I want to stay for?

Candice   Well, think about it. If Ryan sees you, he might let you join his crew, it is what you want. Especially if you help him . . .

Clint   Beat up Alex?

Candice   Exactly. See, it's all good!

Sam   Don't do this.

Candice   This is your chance, man.

Clint   I don't want to join his crew now.

Candice   Since when?

Clint   Since now.

Candice   Lie!

Clint   Not if I have to be a skank.

Candice   Like me?

Clint   I didn't say that.

Candice   Look, I ain't his skank – yeah, I love Ryan, and he loves me. I know you are scared witless of him, Clint, so don't chat rubbish to me.

Clint *receives a text.*

Candice   I do as I do, I mean what I say.

Clint   When did you say Alex is coming?

Candice   Any second, I told you.

Clint   And Ryan?

Candice   Any second after.

She gets a text which she reads.

See, that's him.

Clint   Alex?

Candice   Yeah.

Clint   He just texted you?

Candice   That's what I said. He's nearly here, and I have to wait. You don't have to go right now, you know. We gotta bit of time.

Clint   Time for what?

Candice   You and me, ennit?

Clint   Are you chirpsin me?

Candice   What if I was? Are you man enough for me?

Clint   What about Ryan?

Candice   What about him?

Sam   Candice, don't.

Candice   He don't need to know.

Sam   Let him go.

Clint   What if Alex comes?

Candice   He's running late.

Clint   You said he was nearly here.

Candice   He is, but he's running late.

Clint   Why are you lying to me?

Candice   Who says I'm lying?

Clint   I am. Alex is in jail, Candice.

Candice   No, he ain't.

Clint   I just got a text from Nathan. He said he just saw Alex on the streets, getting arrested by the feds. So how could Alex have just told you he's running late?

Candice   Duh! He musta sent the text before he was arrested, ennit?

Clint   Him and Nathan were raiding JD Sports before he was arrested. You telling me Alex stopped to send you a text?

Candice   Obviously!

Clint   Why don't I call Nathan right now?

Candice   Do what you want.

Clint   Ask him if he saw Alex send a text to anyone.

Candice   If you not interested in me, Clint, you only have to say. It's not your fault if you ain't man enough.

Clint   Who sent you that text, Candice?

Candice   Alex, yer deaf?

Clint   Let me see.

Candice   No.

Clint   Pass me it.

Candice   Move!

Clint *grabs the phone off her.*

Candice   Pass it back.

Clint (*reads*)   From Ryan.

Candice   Don't make me hurt you, Clint.

Clint (*reads*)   'B THERE IN 5, KEEP IM DEH'! Keep who here?

Sam   Tell him.

Clint   Keep who here? If it ain't Alex, who, who is it?

Sam   Tell him.

Clint   It's me, ennit? Isn't it? That's why you were chirpsin me, that's why you kept wanting me to come back, ennit? Candice? Are you just going to stand there and say nuttin? Why me? Why me, what have I done?

Candice   What have you done?

Sam   Yeah?

Candice   You don't even like football.

Clint   Football?

Candice   Can't play to save your life, can you? Where you play, right back? Yes, right back to the dressing room.

Clint   What you saying?

Candice   Why did you cuss him?

Clint   Who?

Candice   Ryan, who else?

Clint   I never cussed Ryan.

Candice   You did.

Clint   When?

Candice   The other day in school, I heard you.

Clint   Saying what?

Candice   Laughing wid yer brers, cos Sergio Aguero scored two past Man U on Saturday.

Clint   Yeah, so?

Candice   'Yeah, so?'

Clint   The game was sic.

Candice   Are you stupid or summin?

Clint   I support Man City.

Candice   What you mean you support Man City? You have never even been to Manchester.

Clint   I still follow them though. I don't see Ryan traipsing up to watch Fergie's boys every other Saturday.

Candice See, that's what I am talking about. You know how loved up he is about Man U, from the time he learned how to walk, he had been a red through and through. You can't say things like that to him.

Clint I didn't though. He wasn't even there.

Candice He doesn't have to be. He heard what you said, and he ain't happy.

Clint So for that I'm gonna get shanked? Ryan is coming to shank me?

Candice It won't come to that.

Clint Tell that to Jermaine Thomas, and his family.

Candice You don't know he did that.

Clint I know. The feds know. The whole estate knows. You know! That's why you wanted me to come back. Sending me all dem texts, making out yer into me. So what was Alex?

Candice The first name that came into my head.

Clint Yer unreal, you know that? You are bloody unreal! Can't you get me out of this, can't you do that?

Candice No.

Sam Candice?

Candice No!

Clint Did you ever like me?

Candice What?

Clint Even once?

Candice Open your ears, Clint, and listen up, listen good. I could choose any brer on this estate, you know that. Ryan is ten times better looking than you. I love him, he loves me, what makes you think I would like a thieving little weasel like you? Cos I wouldn't, not now, not ever! I've known you since I was three years old, and all you've ever done since is follow me around. I'm sick of the sight of you, do you understand, do you get me?

Clint   How far would you have gone to keep me here?

Candice   All the way if needs be.

Clint   Ho!

Candice   I ain't no ho, Clint.

Clint   Yer Ryan's ho!

Candice   He loves me. He doesn't make me do anything that I don't want to do.

Sam   Candice?

Candice   Nobody makes me do anything I don't want to do. Look, Ryan ain't gonna shank you. It's not like you stole money from him, or stepped into the wrong endz is it?

Clint   Is that what Jermaine did?

Candice   Never mind Jermaine.

Clint   Did you chirps him too, set him up for Ryan, did you?

Candice   Will you shut up about him? Ryan just wants to scare you, beat you up a little, what's wrong with that?

Clint   Are you for real?

Candice   I'll be here, make sure they don't get carried away or nuttin. Ryan will listen to me.

Clint   They, who is they?

Candice   Well it's not going to be just Ryan, is it? He's bringing his whole crew.

Clint   To deal wid me? All this cos I follow Man City?

Candice   You shouldn't have said it. What are you doing, where do you think you are going?

Clint   I'm gone.

Candice   Gone where?

Clint   You think I'm gonna tell you. I ain't hanging around here to get beat up!

Candice   I don't think you understand, Clint.

Clint   I understand, I ain't stupid.

Candice   If you ain't here when he comes . . .

Clint   What? What? He'll beat me up?

Candice   He'll find you, he'll find you and he'll shank you. He will dead you, Clint. And that's nuttin compared to what he will do to me.

Clint   I thought you weren't scared.

Candice   I ain't scared, I ain't scared of anyone, I just don't need this madness.

Clint   You are mad up in the head.

Candice   You shouldn't have said what you said, now will you please, stop acting like some pussy and take your beating! I ain't playing wid you, Clint.

Clint   No, Candice.

Candice   Clint?

Clint   No! What happened to you, man?

Candice   Nuttin!

Clint   This ain't you.

Candice   It is me.

Clint   Since you got involved with Ryan, it is. Just get away from him.

Candice   I can't.

Clint   I thought you weren't scared.

Candice   I ain't.

Clint   Well, what you want then? What do you expect me to do? Just stand there and let him shank me?

Candice   I told you, he's not going to do that.

Clint   But you want me to get beat up though?

Candice   Well, what else do you want me to do?

Clint   Tell me what happened?

Candice   What?

Clint   Lauren's eighteenth birthday party. Tell me what happened.

Candice   Nuttin happened.

Clint   Least you can do right now is tell me the truth about that.

Candice   I am telling you the truth.

Clint   What did Ryan do to make you do?

Candice   He didn't make me do anything.

Sam   Yes he did.

Candice   No.

Sam   Say it.

Candice   Stop it, man.

Clint   Tell me . . . tell me, or I'm gone. (*He starts to leave.*)

Candice   Alright, I'm scared, I saw what Ryan did to Jermaine, and it scares me. Happy?

Clint   What else?

Candice   There is nothing else.

Clint   Why can't you tell me?

Sam   Tell him.

Candice   Why are you doing this to me?

Clint   It's true, ennit? It's bloody true, what I heard.

Candice   Heard what?

Clint   At the party.

Candice   Yeah?

Clint   His brers came.

Candice   Course they came, it was a party!

Clint   They took you upstairs, ennit?

Candice   They didn't take me anywhere. I go where I want.

Clint   He told you to do it with them.

Candice   Shut up.

Clint   Each one of them.

Candice   He never!

Clint   Ennit?

Candice   Ryan wouldn't do that.

Clint   Wouldn't do what, Candice?

Candice   He's my boyfriend.

Clint   Did he give you to them?

Candice   He's my boyfriend!

Clint   One by one?

Sam   That piece of –

Candice   See, this is what you don't understand.

Clint   Tell me . . . Tell me or I'm gone.

He starts to leave.

Candice   Ryan was desperate to join the crew. It meant everything to him. Join a crew; you get a family. Yer get brers who will die for you. Stand up for you. You get respect! He had to show how loyal he could be! It's alright, I didn't mind,

I wanted to help him. And I did help him, yeah, and that don't shame me. You don't know what you are talking about, so shut up. Nobody makes me do summin I don't want to do, get that in yer head.

Clint   Candice, they were laughing, man.

Candice   What?

Clint   About you.

Candice   Who was laughing?

Clint   What do you care?

Candice   What you saying?

Clint   It shouldn't matter, if he didn't do anything.

Candice   Tell me.

Clint   Ryan and his brers at school, flapping their gums about they couldn't believe their luck, that you would free it up that easy for them. They said you was crying like a baby, cos you couldn't keep up wid them.

Candice   Keep up wid dem?

Clint   Yeah. See, that's you all over, Candice, from the time you were five, you've been like this. That time when you were twelve, going on and on about that you could beat Donna Fraser in a race. And when it came down to it, she dashed you, she left you behind, cos you couldn't keep up. All you ever do is talk the talk.

Candice   Are you completely stupid or summin? You think racing Donna Fraser as the same as me getting ra –

Clint   What? What, Candice?

Sam   Say it.

Candice   You think you're smart now, Clint?

Clint   Tell me what they did to you, man.

Sam   Don't be afraid.

Candice   Why should I, you don't believe me.

Clint   You think I believe a word that comes out of Ryan's mouth? He don't care about you.

Candice   He does care about me.

Clint   Oh come on, man.

Candice   He's the only one that ever did care.

Clint   That don't mean he has give you to his brers, force you to . . .

Candice   He didn't do that, stop saying that.

Clint   'A stupid crying little sket!'

Candice   Say?

Clint   That's what he called you! A *sket*! And a *hoodrat*!

Candice   No.

Clint   I ain't lying.

Candice   Yes you are. He didn't say that.

Clint   I was there.

Candice   Why you saying this?

Clint   Cos I'm your friend, from when we were at nursery together. Cos I care. I always have.

Sam   Listen to him.

Clint   Gimme a chance.

Candice   Don't play me, yeah.

Clint   I won't.

Candice   Not you, Clint, I will dead you.

Clint   I won't.

Candice   You understand?

Clint   Yes!

Candice   Not you, yeah, not you.

Clint   Am I right? Tell me I'm right.

Sam   Tell him.

Candice   No.

Clint   Candice?

Candice   You're wrong. I did want it. It was easy. Ryan told me to close my eyes and pretend it was him, so that's what I did.

Clint   That's what he made you do.

Candice   That's what I did.

Clint   He made you do it, Candice.

Candice   No.

Clint   Yes.

Candice   That's what I did. That's what I did, that's what I did, that's what I did . . .

She is close to breaking down. **Clint** *is unsure what to do.*

Candice   No. Stay away, just get away from me.

Sam   You can do this, my darling.

Candice   Shut up.

Sam   Let it go.

Clint   Candice?

Candice   'Candice' what? What do you want from me, Clint? What do you want, the truth? The truth? Alright, I'll give you the truth seeing you are so desperate to hear. I was begging him, over and over, please don't make me do it. And in that bedroom, with his brers, one by one as you put it, I was begging him again, in my head, I was begging for Ryan to come and get me, to kick the door down and drag me out of there, but he never came, not until they were all done wid me.

He took me home, but he never looked at me, not once. Like he was ashamed, ashamed of me. I don't love him, I hate him, I hate him, I hate him, he makes me sick, but I can't leave him. So what I am supposed to do? Ryan is still coming, he's on his way, what are we supposed to do?

Clint   I dunno.

Candice   Just as I thought.

Clint   Just let me think.

Candice   Think about what, there's nothing else to do.

Sam   Yes there is. You just need to remember.

Candice (*aside to* **Sam**)   Remember what?

Sam   What I told you, the last time I saw my brother.

Kenny *appears.*

Kenny   Have you done it yet?

Sam   Done what?

Kenny   Told that black girl to sling her hook, of course?

Sam   No, I haven't, and I ain't going to.

Kenny   Sammy!

Sam   If you don't leave me alone, Kenny, I'll go to the police. I will tell them what you did.

Kenny   You'll grass me up?

Sam   Yeah, I would.

Kenny   You're forgetting something, you'll go down as well, mate.

Sam   I don't care. I'll tell them what you did, Ken, what we both did, I swear.

Kenny   I can't believe you are saying this to me.

Sam   Believe it.

Kenny   You're a stranger me, a total bloody stranger.

Sam   Yeah, I must be.

Kenny   Well then, you had best be on your way then, hadn't yer?

Sam   I suppose so.

Kenny   I don't want to set eyes on you ever again.

Sam   Right.

Kenny   Don't go home, don't you ever go home again, do you understand me? You're on your own.

Sam   I know.

Kenny   I'll square things with Mum and Dad?

Sam   Tell them I love them.

Kenny *takes out all of his money from his wallet.*

Kenny   Here, take this.

Sam   I don't want yer money.

Kenny   I know you don't want it, but you need it.

Sam   You don't have to keep worrying about me.

Kenny   You're my little brother. Of course I worry. Now take it!

Sam *takes the money.*

Kenny   Now come here.

The brothers embrace. **Kenny** *is first to pull away.*

Kenny   Now I have to turn my back on yer.

Sam (*tearful*)   Kenny?

Kenny   No! Yer dead to me.

He leaves. **Sam** *watches him go.*

Candice   Sam?

Sam (*in tears*)   Do you see? Do you see now?

Clint *turns to face* **Candice**.

Clint   I don't want to get shanked.

Candice   Say again?

Clint   I don't want to get shanked. A beating. That's all I'm gonna get, you said. Just a beating. I can handle that.

Candice   Are you mad or what, Clint?

Clint   Where am I gonna run to? What's gonna happen to you? I don't want summin else bad happening to you.

Candice (*sighs*)   My phone is dead, gimme yours.

Clint   Why, what you gonna do?

Candice   Phone, gimme!

Clint *hands her his phone.* **Candice** *dials a number.*

Candice   Yo, Ryan, where are you? Well, do me a favour yeah, turn right around and go right home, cos Clint ain't here.

Clint (*protests*)   Candice!

Candice *motions* **Clint** *to shut up.*

Candice   I said he ain't here. Yeah, I know what you wanted, but he ain't here! In fact not only is not here, I ain't gonna bring him to you.

Clint   She's dead.

Candice   I want you to leave him alone. You heard me! Leave him. He's a Man City supporter, so what? Deal wid it. Ryan, I don't think you heard me. Well, you need to, you really need to, cos if you don't, I'm calling the feds! You know what for, you know what for, you bloody well know! Listen yeah, no, shut up, yeah, shut up, as in close yer mout and stop talking, *shut up*! You go anywhere near Clint, you touch a hair on his head, and I'm gonna straight to Five-O, I will tell them

everything, about Jermaine, about me, you understand?
Everything! Yes, I bloody will. Clint ain't nuttin, nor am I. It's
not like I am yer only girl, innit? You think I don't know about
you and Jessica? How stupid do I look? And don't even get me
started on that Carly! Why don't you use your brain for once,
Ryan, is all this really worth the aggravation yer gonna get?
Yer done with, Clint, yer done! And I am done wid you! Don't
ever come near me again. That's noneya business, not your
problem. Don't play me, Ryan. I'm serious. Why did you
make me do it? You know what I am talking about, don't lie
to me, why did you make me do it? The party, Ryan, Lauren's
eighteenth, why did you make me do it? No, I didn't, no, no,
listen, yeah, listen to me, just shut up for a second . . .

Sam   You can do it.

Candice   I DIDN'T WANT THAT, RYAN!

Sam   That's my girl!

Candice   I didn't want that. I didn't want that, I didn't want
that, no girl would want that. It's not my fault. I didn't want
that, and it's not my fault, are you hearing me, Ryan, it was
not my fault! It wasn't my fault. We are done, right?

She hangs up. She throws the phone back to **Clint** *who drops it.*

Candice   Seventeen years old, and you still can't catch.

Clint   Are you mad?

Candice   It's over, Clint.

Clint   But it ain't right though, what he did to you.

Candice   It's over! You should go home now.

Clint   No, I want to stay wid you.

Candice   Clint, I'm alright. I just need to be on my own for
a while, just go home please, I'll see you tomorrow. I'm alright,
and so are you. More than in fact.

Clint   I'll catch you later then.

Candice   Thanks, yeah.

She smiles, **Clint** *smiles back before leaving.*

Candice   I have to leave. Don't I?

Sam   You know you do.

Candice   Up north, to see Aunt Cheryl?

Sam   You always liked her. I have something at home for you, something I wanted to give to you. Five-one-nine-four. Your birthday.

Candice   Yeah, I know.

Sam   That's the PIN. My account number is at home. It's not much, about four grand. It's yours.

Candice   Sam?

Sam   Bedside table, picture of your gran . . .

Candice   Picture of my gran . . .

Sam   I wrote it down . . .

Candice   Written on the back . . . in case you forgot.

Sam   You've seen it?

Candice   Seen it, teifed it, spent it.

Sam   You stole my money?

Candice   No, I borrowed your money.

Sam   Without intending to give it back?

Candice (*giggling*)   Well, yeah. Sorry.

Sam   You spent all of my money? You spent four grand? On what, Candice?

Candice   I dunno, things.

Sam   Like?

Candice   The flat-screen in my room for one.

Sam That bleeding monstrosity in your bedroom cost you four grand?

Candice One grand, actually.

Sam You told me a mate gave it to you.

Candice (*scoffs*) And you believed me.

Sam Well then, would you mind telling me how much is left?

Candice This is exactly as I imagined it, you losing your rag like this. I love it. About eight hundred or summin.

Sam Well it's better than nothing. Use that, use the eight hundred. Buy a train ticket, go stay with your Aunt Cheryl.

Candice All the times I asked you to dash me a tenner, you going on about how bruc you were.

Sam I always had money. I just didn't *have* money.

Candice Why did you never tell Mum?

Sam Is that a joke? The way she spends.

Candice Point. So, what about you?

Sam Me? I've got a date, remember? Taking your gran to the flicks.

Candice Best get going then.

Sam Say nice things about me, you know, next week?

Candice Most def! They're nice threads.

Sam Yes, very funny.

Candice I mean it. Grandad.

Sam *smiles.*

Candice *watches her grandfather leave.*

She addresses the audience.

Thank you all for coming. Until a while ago, I thought I knew everything I needed to know about my grandfather, Sam Mullings. And what I knew, I didn't like. I couldn't wait to get away from him. He was dead to me before he even died. Turns out, he was more alive than I ever thought possible. He was always thinking of me, even when I wasn't thinking of him. If I was, I would have realised how much he gave up for my mum and for me, just to be with us. Sam Mullings did bad things just like us, and good things just like us. He felt the same as me; he felt the same as all of us. At times like this, our saving grace is that the good people in our lives leave good things to the world. They leave good things behind like love. It's what makes us miss them, it's what makes them a blessing. Bless you, Sam Mullings, my grandfather. Live to learn, and learn to live, yeah? Peace.

Clint *returns. He and* **Candice** *embrace each other for the last time.* **Clint** *then hands* **Candice** *her travel bag before going.*

Candice *walks away.*

Death of England

Death of England premiered at the Dorfman Theatre, London, on 6 February 2020, with the following cast and creative team:

Michael   **Rafe Spall**
Understudy Michael   **Cary Crankson**

Director   Clint Dyer
Set and Costume Designers   Sadeysa Greenaway-Bailey
                                           and ULTZ
Lighting Designer   Jackie Shemesh
Co-sound Designers   Pete Malkin and Benjamin
                                           Grant
Movement   Lucy Cullingford
Dialect Coach   Hazel Holder
Staff Director   Sian Ejiwunmi-Le Berre

Death of England was originally commissioned as a micro-play by the Royal Court Theatre and Guardian News and Media Ltd, written by Roy Williams.

Death of England

For Stephen Jeffreys & Barrie Keeffe

Characters

Michael, *White, thirty-nine*

Part One

Flower Stall

Michael *is selling flowers on his dad's stall.*

Michael (*in mid flow*) . . . I must have looked like a cadaver but one with eyes determined not to close . . . ever. Determined to create or re-create the best sell . . . the best service . . . just like him . . . just like he would do. Then a customer pops into view like a long overdue bus. He was a small weaselly kinda fellow . . . in a Burberry knock-off mac . . . He looked somewhere between 80's football hooligan and the manager of a Prêt a fucking Manger . . .

'So, what can I do ya for mate?'

I say with one of my winning smiles . . .

'make-up flowers, wanna get laid flowers or I've spunked me pay on the gee gees' flowers?'

Nothing back from him . . . like talking to a pane of glass. I could almost see my breath on his coldness.

'Oh, judging from that boat race of yours, I would say, it's the please forgive me, I love you flowers. Is that right? I won't ask why or what you've done, I'm not judging you my friend. Let me get these for yer.' (*Cuts the stems off the flowers as he makes a small but impressive bouquet, with complete ease.*)

With my back turned I could hear his eyes rolling at me . . . I had to win him over . . . but my Charlie- and alcohol-ridden body was sweating out my shame.

'It's alright mate, you can trust me, I won't tell a soul. You wanna see me more like coming to confession and paying for some flowers . . . it's like your penance. Whatever it is, like I said, don't tell me, I do not need to know, just, whatever it is if you want my advice, it is up to you at the end of the day, take it or leave it, but it's going for free, so if I was you I'd take it, the advice that is, if I were you, listening to me, saying if I, were you? Get it? No mind, I do go on a bit, and this is usually the bit when I say my missus keeps telling me I go on too much, but seeing as I aint got a missus, I can't. Well, that is not strictly true, I do have a missus of sorts, we are just working stuff out you know how it is, well course you do, you are buying some of my finest *I love you, please forgive me* for your missus.'

I broke him . . . his face creased and then it came like manna from heaven . . . a fucking smile . . . from ear to ear . . . he was mine the cunt . . . he was coming back for sure, Dad would have been proud. 'I mean you wouldn't be buying them for my missus now would yer? (*Looks serious.*) Would yer? (*Laughs.*) Only messing mate, only messing. Now, where was I? Where was? Oh, that's it, my advice to you, in times like this, what you have to do is, throw yourself at the mercy of the court! Whatever it is, whatever you've done, hold your hands up, cough it up, plead guilty, all of that, tell her you love her. It's all about giving her control, they love that, the idea of them having your balls in their hands every once in a while. Works a treat. Let them have it I say, what harm can it do? (*Finishes the bouquet.*) Here you go chief, call it a pony.'

Then just like that his face changed, all downcast, as quick as a finch passing your window and then he said it. Caught me off guard it did . . . I didn't realise . . . he's a fucking regular . . . I hadn't twigged.

Mr Weasel   My condolences.

– He says, rubbing his greying beard like it's the cure for cancer. Shit my eyes started to well . . . I begged them to recede . . . just for a bit till he's gone . . . don't . . . don't cry I told myself.

Michael   Thank you mate, that means a lot, cheers.

Mr Weasel   When's the funeral?

– He asked like ordering a pizza at Franca fucking Manca. I wanted him gone. Now . . . fuck off will ya.

Michael   A week on Wednesday. We're hoping it draws a big crowd, well you know what kind of a man he is, or was, I should say. I hope to see you there, at the church.

Then he looks to the floor and I could see him biting his lip and his brow furrowed like a British bulldog.

Mr Weasel   He was proper your dad . . . I had a lot of respect for him . . . wished I had a dad like him . . .

He then shoved the money in my hands and was off. *Usain Bolt* style . . . It was gonna be a long day.

The lights go down.

The lights come up and **Michael** *addresses the audience again.*

Michael   If we'd a shop I swear the sign would never be shit. I've never got it you know. I'm standing outside with a little bit of shelter from the weather with these stalls . . . and I'm looking in front, across the road. And it's a fruit and veg shop. And the sign is half falling off. I mean it's your signature innit, it's your moniker you know . . . it's like a man and his shoes innit. Shit shoes shit moves, every girl knows that, am I right? You dun know. Same with signs. If my dad could have gotten a shop . . . the sign would have been mint . . . (*he starts to laugh*) my school had a great sign . . . tell ya a story about a sign. It was the big sign that they had hanging over the gates to our school, the school crest. Now before I begin, it was Delroy's idea, not mine, oh no, Delroy, he was the mastermind that wanted to pull it down. Dad used to go to the school as well, and he was talking of boys, pulling it down and running off with it, it was sort of the school ritual, back in the day, although it hadn't been done in years, according to our history teacher, Mister Quinn. The way Delroy saw it, it was like Mister Quinn was daring us, if not the whole class, to do it, to take that sign. It was our last year at school, we might as well be remembered for something. So, we nicked it. We 'borrowed' a ladder from the school caretaker. I held it from the bottom, as Delroy climbed his way up. Easier than I thought, the

emblem wasn't even fastened that well onto the wall anyway.
Bit of sticky tape. Held together from the last time some boys
took the sign down. That sums up how cheap our school
was, don't it? The way I think it, me and Delroy saved
someone's life by taking it, cos Delroy was going on at the
top of the ladder about it being all wobbly and that. That
school owed us, and how they pay us back? They end up
giving a two days' suspension and double detention when we
got back. It was a nice little thing, with a large crow in full
flight in the middle, made of brass, heavy as fuck. Delroy
told me to 'hold my hands out' with that laid-back roadman
flick of the chin, not to be outdone in roadman cool, I rolled
a middle finger out of me fist and said 'dream on rude bwoi'
while checking for any Babylon . . . I had to climb up the
ladder and we both had to bring it down gently. We just
wanted to nick it, we were not vandals or anything. Fuck
knows what we both wanted to do with it after we got it
down, no point in putting it back up, no point at all, if no
one knows about what you did. The teachers had to notice it
was gone, the headmaster got to at least pull a stroke and
that, so we took it to the park, shared a ciggie, like we always
do and waited. Now, the best part of any plan, actually the
worst part of any plan, is the unknown factor. Something
that you couldn't ever predict, no matter how smart you are,
comes into play. Now, I aint saying, me and Delroy are a
couple of Stephen Hawkings here, but we did a pretty swish
job, if I may so say so, of taking down that school sign
without anyone noticing, all during the school lunch break.
Anyhow, where was? Oh yes, the unknown factor, in other
words, Delroy's mum. She saw us in the park, all five feet ten
of her, full of noise, like all of them black women on full
volume are. After what I thought was a small encounter she
marched me all the way to my dad's stall. This was not the
usual move for a woman . . . but this was Denise, British
born but was taken to Jamaica on a regs like. Loved her
lovers' rock but could kill some dutta ragga on the dance
floor I bet. She had a gold tooth that you only saw when she
smiled . . . which for me was not often. Thin well-kept long

dreads . . . and she was fit as in hot . . . even then I'd have loved to have gone a few rounds, but I knew I'd be going down in the first. . . no split decision there. Anyway . . . she flicked a dread from her face and launched in.

Denise   Your boy and my bwoi weren't at school today, you know why?

– in that half cockney half patwa way.

My dad shakes his head and folds his arms, not even looking at me.

Alan   No, but I don't need Mystic Meg to know you are going to tell me why.

With a rude girl tilt of her head and lift of an eyebrow she replied:

Denise   You see that big sign they have at school over the main gates, the crest?

Alan   Yes, I know it, I went to school there as well.

Denise   Well it aint there now. It's gone, it's been nicked. Someone pulled it down. Your son nicked that sign and dragged my boy into it.

Finally, he takes me in with a glare of disapproval and pride. I looked away, playing with the chrysanthemum like I'd found love.

Alan   How do you know it was even him? It could have been your boy's idea? Why are you dragging my lad into it? No offence.

I didn't know which was annoying her more, her dreadlock falling across her face or my dad . . . giving the lock a hard brush from her now hot face.

Denise   No offence what?

– she shot back at him.

Alan   No offence nothing. It's what we say isn't it?

Denise   We?

Alan   Yes, we, you, me everyone! Don't be so touchy.

Her feet parted, and I could feel the temperature rise.

Denise   I aint touchy. It's not even about the *sign,* me and Delroy have had words about that. I saw dem, our boys in the park. Smoking God knows what, laughing about what they did. When I challenged them on it, your son, your little boy called me a black bitch. To mi face!

Now, now I admit, not right, I know. But fair do's, I was only 15, and Delroy's mum does love to go on, when she gets a roll going, it's hard to break her up. Only something personal, like calling her that, would do it. I aint saying it's right, but it worked, it shut her up, good.

Alan   Whoa! Danger, Will Robinson, whoa! Whoa! That is hardcore.

Her voice started to wobble and like a stitch after running I felt a pang of guilt.

Denise   I was cussing my boy when him say that. For bunking off school and stealing things that don't belong to him. I didn't even business wid yer boy, till he come out with that. My bwoi, goes to church.

Alan   Fucking Hitler went to church.

To cut a long story, it was all about to kick off.

Alan   Why don't you go and protest outside the town hall, like the rest of your mob, leave me alone and let me graft will yer?

Denise   I know what yer about.

– she growled, now letting the stray dreadlock fall on her face.

Rights for whites, England first, all that bullshit.

Alan   Oh, take yer swing and fuck off. Giving the big I am, I mean who the fuck? I mean, Jesus, H!

They were now almost touching they was so close.

Denise   Like you want to tek a swing.

– she inquired. Dad pulls his neck right in, a little ashamed of himself.

Alan   Leave off I am better than that.

Denise just laughs loudly in his face.

Denise   Yer better than that?

Alan   That's right, now fuck off.

Denise   And you wonder why we're forever at the town hall protesting.

She didn't say it but all he heard was 'you racist' and that got to 'im, coz his tic started . . . little thing his lip did when he felt on the ropes.

Alan   Here we go, every time. It's regular!

– He put to her with much disdain.

Denise   I've been living in Essex all my life, I am not having it from you.

Alan   Pipe down.

Denise   Talk to yer bwoi.

They look straight at me, I just wanted to be swaddled and put in a pram.

Alan   Don't tell me what to do.

Denise   Will you please talk to your bwoi?

– she insisted.

Alan   You bet your sweet life I am talking to him. You think I want wars at my stall, with my neighbours?

– his tic now a permanent wobbling grimace.

Denise   My boy will get the blame for this. You know that, my boy will get the blame.

And she was right, I knew it, Dad knew it, we all knew it.

Alan   I remember yer boy. Good footballer.

She cocked her head back with a knowing look and replied –

Denise   He is also good at maths.

Alan   I will speak with Michael.

– he answered, looking across at me with disdain.

Denise   You do that.

– also looking at me with disdain.

Alan   btw . . . Yer hair's nice.

Denise   Fuck you.

(*Laughs.*) And that was it, from then on, me and Delroy, both of our families, became entwined. I would go round to Delroy's, and his mum would feed me the hottest Jamaican patties ever, I'm no expert on Jamaican patties or anything but jeez they were hot. I thought she was doing it on purpose, you know, pay back for the school and that, but I then look over at Delroy's face, and he was suffering an all, make your arse burn and everything. Tasty though, has to be said. You won't want to eat anything else that day, after one of Delroy's mum's patties. I almost felt ashamed when he would come round to ours. I love my mum, but she was not the best cook, it has to be said. It was Dad, he was the dogs in the kitchen, Sunday lunch was his triumph. He could do a mean roast lamb our dad. But you can't have roast lamb every day though, can yer? Most nights, it was fish and chips, pizza, and whatever was left in the freezer. Delroy was always good at pretending he was enjoying our food. I felt for him. Not only did he have to deal with that, but he had my bleeding sister Carly giving him earache. Right fucking bully, Carly. The amount of times Mum and

Dad had to go to the school and speak to the teacher about her. Delroy was a Gent, you don't hit girls, but boy there were times when I wanted him to make an exception in Carly's case, especially when she was dropping one bad joke after another about him being 'coloured'. She thinks she's got the licence cos Dad does it but at least he's subtle, not in front of the boys. *'Time and place for that'*, he always said. Carly was full of shit though. She had the serious melt for Delroy from the moment she clapped eyes, can't get enough of him, all that racist lark was a front cos she knows Dad would lose his nut. Crazy bitch. She always wanted approval from him. Then again, we all did. *'Time and place though.'* Dad was all about time and place. Whenever him and right-wing nut job mates would come round the house and discuss how they would take the country back from the Blacks, Mum would send us out with a tenner, to buy a McDonald's and stay there, time and place. When Delroy and I had a falling out over who broke my Nintendo, and we had a fight about it, Dad made me go back out and fight him again and keep fighting him until I won. I never did. Time and place. All those times he would cover my ears at Leyton Orient, whenever they aimed their shit at a black player, time and place. But never at his stall. Black, Asian, yellow, it didn't matter to him who bought flowers, not a jot. He kept his black this, chinky that shit to himself then, time and place. But when we were told we were going to have a referendum at long bleeding last on Europe, oh, no stopping him, no stopping any of them. It was like he was let out of prison, they all were, we're going to get our country back, immigrants out, all of that. It meant fuck all to me, but him, oh my word. Every conversation he had on the stall. The month leading up to it, he did the worst business for years, and never wondered why, or he refused to. The leave voters win and now the Tories don't know their arse from their elbow. Nationalism, eh? Well he paid for that. . . *'England for the English'* he'd say like he'd never read a fucking book . . . like he'd never watched *Passage to* fucking *India*. He bloody cried. Tried to make out he didn't but I saw him . . . like he didn't love Mo Farah. Nationalism . . . Brexit and then came the World Cup. Southgate and his men, well boys, and we start so well don't we (*sardonic laugh*). Sorry, it's just . . . well . . . you know. Semi-final. I had clocked off from work at 5, Dad was already in the Duke, making sure he could reserve a couple of stools in the front. Dad hated standing up, I told him we could watch the game at home, but he weren't interested, he wanted to see it on the big screen, and he was desperate for some English glory. Not his own glory, not something that he had earned himself . . . worked for himself . . . made himself . . . proxy glory. The kind where all you have to do is shout a bit and you can claim you did it, type of glory. He wanted it, he needed it. Nationalism . . . not to confused with patriotism . . . he wanted to feel better than the rest, more powerful, more dominant. . . like the old days . . . But I'm happy too, the whole pub is jubilant.

Alan   Look at their shirts. They look like table cloths.

– he joked.

Can't believe he's still playing Sterling he's shit for England.

– now looking serious, almost violent. I thought I'd try and calm him down.

Michael   He's low on confidence aint he?

Alan   He's low on fucking Englishness.

– he sharply replied, swigging his third pint.

Michael   All them racist threats and stuff on Twitter can't help can it?

– he turned and looked at me with such . . . well, disgust, I laughed out of embarrassment . . .

Alan   Let's just watch the game son.

Five minutes in. Five fucking minutes! Trippier was up for the free kick. I thought I could read him. He plays for bloody *Spurs*, you can read them lot like a book. He was on target and he was going to kick it low and he was going to kick it hard, but nowhere near the sodding goal, I just bloody know it.

He relives it. Trippier scores. Crowd erupts.

Who knew? Who the fuck knew he was going to sweep the ball over the wall like that and into the top corner, fucking who? Dad was beaming like a Christmas tree! We'd won the referendum, and football, finally, was coming home! We were English! We believed! Yes, but . . .

Croatia scores.

(*Sighs.*) And English being bloody English, we spent so much time patting ourselves in the back, we let the bleeding Croats slowly crawl themselves back up our arse to cause untold damage. And damage they did. 22 minutes left, 22 bleeding minutes away from being in our first final since '66. Twenty-two, and they worked us, they played us, right off the pitch. As soon as I turned my back to the game as I was going for an overdue slash, Croatia scored. It was like someone turned a tap at my dad's ankles releasing all his blood.

Michael   Dad it's ok, we can pull it back.

But then we start playing like old England . . . long balls and bad touches and Dad was getting more and more wound up.

Alan   Somebody show a little quality will ya!!! We're better than this!!! We're English!!!

Dad's heart broke when the next went one in. That should have been my first clue, he was starting to sweat, and loosening another button on his shirt. Hindsight, eh? The rest of the game was torture, absolute torture. Three Lions? More like three kittens. I joked with Dad about this could be a metaphor for us leaving the EU. Again, he gave me one of his devil stares. He was not amused, like I wanted Remain or something, he still wanted to know which way I voted . . . I'd been telling him it was my business . . . but he looked so down. 'Leave, Dad. Leave of course' my eye quivering under the weight of my lie, but he didn't buy it. I kept telling him I was Leave all the way. I think if I had told him I didn't vote at all that would have finished him off. I didn't have time for the way he used to get my back up about it. Leave? Remain? Who gives a shit? I said whatever to shut him up, All I wanted was for that sorry excuse for the game to end.

Alan   Torture!

– he said leaning right up against me, like he was going to sleep, which is what I thought he was. Mum went crackers when I told her that. 'How could you think he was sleeping?' she whispered, broken. 'I'm not a bleeding doctor' . . . that's why he looked peaceful. Just lying on me. All tragic and that, cos the way he felt about the football . . . England. I should have known. I gave him a minute, plenty of time for the rest of the pub to clear out, then we would go. It didn't take me long, I swear, to know Dad weren't sleeping. Well, he was sleeping, in a way, you know what I mean. According to the doc, it was his heart just gave out. No drama. It just stopped beating. Sayonara and all that. It happens. More than you think. The heart stops. You stop. Dad stopped. Fucking England. You think they'd fucking give him a proper send off, you know, if that was his time to go. The World Cup Final, us vs France. Something like that, I mean. That is all they could muster for my dad, after years of watching, total belonging. That shower was to be his last game. *Alan Fletcher!* Thank You God. By the way you have one fucked-up sense of humour, you know that? You come for him at an England game, that England game? What a vicious cunt you are. I mean it's wrong.

I'm not sure how long I held him in my arms, while waiting for the ambulance. I didn't cry. That came later. Everything came later.

Part Two

Family Kitchen

Michael *just sits at the kitchen table and stares at his phone that continues to ring. He does not answer. Just stares.*

Michael That is how it was that night. My phone just kept ringing and ringing. It was Mum, wondering where the two of us were, what was keeping us? She knew what the score was and knew Dad would not be happy. I don't know why I didn't answer, kept her hanging. I suppose I couldn't believe it. I needed a breather to take it all in. Is that so wrong? Who the fuck wants to tell their mum their husband keeled over without a warning? I didn't wanna see that face she does. All me life . . . like I remember when . . . I mean . . . me bike, When Delroy broke it, I knew he didn't do it on purpose. I didn't care. But the old man was not having any of it. I stood here, right in the middle of this kitchen as he lectured me on it's our country, not theirs they should learn their place, all the usual. Mum just stood behind like she does, and she did not say a word, she just stood. With that disapproving look on her face. She drove me mad with it. That was the same face she had on, when I walked in here that night to tell her about Dad. She wanted to know if I was on the piss again, and before I could even answer, she's telling me she does not blame Evelyn, my wife, ex-wife I mean, for leaving me. Mum knows where to strike, believe me she does, mentioning my bitch of an ex-wife is going to get me going and Mum knew that. But it wasn't the time for that, I had to tell her about Dad, I had to cut her off from all of the usual shit, i.e. pick on Michael day.

Michael Mum. Don't you want to know where Dad is?

– I said trying to sound like a grown up but sounding younger and younger with each syllable.

You can put my head on a stick later, alright?

My eyes started to well and I could see she noticed . . . she became so still, like a wax-work as she asked –

Mum Where?

Michael That is what I am trying to tell you. Mum, give me your hand?

I hadn't held my mum's hands since the noughties and she knew that . . . and just looked blankly at my sweaty palm.

Michael Just give me your hand, Mum.

Mum Why?

– she whispered.

Michael Mum, please just give me your hand. Something bad happened.

I wanted to just curl up in a ball. I wanted to just have her hold me and to tell me . . . I don't know what but something, anything that meant I was not an adult . . . a man. I froze.

Mum Michael! For fuck's sake.

– she exclaimed now, scared out of her mind . . . her eyes darting at what might follow.

Michael Dad was in the pub.

Mum I know he was in the pub, he was in the sodding pub with you.

Michael He had a heart attack or something.

She just stared at me, eyes wide.

Heart attack, he had a bleeding heart attack, it came out of nowhere, and he died . . .

I said it, it fell out of my mouth like a large black lump of iron, but her face didn't move an inch.

He's dead. I'm sorry. Mum? Mum, did you hear?

And there it was, the same look she had when I told her and
Dad about Delroy busting my bike. The same look she had
when I told her Evelyn wanted a divorce. Like I had done
something, like I had killed Dad. I mean what the fuck? And
if that weren't enough, I had Carly standing there with her,
either side of me, hate in stereo . . . bitches in stereo . . . I
know, out of order, but it's how I felt.

Mum   What happened?

Michael   I don't know Mum. His heart just gave out.

Mum   Why didn't you call?

Michael   I don't know.

I knew. I was scared of you! But I wasn't gonna say that
was I?

Mum   You don't know?

– she quizzed as Carly started to pace around like a
Doberman dog trying to work out who to bite first.

Michael   I needed to think.

Mum   He's my husband

– she said, now clearly finding it hard to breathe.

Michael   Mum, I know, don't you think I know, he's your
husband, but he was my dad.

Carly   He was my dad as well!!!

– Carly yelled, her face full with blood.

Michael   Oh, here it comes, here comes Carly.

– I parried meekly with.

Carly   Michael?

Michael   Well don't start, alright? Just don't start. I weren't
thinking.

Carly   You never think.

– Carly jabbed.

Michael   Well alright then. Yer right Carly, yer bang on, I wasn't bloody thinking.

I turned to Mum and she was wilting badly, aging by the second like in some fairy tale.

Mum? Mum? Just let me hold your hand, will yer?

Mum   I wanna see him.

– she said moving away from me.

Michael   Of course. Of course, d'you want me to take ya?

Mum   I'll take a taxi.

She looked up at me, hollow with grief like I did it . . . like I had in a fit of Oedipal rage struck my father down to claim his space.

Michael   Mum, come on please, you don't need a taxi, I'll take you to him, just let me please. I'm sorry.

Carly   I can't believe that is all you have to say.

– piped in Carly, smelling blood.

Michael   Oh erm . . . it'll be alright Mum . . . no, of course it won't be alright, see I beat you to it Carly . . . I should have known you'd say something like that, yeah, fuck you an all sis! Sorry Mum, so sorry. I'm just sorry I didn't know what to do. Do you want to see him or what?'

Carly   Wanker.

Michael   Carly, Carly, can you do me a favour please, Carly! Just close your mouth, Carly, just stop talking. He was my dad as well! I'm sorry Mum, I know I keep saying it, but what else you want me to say? What else eh? Yeah, yeah, I knew, I bloody knew, you would take her side, sweet little Carly. Always the way, not so sweet, going behind you and Dad's back. Yeah, tell Mum that sis, tell them all about it. You and Delroy, and your weekends away in Blackpool. Yeah Mum, her and him. What are you going to say about that?

It's like we can't help ourselves, we Fletchers, we always love a ruck no matter what, where, or with who, mostly with each other. Though I couldn't believe how silent we all were when I drove them to the hospital, Carly with her death ray stares at me. Mum, doing nothing, just staring out into space. Not a single expression on her face, even when she saw him, when she leaned in and gave him a kiss on the head. She asked me again, 'what happened?' over and over. I mean, what the fuck did she want me to say, the old man and I had another fight? We went right at it, causing him to keel over or something, and I went in for the kill, and then his heart gave in. Does that paint a prettier picture for her? I'm sick and tired of not knowing what she wants. You could have knocked me down with the number 3 bus when she started laughing. It happened after I brought her home. Made her tea, told her I would take after Dad. I would look after her, the whole family, make her proud, make the old man proud, I would be Alan Fletcher's son. I have never seen her laugh so much, not since *Only Fools* was on. The episode with Del-Boy falling arse over tit through the bar. *'Yer cramping my style Trigger'*. That did it for her every time. *'You'*, she said, over and over, would not stop. I saw tears in her eyes, from all the laughing, the fucking laughing, at me. Even Carly didn't know what to do with her herself. I didn't want another ruck, far from it, I didn't have the strength.

Michael   What Mum? What, what is it? What's so funny?

She came with it. All of it, both barrels.

Mum   You looking after me? Look after the family? You can't even look after yourself!

– that I may be Alan Fletcher's son, his only boy but I am not him. I will never be him. All I am is a disappointment, all I do is fuck things up. My job. My wife.

Mum   What do you believe in Michael? Tell me? What do you stand for, like your dad stood for, what do you believe?

She had me there, she really had me.

What do I believe in? I don't know. All that stuff he said, immigrants, blacks, Muslims, Fucking Brexit! Conservative, Labour, the UN, global warming, bloody Corbyn, harvesting Mars, free trade, the IMF, war on terror, NHS, porn laws, burkas, *MeToo*, minimum wage, paedo priests, *Donald Orange Trump*. I heard! I nodded, but what do I believe? Fuck knows. How he did I don't know. I mean at the end of the day, what does it matter?

Michael   I don't know Mum, so what does it matter what I do or don't do or what I do and don't believe? We're family and I love you, I love you all, even mouthy Carly over there, I love you all, I want to take care of you. I want to take care of the stall.

Now Mum was listening all through that, I could tell she was listening, she never butted in, like she does like she usually does, but I had to go and say it, I had to talk about the stall, Dad's flower stall. If her first rant was bad, this was a pure Incredible Hulk rant, all million pounds of it coming down on me, from Mum's mouth to my ears.

Mum   The stall is nothing to you, you had your chance to run it, you had your chance to look after it, when he was alive, you broke your dad's heart, that you didn't want it, coming out with ya 'want to find your own way in life' the stall you said was not good enough for yer. You would rather piss your life running around after Delroy, acting like a bleeding black man, that was you, with the chat!

Mum weren't thinking, Mum weren't making any sense, she was just launching. Everything coming out of her head, on me, pure Hulk!

Mum   You didn't want it before, what makes you think I am going to give it to you now? What is it that you think you can do? Be a better seller than your dad? Only in your mind, boy! Go on, get out, get out of my sight, go back to your black mates, go back to Delroy's be one of them, carrying on with their noise, thinking the whole world owes them a living, be like the rest of them, who think they are better than the rest of us, they bleeding well act like it and all. Well. Go on Michael. What are you waiting for, don't stand there like you have wet yourself? Go, I want you out of here, just go!

Even Carly had to calm her down. She was shouting at me so much, Mum lost the power of speech, shocking! Carly had to take her to the living room, put her feet up on the sofa. It's funny, I mean I knew she loved him, but I didn't realise that much. That it was so tight, the two of them. They were a unit. How any of us could do that, I wonder, be that tight with someone, no one else matters. I know I couldn't, course not, got fucking divorced! Who am I good for? Who's gonna want me? Need me? Who? What's the use of me?

Part Three

The Funeral Chapel

Michael, *now dressed in black, can longer contain himself. He stands up to face his family and friends.*

Michael Look, just get off yeah, I got things to say, he was my dad as well, alright. Just rein it in everyone, just calm it down. Alright? I have things I want to say. So, take a seat, please, just sit yourselves down. Go on! Thank you. That wasn't so hard now, was it? Nice to see everyone, I mean it. I always knew my dad was a popular bloke. And here you all are. Family and friends, how nice. It fills me right up. That you all believed that my dad, the salt of the earth, was top draw. I mean look at yer. It's not about who knew my dad, who didn't know him, more like? Yeah, there was a lot to love about my dad, that old bastard. (**Carly** *protests at the use of his language.*) Oh, put your face back Carly, will yer! My sister, the fusspot! I only said bastard, it's a word, it's in the dictionary, look it up. Anyhow, where was? Oh yes, My dad. The proper. Let me give you an example. When I was little, and he took me to the footie, he would cover my ears like this, whenever the other blokes would shout black this, black that to all of the coloured players. He could stop me hearing but he couldn't stop me from seeing bananas being thrown at them. I mean what was that, my dad would say, where was the sense? On and on, he would go on about that, all the way home every game. Time and place he'd say. Even when that stopped, he would go on about it. It got to the point, that when I got older, I thought, if you hated it so bad, why didn't you say something? Why didn't you tell your mates to stop, never mind covering my bleeding ears! (*Sees his sister get up from her seat in protest.*) Sis, will you just sit down! What is the matter with yer? Where was I? See, you made me miss my chain of thought, or is it train, I dunno. Anyhow. Suppose, what I mean is, Dad loved his footie. He lived for The Orient. World Cup, Euros, all that. (*Stops himself from* *talking about the game.*) Yeah. I mean, cos, cos we still believe, we still have hope cos we are England, cos we invented the game, it's ours, it belongs to us, right? All that crap, and like dogs, we lick it up. We lick it clean. Seriously though, let's face it, let's face some facts, we are shit, we are shit at everything! Not my words, the old man's. Because England now is nothing but an island of shit, crawling its way up the arse of the likes of Theresa May, Fucking Farage, Red bleeding Corbyn, and don't even get me started on that fat orange cunt in the White House! Ooh was that a bad word? Should I have not said that, what orange? (*Laughs.*) Orange! The rest of us, nothing but flakes, flakes of shit trying desperately to hang on. It's no use looking at me like that sis, it was his words, not mine, you know that. Only when he was pissed . . . that's when the truth came out . . . You want to know what else he thought, about all of you? Yeah? Well, get ready to have your minds blown, he hated you. He hated every single one of you. I mean, take you Carly. His own daughter, my sister! He couldn't stand seeing you living off benefits for the rest of your life, bleeding this country dry! Dropping your knickers at the first sight of a bit of black cock. Dad's words Carly, are you listening to me? Your new bloke Andy, first white bloke you've ever dated who blames the immigrants for everything, going on and on about foreign players running the English game, killing it, Andy, what are you talking about, the only reason foreign players came over here is because English players are so rubbish, we've been rubbish since 1966, wake up will yer! Who do you think built your house, 14 hours a day, below the minimum wage, English? You are having a laugh. If our English players weren't so up themselves all the time, picking up their fat cheques at the end of the week, they would learn from the foreign players, like learning how to pass the bleeding ball as well as keep it! Maintain the midfield, be creative, fucking press! Don't throw a wobbly now, this is Dad's drunk talking, not me. Delroy, my best mate, his parents came over here from Jamaica, but he went and voted for fucking Brexit. Fucking leaver, he is, I mean

Jesus H, Delroy, I mean what is the matter with you? When they want a curb on immigration, who do you think they are talking about? Delroy, I love you, like a brother, but you may sound like us, act like us, but you will never be one of us, and deep down you know it, you have to, cos this is England we are talking about. Banana throwing on the pitch is not regular but mark my words, that anger is still there, it's coming out in droves, it's making a comeback, or maybe you choose not to. Eh? Delroy? Delroy mate, it's not me, it's my dad talking. Or maybe it aint, I dunno anymore. Anyhow start as I mean, I suppose. (**Michael** *points to another woman watching.*) My other sister Lisa, and her ever so friendly but so patronising it hurts liberal leftie uni mates, who think they know us, so down with us, yet seem to care less about us than the bleeding Tories! Liberals who think a cockney accent is verbal suicide, a council flat destitution and whose greatest marker of success is how far they can live away from us. And you know what, this is going to make you all laugh, it really will, it wasn't just you Dad hated, Dad hated himself! And so, he should. Always upset, always complaining, but never once got up from his arse and did anything about it. He never marched for anything or anyone. He would cover my ears in the terraces, but he would never tell his mates to stop. I'm no better, Dad hated me cos I'm gutless. Because I would rather have ten pints than stand for something, and Dad wanted me to stand for something, he wanted me to be better than him. How the hell was I supposed to do that, Dad? Who gives a toss what the likes of us think, because they don't care. They don't want to know what we say, they wanna know what we do, and we fight . . . don't we? Because that is the only thing we are good at doing! Smashing things up, people's claret everywhere, blaming everyone who are not English for our troubles, when it comes to that, we are world bleeding champions! And Carly, that is not Dad talking, that is me, your brother! But don't worry, don't you fret, because come tomorrow, I won't remember a thing about this. No one will. I mean, I'm just another stupid drunk Englishman, who cares about him? We might as well have a ruck in that case. It's the English thing to do, isn't it? (*Screams.*) So, let's have it!

Blackout on sounds of tables thrown and glasses smashed. Sound of total carnage.

Part Four

A Park Bench

Michael, *still in his black suit, sits alone on a park bench.*

Michael   I say one thing for Delroy, he can hit, I mean
fucking hell! It was all of that boxing he did when we were
kids. The Repton club, every Tuesday night, for a year.
Delroy could have turned professional, if he hadn't have
fucked up that last fight of his. Under 16, ABA. The first two
rounds he had in the bag, Delroy's uppercut is a thing of
beauty. He was laying one after the other on this guy.
Fucking class! He had him, he really had him. And he would
have kept him, kept him right in that corner, right where he
had him, woulda have been him wearing that belt, if only he
kept himself on the job. He took a step back, one step too
many, gave the kid plenty of room to get himself back into
the fight. It was jab, jab and jab, uppercut! He fucking
floored him. Delroy was down. No way was he getting back
up. He couldn't believe it, we couldn't believe it. The whole
lot of us was there, Dad, Mum, Carly, of course. Dad
borrowed a mate's van and everything. We crossed the
fucking river for that fight. And for what? See what? Delroy's
busted-up face lying on the canvas, covered in blood and
sweat. What a let-down that night was. The only one of us
who could be bothered to look at him was Carly. Her eyes
were all over him. Like the state he was in, was a real turn on
for her. I mean, really? Delroy was stacked, he looked after
himself, but all of that shiny sweat on his ripped black skin
was a real turn on for her? I mean, sweat smells . . . it really
stinks and that, and 'that' got my little sister to pull a face,
like she was 'going live'? Whatever flicks her switch I
suppose. Whilst Delroy was going at it on my face earlier, I
could see Carly from the corner of my eye, glaring over,
nothing was coming out of her mouth, no, 'Delroy stop, he's
still my brother, don't hurt him.' If I didn't know better, I'd
say she was grinning, like she wanted Delroy to hammer the

granny out of me. I mean, thanks sis, I know we are not
close and that, but you know, blood is still blood. It's my face
he is caving in. Ah, what the fuck was I complaining about, I
deserved every punch for what I did. I managed to get one
slap in though. It landed right on the side of Delroy's nose, it
knocked him back a little, but more importantly, it gave me
time to pull away and get the fuck out of dodge! I could hear
Mum screaming, *'you're a disgrace, your father would be
ashamed.'* Now let me tell you, if I had known then what I
know now. About Dad, our wonderful old man, my little rant
would have been . . . let's just say . . . a little different . . .
yeah . . . it would have been a right royal fuck off one. A
proper rant! It all started here in fact . . . here, right here,
while nursing my wounds, with Mum's screaming still
ringing in my ears, feeling like I'd made a proper arse out of
myself, ruining the memory of Dad, in front of everyone he
loved and who'd loved him . . . I could see him coming,
walking up to me . . . He was roughly about 80 seconds away
this bloke, 80 seconds, from turning my life upside down
when I saw him. I didn't think much, I didn't think anything
at all, to me, all he was was some fat old Asian bloke walking
towards, jogging on to wherever he was going. Like I gave a
fuck. But as he was coming closer and closer to me, I started
to give a fuck. I never laid eyes on the geezer, but he was
coming at me, gearing for a conversation, about what, I
didn't have a clue about, he put out his hand, all polite and
that, he knew my name. He wanted to extend his
condolences, I thought he was taking the piss.

Who are you mate, what do you want? A mate of my dad's? I
don't think so, somehow. Jog on? Did you not hear?

He then spends the next 60 seconds of my life coming out
with some guff about us buying regular takeaways on the
high street, *The Bengal Tiger.* We even sat down and ordered
a table every once in a while, birthdays and that. I mean so
what, are we supposed to remember all of their faces?

Michael   Look, I don't mean nothing by this fella, my dad may have bought me more than a few Lamb Biryanis in his time, but that don't mean you have the right to say you and he were mates.

– I said, slightly riled now with my head was beginning pound.

Riz   I'm not surprised you don't remember me.

– he says with a deep sincerity, his large brown eyes looking hurt but resilient.

Michael   It's not happening, it never happened, do you understand me? Do you understand me? You do. So, why are you not moving then?

– he put his face to the ground as if just waiting for me to puff myself out.

Michael   No way were you and my dad pals? I mean, how?

Softly he leaned his head to the side and asked –

Riz   What you mean how?

Michael   H'you know my dad? You know who he is? Do you have any idea what he says about you lot?

His eyes half shut on me as he prepared himself. Straightening his head.

Riz   No.

I'm not sure why I didn't just pull my neck in . . . why I felt it was ok . . . why respect left me . . .

Michael   Right, here you go, don't say you weren't warned. What do you get when you cross a Paki with a black geezer? A car thief who can't drive. That was one of his favourites. What you still here? You want more?

He took a deep breath in and looked about him as though checking if the coast was clear . . . but not for himself . . . it seems like he was out to protect me.

Michael   Oh, you must be loving this.

– said I with my teeth chomping at the bit.

This will make you stop, guaranteed. What do you call a Muslim who's drunk? Mo Hammered! He told us that on Xmas Day.

But he was not perturbed one bit. Well not that a stupid racist cunt like me could see anyway.

On your way now?

– He stood firm.

Oh, what is your beef eh? What's the strife here?

Riz   I'm not Muslim.

– he said, watching my every move with laser precision.

Michael   You're not. My problem how? Yeah, well whatever mate.

Riz   I have something for you.

Michael   For me? What can you possibly have for me?

He dug into his over-starched trouser pocket and pulled out –

Riz   Front door keys.

Well he got me there . . . I blinked wildly at them . . . I felt a bead of sweat roll down my spine.

Michael   To what mate, you're not making any sense here?

He looked at me guilt-ridden. Now he was beginning to look rattled . . . all that I said before hadn't touched him but now . . . nervous tic in his hand . . . he began shifting his weight on each leg, uncomfortable.

Riz   A room?

I enquired with haste and trepidation –

Michael   What bleeding room?

Riz   Your dad's room?

He might as well as punched me in my kidney cause my legs wanted to buckle.

Michael   Alright chief, you need to start making some sense to me, like right fucking now?

Riz   Come.

– and with that he strode off like fucking Tonto, his long hair blowing in the wind, chin raised with a righteous poise. I followed, silent, my curiosity stifled by fear. And so, he took me, to this room he had above his Indian restaurant. It didn't look all that from the outside. Just some tatty door. But the inside? The inside was about to change my fucking life. I had no idea at the time it would, but as soon as he used those keys he gave me, straight off, I could smell him, I could smell my dad, I knew he had been in there. There was a tele, a sofa, fridge at the back, a pint of milk still in there, and a half-eaten pack of chocolate hob nobs . . . his favourite. There wasn't a carpet, but a rug, on it some little dining table. Fucking room! It was a flat, a crummy little bed-sit, truth be told. All that was missing was a bed, and he'd be laughing, there was a cassette player on the window sill, some of Dad's tapes, Rod Stewart, Squeeze . . . Oasis.

Michael   Well, no argument now? What did he do?

He looked at me as though he was trying to stroke me . . . and though I could tell he was trying to be kind in this moment I fucking hated him. It was like he suddenly had one over me . . . as though he had a right to my dad's legacy . . . You know?

Michael   You tell me right now what my dad was doing here.

Riz   Nothing.

– he replied compassionately.

Michael   Was it a woman? Did you fix him up with a brass or something?

Riz   Nothing. No nothing like that.

Michael   No? Well what when?

Riz   Sometimes we just talked.

Panic was setting in fast . . . I could feel my eye twitching . . . my fist clenching. My blood pumping.

Michael   Talked? What do you mean talk? What could the two of you . . . what did you talk about? Tell me, what did he say, what did you say . . . tell me what you bloody well talked about?

Riz   Life . . . as people do . . . you know.

The more decent he was the more I wanted to punch him . . . I mean what is that?

Riz   My name is Riz, by the way, Rizwan Murad. Fifty-five-year-old, father of three.

He sat down with the ease of familiarity . . . then ushered me to do the same . . . I stood . . . uncomfortably.

Riz   I've been running The Bengal Tiger for the last twenty-five years and your father rents . . . rented the plot for the stall from me, I suspected my wife was cheating on me . . . with a cousin of mine, your dad said to me, 'I didn't know Asian women had it in them, to cheat on their husbands.'

He laughed, pleased with his take on my dad . . . that was when I sat because the fucker had him down to a 't'. Then he did that thing with his eyes again . . . but this time it was working on me . . . I could feel his kindness like a wool blanket on a cold night.

Riz   Said to me 'you wanna see me like going to confession . . . sold me white and pink lilies and three ladies fingers and convinced me to stay with her . . . and we became friends . . . We are all people

– he said.

We do people things.

It's not what he said but it was the way he said it. '*We do* people *things*.' It was deep, the way he put it, like you couldn't help but listen to his voice. There was a shelf in that flat as well, with books, books! I never saw my dad read a book in his life, yet there they were. Loads of them, history books, history of Britain, going as far back as when the Romans were giving it large. The King James Bible! Milton's *Paradise Lost. David Copperfield* by Charles Dickens. Salman Rushdie, *Satanic Verses. Crime & Punishment*, Owen what? Owen fucking Jones/chavs, The demonisation of the working classes . . . Akala!!!! What the fuck is this about?

Michael   Oi, my dad read all of this?

Riz   No no . . . but he tried . . . he tried to, sometimes out loud, sometimes to me.

Michael   To you?

This is getting weirder and weirder I thought.

Riz   We disagreed . . . a lot . . . but he said he was thinking more . . . understanding more but was stuck.

Michael   But he never said . . . wait a minute.

Fear leapt in my throat like a nut jammed down ya wind pipe. Were these two at it or something?

Michael   Did Dad like it up him?

– Is that what he was about to tell me?

Riz, come on, tell me.

My eyes betrayed me as a tear just fell down my cheek. I wiped it away as quickly as I could hoping he didn't see it.

Riz   No . . . no jiggy-jiggy.

– he answered, shaking his head furiously.

Michael   Well, thank fuck for that!! Now, you tell me what is going on here. Why was Dad here, why was he reading these books, why was he talking to you, what was he talking about?

Riz   Life, Michael.

That was the first time he had said my name. What did he know? What had Dad said about me? Reluctantly I asked –

Michael   What did he tell you? About me?

Riz   As much as he could.

– Off came the blanket.

He wanted you to be a better man.

His eyes went cold for a moment as he said it.

He wanted to be a better man himself. He was lied to. Just like you are being lied to.

Michael   Lied to? About what?

Riz   Everything.

Michael   So, he would come here, to know the truth, be a better man?

Riz   Maybe.

– he retorted.

Michael   Listen, Riz. Bloody. Wan. My dad, he had everything he needed.

He just fell silent . . . like the end of a LP when you hear that crackle as the needle plays nothing, just going round and round but playing nothing . . . This is bollocks I thought . . . This is total bollocks.

When exactly did he find time to hang out here, to read and chat with you?

Riz   Every other Saturday, he would leave your house at 3 am to give himself time to drive to the wholesalers and buy flowers before 4 am, yes?

Michael   Yea.

Riz   Your father did not set up his stall until 7.30. He gave himself a three-hour window to be here.

Michael   Why though? Why was he here?

– my voice cracking with the pain.

Riz   Your father was a confused man, a lonely man, much like his country.

Michael   His country? You're talking about England, right? My country?

Riz   Yes Michael, I am talking about England. Your country.

Michael   Talking bollocks is what you are doing. My dad wasn't lonely. He had friends who would lay down in traffic for him. He had a family.

Riz   And yet he was still lonely. He was worried that he had no space in his own life to grow . . . change, worried that you wouldn't either.

Michael   He said that about me?

Riz   All of the time. Spoke about your mother as well, and your sisters, but mostly you.

Michael   What the fuck is he worried about me for?

– I managed that sentence without no sense of irony too.

Riz   Michael, I was at the funeral. I stood at the back, I heard every word you said.

Michael   Fuck off, just fuck off Gandhi, alright! I said fuck off! Fuck off.

He just sat there, this self-righteous prick was just sitting there. Pulling my life apart like it did not mean anything to him, just sitting there.

Riz   I own this room, Michael. Why should I leave?

(*Chuckles.*) Yeah, he had me there.

Riz   Your father needed help, Michael.

Michael   Your help?

Riz   No, just help.

Michael   What kind of help?

Riz   We all need help to . . .

Michael   You know nothing about me, mate. I know what I have said. I was drunk.

Riz   No, you were rat-arsed.

– he said knowingly.

Michael   You enjoying that, Rizwan?

Riz   Not for a moment, Michael. You lost a father, I lost a friend.

Michael   Yeah, triffic, a fucking catastrophe for the both of us, but what am I supposed to do now? Come here every other Saturday and read books as well . . . talk to you?

Riz   That is up to you, or you could listen to your father?

Michael   Oh, really and you know there is a way of me doing that do yer Einstein?

And without saying a word or missing a beat he just takes out his mobile, puts it in the table, presses play.

Riz   You can give that back on the way out.

Alan   Michael. I have never been able to say this to your face. Too bleeding scared . . . truth be told. I bet you could never imagine that, me being scared of you. My own boy.

Well I was. I mean, I am. I am letting my new mate Rizwan here, record all of this on his phone. He reckons it will help, fuck knows how. (*To* **Riz**.) This is stupid.

Riz   Come on, keep going.

Alan   Thing is, according to the doctors there's a problem with my old ticker. My heart could give out at any sec, if I don't get treatment. Talk about drama, I mean what do they know?

Michael   More than you, stupid cunt.

Alan   You've seen how hard I graft on the stall, morning, noon and night, that's me. You won't find many blokes my age as fit as me, that's for sure. My heart is fine, made of Teflon. Fucking doctors, any excuse to get you under the knife, they take it . . .

Riz   Alan, come on.

Alan   Alright. 'Kin 'ell. (*Sighs.*) Thing is, my gran always used to say, 'Better safe, darlin'. So, here's the main thing, what I want to tell you. I want you to know, I'm sorry for everything I didn't teach you, everything that I should have taught you about being you . . . your Englishness . . . your roots . . . your heritage . . . and that, but I tried . . . you know . . . to be me, as much as I could to show ya instead of telling ya . . . I did that for you, not that you should follow me, but that you should be better than me. That you should do better, than me, but they probably won't let you, the powers that be, they'll fight you, they want to keep you down, to stay down, they will never think much of you, except when they want your vote that is. You gotta fight them back boy, with everything you have. You gotta show meaning, don't let them walk over yer. I have been so wrong about so many things.

Michael   I'm not listening to this.

Alan   I don't think immigrants are to blame.

Michael   Eh?

Alan It's the powers that have something to answer for.

Michael Shut up.

Alan They're selling out our country, right from under us.

Michael Jesus, Dad.

Alan What I am, what's left of England now, it's all for you.
Except the stall. Not my beloved stall, you can keep your
fucking mitts off that. (*Laughs.*) That's coming with me,
they're fucking burying me with that. I mean the country,
the world, it's yours. You know what I mean right, whatever
it is, you know in your life. No matter how small it is, make it
right, make a difference.

Riz Alan? You haven't told him. You have to tell him.

Alan Yes, alright! I love you, boy. I truly love ya . . . oh, and
I'm joking obviously about the stall . . . do what you will with
it . . . no pressure. There you go, Riz . . . You happy, now?
Gonna crack a smile at last?

Riz Well done, my friend.

Dad Fuck's sake. Waste of time this, I'll tell him, one day
. . . I'll tell him myself . . .

Michael *turns off the recording.*

It was then I saw it . . . shining in the corner of the room.
Closed but so inviting . . . I stared at it. Realizing that this
could be the most honest thing about him . . . it panicked
me. I looked around the room even though I knew I was
alone. My tears dried up immediately . . . it was a laptop . . .
in his secret pad . . . on his secret table a secret laptop. I
stood but still made no steps towards it . . . see he had a
desktop at home . . . so this . . . this one . . . was a secret . . .
and why? I wondered . . . I mean they're not cheap right . . .
it was an Apple . . . and new at that . . . good money that cost
. . . so why is it a secret? Show a man's Google search and it'll

show you the man . . . shit. . . I found myself walking
towards it. Picking it up and opening it. There was loads of
shit on the desktop like he'd never heard of a folder. . . I
begin to click . . . first . . . a picture of *Bin Laden* . . . dead . . .
Pavo-fucking-rotti . . . click Trump . . . Trump? Pictures of
Donald Trump . . . like loads of them . . . he said he
respected his . . . his honesty . . . Click Oswald Mosley
interview . . . click Steve Bannon speech . . . Tommy fucking
Robinson. click click click!

Is this what you want for me, Dad? Is this what you want me
to learn? You noticed I hadn't looked at his Google search
. . . I pondered it for a long while. Did I want to know, really
. . . cause I knew it would be worse than what he's saved . . .
I knew . . . ya know. It made me angry . . . Because I knew I
wasn't gonna search the history . . . because I knew it would
be worse!!! I knew I was too weak to face my dad's truth . . .
too weak to own my heritage . . . too weak to admit what I
embody . . . too weak too weak . . . too weak! DADDY!!! It
was like a fight was going on inside his head. And he couldn't
tell us. He couldn't tell me. Embarrassed. What's so wrong
with being honest, really honest? What is so shameful about
being a victim of it all, about wanting to know more, wanting
to be more, we all do, it's how people live, innit . . . it's how
we go on . . . it's how we all go on . . . as . . . people . . . by . . .
learning . . . by understanding . . . as a people . . . that is how
. . . what is the problem? (*In a rage, followed by tears.*)
WHY COULDN'T YOU TELL ME?

Part Five

Leyton Orient Football Ground

Michael, *holding his dad's ashes, stands in the middle of the football pitch.*

Michael The plan was, after the service, we'd all go to the hall, for a bite to eat. After my shennagins, I thought that was well and truly fucked up. And after what I'd just seen I just kept on walking, don't ask me for how long . . . I didn't think there'd be anybody there at the hall, in fact, I was hoping there wouldn't be. But there she was, Delroy's mum, getting the tables ready, putting foil over the plates of Jamaican patties she had made especially for us. Delroy's mum don't do funerals, on the account she lost her dad, Mum, 1 brother and her cousins all within 18 months a few years back. I mean that's bound to put someone off churches forever. I saw her, and I knew she clocked me. Her and that scowling face of hers. She obviously must have heard what happened. All she could do is suck her teeth real loud and look away. She didn't even say anything when I swiped one of her patties from under the foil, nearest to me. She sucked her teeth, looked away and muttered under her breath, quietly, but loud enough for me to hear, '*Eddyaatt!*' (*Laughs.*) The same look, I swear to God, she had when Delroy nicked the school sign when we were kids. Her patties are still hot, I don't know what, too many hot peppers or summin, but regardless, you just want to finish it all up. It was when she was clocking me trying to reach for another one, that she lost her shit at me. The complete verbal it was, full package.

Denise What was you thinking, typical white bwoi foolishness.

– her words peppered me like a machine gun. All of that and more she yelled. I used to watch her lay into Delroy, when we were kids, Delroy would just stand there, not say a word, like he could get a word in edgeways anyhow. '*Wat de rah you tink you is coming out wid bwoi, yer having a laugh yungsta, don't even tink about bringing dat shit home to me, yer mad?'* Delroy just took it, crying like a bitch, nodding his head. And, so was I, as she laid it out for me.

Denise You come just like yer papa, yu talk, before yu tink. Why you English bwoi like to drink so? How you drink so much? Does someone at school tek you boys aside and teach you how to do it? Answer mi nuh!

After a while, it was just noise to me. The trick is to keep looking into her face, like you're listening. Delroy taught me that. Not that I wasn't sorry for what I said and done, of course I was, but Delroy's mum losing her shit like that, always makes me laugh. Like when she nearly got kicked out of the country last year. Can you believe that? She's lived here all her life. And some twat in the government decides she aint British! Lucky it got sorted, because I'm telling you, no lie, I would have stood with Delroy's mum. Stood! When all of that was kicking off, Delroy asked me if I think the old man would have stood with his mum as well. I didn't know. I hoped so. But he's dead, I'm not. I think he would have liked me standing up for something. I think he would have liked that. You could have heard a pin drop, when Mum, Carly and the rest of our mob stepped in. Everyone else was watching us like it was a bleeding tennis match or summin. First Mum, then me, then back to Mum again. All waiting to see who serves. *Fuck it,* I thought, *just get it out the way.* I think I only made it as far as the word *Mum* was about to leave my lips, when I felt the full force of the back of her hand, landing right across my cheek. *Fuck that hurt,* I didn't mind saying. I felt the back of Dad's hand a few times in my life, but Mum's slap was summin else, it was premium!

And where there is Mum, Carly, my darling little sister sister wasn't too far behind. She was marching right up to me, she had a face on, like she was about to dig me out good and proper, but I was ready, I knew exactly what I wanted to say to her.

Michael   Carly, before you start, there is something I need to say to you, something really important. You see Delroy over there, that big good-looking black bloke scowling his face up by the door, who looks like he wants my face all over his fist again. Do me a favour will you please? Take him by the hand, right now, take him back to your flat right now, or his flat right now, or that hotel room the two of you had in Blackpool for your dirty weekends, it don't matter, just take him back, and will you please in the name of Leyton Orient football, fuck his brains out.

Carly   You what?

Michael   I said fuck his brains out Carly! Like right now. And don't just do it tonight, I want you to be fucking his brains tomorrow night, and the night after that, and the night after, in fact, fuck his brains out for the rest of your life, and don't just fuck him either, I want you to caress him, I want you to kiss him, I want both of you to be waking up in each other's arms, for the rest of your natural. Carly, you know you want to, you know he wants to, so in the words of Will Smith, the Fresh Prince of Bel Air himself, get jiggy wid it! Carly please, just for once, trust your brother on this one. Oh, fuck what Dad used to say, fuck what he used to think. Dad's dead, he's dead, Carly! And believe me, he's no right to tell you how to live. He can't tell you what to do anymore. He can't tell any of us and fuck Andy too! Everyone hates him . . . including you! Delroy's proper, he always has been, and he's mad for yer. Sis? We need to find our own way now.

From the corner of my eye I could see Mum watching me from the corner of her eye, wondering of course, what the hell I was going to do next. I think the other side of the world must have heard Mum's jaw drop to the floor when Carly marched right up to Delroy, grabbed his head with both hands and gave him the longest, sloppiest wet kiss of all time. Even Delroy's mum didn't know where to look. Mum was giving me one of her evil stares. She wanted to say something, she had plenty to say, like she would even dare with Delroy's mum standing right next to her. Does she not get tired . . . I stared back at her wondering if maybe she has a room of her own, somewhere.

So, Carly and Delroy are loved up. Mum is chomping down on another one of Delroy's mum's hot patties. A right royal crowded house for the old man. He was missed. He was loved. But I couldn't help myself. The day needed something more . . . well, something not spoiled by me . . . a finale. I waited, and I waited, Mum had been trying to give up ciggies for months now. I just knew, she couldn't resist the urge to pop outside. As soon as she did, I saw it, the urn, just lying there on the table. That was my chance. I was *Jason,* and that urn was my golden fleece. It's coming with me. As I dashed out, I made a point of showing I had it to everyone. No point in everyone fretting. She knew where I was going, if anyone wanted to come, they only had to follow.

Getting into the ground was no problem, one of Dad's mates was a groundsman . . . well he was a mate of a mate of his, proper wanker. Going on about not to step onto the grass until he was finished mowing, bleeding moaning more like.

We stood there, centre of the pitch, like we're ready for kick off. It seemed appropriate. Mum said her bit, 'gone but never forgotten' with the stateliness of the Queen. Carly just wept loudly . . . and I . . . I hold the urn up . . . 'a Fletcher is dead (*Begins pouring the ashes onto the grass.*) *Long live, The Fletchers.*'

Blackout.

Death of England: Delroy

Death of England: Delroy was first performed at the Olivier Theatre, London, on 21 October 2020, with the following cast and creatives:

Delroy	**Michael Balogun**
Understudy Delroy	**Lace Akpojaro**
Voiceover	**Amy Newton**

Director	Clint Dyer
Set and Costume Designers	Sadeysa Greenaway- Bailey and ULTZ
Lighting Designer	Jackie Shemesh
Sound Designers	Pete Malkin and Benjamin Grant
Staff Director	Sian Ejiwunmi-Le Berre
Project Producers	Christine Gettins and Fran Miller
Production Managers	Anna Fox and Richard Eustace
Stage Manager	Ian Farmery
Stage Manager on the book	Ben Donoghue
Assistant Stage Manager	Jo Phipps
Project Draughting	Tom Atkinson
Costume Supervisor	Iona Kenrick
Prop Supervisor	Kirsten Shiell
Lighting Supervisors	Jack Champion and Jack Williams
Lighting Programmers	Will Frost and Laura Choules
Production Sound Engineer	Alex Caplen
Sound Operator	Ben Vernon
Stage Supervisors	Barry Peavot and LeeHarrington
Construction Supervisor	Barrie Nield
Scenic Art Supervisor	Cass Kirchner
Assistant Designer	Shankho Chaudhuri
Rehearsal Photographer	Cameron Slater

Taking inspiration from the short film, *Dim Sum*, written by Clint Dyer, produced by Headlong and the *Guardian*.

Commissioned and developed by the National Theatre's New Work Department.

Death of England: Delroy

Scene One

Front Room

Delroy *stands laughing loudly with a Guinness in his hand. He is clearly drunk.*

Delroy It was as if things weren't bad enough. It was the punch in Punch and Judy, the real in surreal . . . I mean, like I didn't know, understand, get, how twisted, corked, mash-up life can be already. They was gonna take my dignity too . . . my dignity, man . . . but I wasn't gonna let him know that.

Wasn't gonna give him, them, the pleasure. Though to be fair he was nice . . . well as you can be in the circumstances, considering. I mean like, he would never have known the size of the crater on my heart.

He's got as shit a job as mine I guess. So maybe I should just enjoy the fact I had a white man doing a Kaepernick. I am guessing everyone knows what I'm on about? Colin Kaepernick. You'd have to be the biggest tosser in the world not to know, right. You'd have to have your head so stuck up your privilege not to know, you'd need Nelson Mandela to rise from the dead and twerk, naked, on the finish line at Ascot to actually see black people exist. So he's kneeling there . . . in front of me . . . and he's telling me, showing me, explaining how I'm gonna have to manage this shit. But even though it was killing me . . . all I'm thinking of really is her . . . her, who is she? Where is she? Is she ok? but I have to engage . . . but I keep drifting off . . . thinking about her . . . wanting to hold her, smell her . . . then he's says the words 'breach'.

Man *You'll be in breach.*

Delroy And my mind whip pans to his will.

I'll breach?

Man *Yeah and that can . . . well that's like, you're fucked! They could bang you up for that.*

Delroy I nodded like a schoolboy being a chastised by his headmaster. He could see my ego sliding off under the door. So in an effort to lighten the mood he asked

Man *What do you do?*

Delroy I paused to try and work out if he was the right kind of person to tell. Noticing my reticence, he looked down to my ankle and clicked it in place thoughtfully and then asked.

Man *Alright, what's the funniest thing about your job?*

Delroy And I just go into one . . . must be the nerves, the anger, the shame . . . yeah the utter shame of it all . . .

The surprise

I say as he stands up and plugs me into the wall.

The surprise . . . yeah, the surprise . . . I think people fink, they're kinda untouchable, well not untouchable just . . . just that it won't go 'that' wrong for 'em. Well, until we bailiffs rattle their cage . . . yeah, bruv, I used to come in and shatter that shit good.

> *He laughs his infectious laugh fully again.*

Cheez . . . the look on the their faces . . . it's like all the muscles in their face just give up . . . like some hundred-year-old man's scrotum, all lifeless and southbound.

He goes for his bag and starts packing his stuff up but keeping eye contact with me, like he's fully engaged, interested, when he must've been dying for me to shut the fuck up.

> *He giggles childishly.*

Every time same shit, like it's some kinda 'surprise'. They haven't paid! The rent, the mortgage or whatever, they ain't paid! So where's the fucking surprise.

Cracks me up.

Posh Man   *GET OUT!*

Working-Class Woman   *Leave me stuff alone.*

Delroy   *This student said my favourite. Stood there . . . this guy, made a grunge attire look well dressed he did.*

Student   *HOW DARE YOU!*

Delroy   *That's my favourite . . . he ain't paid his bills and I'm the scum. 'How dare you!' Jokes, man.*

He drinks down the last of the Guinness and opens another.

Then . . . he wants my sympathy . . . I mean what the actual fuck . . . I was like Mate, I'm a black man. Of West Indian descent, claiming some kinda Britishness . . . on the account of the fact that I was born here and my grandparents was born in a British colony that 'reach inna England' with a British passport in the fifties, and had learnt all the British values there, of not giving a shit about anybody! Part from their kin . . . I'm a product of this country!

Student   *Come on 'man' you could help me. We could 'keep it on a downlow'.*

Delroy   *I said to him, Boss man, you're tripping.*

He's got his coat on now, this tagman fellow, and he's holding the door knob hinting desperately at me that he wants to talk . . . but I don't wanna hear what he's got say . . . I don't wanna hear the truth of what he has to say so I carry on.

He laughs taking a large swig of Guinness.

Here's the rub . . . if there are no evictions, I don't get paid and I need to get paid or I'm not a good member of society, right?

That's capitalism ain't it? Or consumerism . . . one of the two . . . someone has to pay for me to live rich . . . that's British values, no? . . . all this.

Michael   *We're in it together.*

Delroy   *Dat's what Michael . . . my mate Michael gives it.*

Michael   *We're in it together, Delroy.*

Delroy *laughs.*

Delroy   *He says, white guy.*

I've known him since school. My best friend to be honest . . . but it's been on the ropes . . . the friendship . . . he mugged me right off a while back and, well, they hated me doing this job, goes against . . . well . . . I'm not sure but . . . I was like 'I'm British!' . . . all we do is clap, pull down a few statues and discuss.

'Bout their looking at me for sympathy, who's Michael to think I should have sympathy. I'm like, 'Get de fuck out of de yard!'

Man   *It takes about a hour and half to charge.*

He says, not taking a breath in case I start popping off again. But I'm on a roll.

Delroy   *And my daughter! She was born eight weeks ago, and I ain't even seen her. They've made no effort to make things right . . .*

It came like vomit from deep inside me, unannounced and visceral as fuck.

None of them! No effort! . . . they didn't even come to court!

Man   *I gotta go, mate . . .*

Delroy   His knitted brow making it clear he'd got the arse with me now.

Man   *Remember if it bleeps you're in breach . . . so you've got to keep it charged . . . right?*

Delroy   I nodded again like the schoolboy from before.

Man   *Charge it every day . . . right.*

Delroy   And with dat . . . he was gone like some CIA operative . . . all he needed was a plume of smoke and I would have thought I'd imagined it. I looked down at it . . . my tag, my fucking tag and laughed.

He laughs loudly. He takes a big swig.

To be honest though I never gave a fuck who it was we evicted, black, white, Indian, Chinese . . . European . . . though that's white still though, right? . . . sometimes I find that shit funny too . . . Whites hating whites cos they got a different accent . . . funny bwoy . . . when they know, unlike us, blacks, if they breed here, their kids will be considered more English then me! Who's got generations of Britishness but that's being British innit . . . well that's what works for most of us apart from that lot . . . the Kumbaya lot who just love to march, while singing and partying.

He laughs, mimicking them.

Thinking that it can make changes, jokers . . . love to travel that lot, think they're better than us for it too . . . fuck dat, staying right here, earning my corn, get a nice car, lickle flat, big flat-screen TV . . . and I'm set.

Fuck dat and fuck dem, fuck Michael . . . Carly, all of dem island mentality innit. All that European shit . . . don't connect to me, man, as long as my tax ain't too high, why should I care? . . . no one cares bout me.

Had no European Union questioning the police stop and search figures for black people here. Checking up on our black deaths in custodies, black mental health figures . . . no European law on dat is there. 'Bout he's cussing me out at his dad's funeral for voting Brexit.

Michael   *In it together.*

Delroy   Look at this fucking tag! In it together . . . I'm just doing as British do innit, look out for your own. I'm about as European as a dim fucking sum.

. . . tell you what though, if I hadn't lost my job, I woulda bin be busy like rass now though . . . everybody bruc. Coulda earn some 'p' mate . . . people broke like . . . like oh what's his name? . . . Did all dem Spike Lee films back in the day . . . and thought tax was beneath him or summin . . . Wesley Snipes . . . lots people who thought their shit didn't stink

feeling it now . . . I'm still gonna have to bail out Carly I bet
. . . all that shit she said to me . . . all that's gonna be
forgotten . . . all water . . . yeah, all big-time sorries cos she
needs me yeah . . . well she can go fuck herself, leaving me
here on my tod . . . didn't even come to the court, man. But
she's getting through . . . I hear . . . whole new her, her mum
tells me changed for ever . . . but she's got family helping her
get through I've got . . . don't worry I won't expect you to be
on my side . . . bailiffs don't engender much sympathy, and a
black one . . . well dat . . . dat's a Black Lives Matter march
too many . . . just fucking off key!

Right?

Carly, man . . . she's a trip . . . oh she's my . . . well I don't
know any more it's complicated . . . always been complicated
with her . . . right from the off . . . she's my best mate's sister
. . . Michael's sister. Carly Fletcher? Their dad was Alan . . .
Fletcher who owned the Fletcher's flower stall on Hermit
Road? Died a couple of years back . . . well anyway . . . I'll
tell you about Carly first, though they all come with a
government health warning and are highly addictive and it's
got to be said, a good crack! But she . . . she's, I don't know
. . . it's chemistry innit . . . some people . . . don't matter
what they look like, they just . . . well, they make you wanna
go deep-sea diving . . . where breathing ain't easy and you
may well drown but you can't help but wanna dive in again
and again and again . . . you feel me?

My mum can't stand her . . . well that's not entirely true it's . . .
It wasn't that she didn't like white people . . . she's a care
attendant, she works with loads, looks after loads and loads of
her mates are white. But she just didn't, well, she just wanted
me to have a black girlfriend . . . like her I guess . . . I think
she just thought, well, after all the years of pain we suffer from
them . . . all the mistreatment, disrespect, all the centuries of
colonialism, that I should wanna date someone who really
understood that. That got it . . . that knew it . . . felt it.

And bwoy did she let me know it.

Denise   *Her?*

Delroy   *Yes.*

Denise   *Her?*

Delroy   She said, sipping on her *Wrey & Nephew* for fuel.
Yes, Mum!

Denise   *But she can't cook jerk chicken.*

Delroy   She slammed that one down like a winning
domino. She can't cook pasta!

Denise   *Ackee & saltfish? Fried dumpling?*
Plantain? My Jamaican patties?

Delroy   *Mum, this ain't* Masterchef, *you know!*

Denise   *All the pretty black girls out there and*

Delroy   *I like her.*
I pleaded weakly.

Denise   *you want a white gal?*

Delroy   *I don't just want a white gal, Mum.*

Denise   *You want her?*

Delroy   *Yes. Yes, I do.*

Denise   *But her daddy is a /*

Delroy   *I know.*

Denise   *Alan is a /*

Delroy   *I know.*

She then stood over me so close her nine-carat gold Nefertiti
head round her neck tapped my forehead annoyingly.

Denise   *Racist.*

Delroy   It landed like a stink bomb staining the whole room.

Yeah. I know

Denise   *So what di 'ell you playing at?*

Delroy   *I like her /*

Denise   *She's not gonna know why you don't like your hair being touched.*

Delroy   *I could tell her?*

Denise   *She's not /*

Delroy   *I get yer, Mum . . . I just like her . . . she's messed-up and mouthy and /*

Denise   *Arrogant?*

Delroy   *Yeah . . . she is she's trying to be better.*

Denise   *Really?*

Delroy   *Yeah . . . and she's funny, she makes me laugh, Mum, and she's so curious about stuff . . . I don't know, Mum, we ain't getting married, ain't having kids! We're just dating.*

Denise   *Her daddy know?*

Delroy   *No . . .*

She kissed her teeth so loudly I thought the glass she was holding might smash.

I knew she was right . . . what the fuck was I doing? I was selling out. I was being a coconut . . . I was but . . . I liked her.

First time we kissed . . . wasn't like romantic, in a normal way, no normal it weren't . . . I mean I remember it fondly but, well, let me tell ya . . . I was walking home from school . . . just got off the 58 . . . and turned to step down Regis Road and there she was. She'd clearly bunked off the last period or something cos she had ditched our school uniform and was now sporting one of those grey low-slung jogging . . . hug me batty tight pants . . . yeah you know dem right?

. . . and a Lycra sports top that if she wasn't fifteen, you'd only get away with on a nudist beach. So, she comes up to me, all bossy like and wid her white gal, road gal stance, and says . . .

Carly   *I hear once you've had a black you never look back.*

Delroy   Now, I know that's a pretty shit ting to say and my heart and pulse rate made it damn sure to me that I didn't like it too. So I lean my head slightly, screwed my face as if I'd smelt something rough and was just about to fling some lyrics in her head, when I felt her hand resting softly on my inner thigh.

And then I registered her pupils enlarge in her green eyes like my house cat on heat. Now I was sixteen and touching me there was like pressing the button on Jack in the box . . . to be honest though really . . . you only had to be a girl with a . . . pulse to climb my summit in those days, and with my heart rate competing with Goldie for beats per minute already, by the time she leant in to kiss me, I'd forgotten what she'd said!

Carly   *Had to say something to get your attention, didn't I? I don't mean anything.*

Delroy   She said, coming up for air, her little finger on the edge of my Calvin Klein boxers . . . there was no tongues though, just tender young lips pressing together . . . blissful, mate. I've been hooked ever since. I know it's a bit Stockholm syndrome, but what can I say.

Scene Two

Hospital

Delroy   It comes to summin *innit* when yer own mudda ain't even on your side. Not that I was expecting much from her anyhow, considering how she loved to give me the arsehole day and night about what I did for a living. Like

was my fault some people don't know how to pay their bills
or get out of debt. My mum has never been in debt, she
never had a credit card until she was thirty-three. Our family
were bruc, like most families are, but we were never poor,
Mum made sure of that. Never was there a day when there
was no food on the table. Mum managed her finances, why
can't others? When I wanted the bike that Michael had,
when we were kids, if she couldn't afford it, it was NO, end
of discussion. Make more of it, you get a slap round the head
for your trouble. And her slaps were premium, no lie! So,
even though we would disagree, I'd see where she is coming
from. So, I don't see how hard it is for her to do the same for
me, to just understand it from my point of view. She's my
mum right? They're meant to understand yer? No? It hurts
when they don't . . . she's cut me a few times but this one . . .
well, when you side with dem over me . . . well, it's not dat
she sided it's that . . . she kinda mugged me off. You know
. . . in front of people too . . . This is what went down yeah, I
just come from a job, some mug fucked it right up for
himself by not paying his tax, I got that a lot, like they're
exempt, no sympathy from me, nada! We got all of the shit
ready to go, laptop, fridge, flat-screen, all loaded up, when I
turn on my phone, I don't like to have it on when I'm
working. Well, actually I'm cool about it, it's just that I had a
new boy working for me, his parents had the nerve to call
him *Elvis*.

Imagine . . . Moroccan fella too . . . bet he loved dat right?
*Cheers, Mum, blinding, Dad. Thanks for naming me Elvis. Eleven
years of bullying at school right there.* Anyhows, I like to school
the new boys in, you know, do as I say, watch and learn,
phones off, when yer working! I like to give it time wid
them, as soon as I feel the love, I relax the rules a bit.
Anyhow, the van is loaded up, we are en route to our next
gig. Elvis is driving, doing as he's told, so fuck it I thought, I
turn on the phone. Nineteen voicemails, eighteen from
Carly's mum. Giving me the arsehole, wanting to know
where I am? So I ring her straight back.

Mrs Fletcher   *Where the fuck you been?*

Delroy   *Eh?*

I said, wishing I hadn't put in on loud speaker.

Mrs Fletcher   *What you got a bloody mobile for if you ain't gonna use it?*

Delroy   Elvis turned his face away but I could still see his cheeks bulging from laughter.

Mrs Fletcher /

Mrs Fletcher   *I told you not to call me that . . . /*

Delroy   *Sorry, Maggie! What is it? Is Carly ok?*

Mrs Fletcher   *Haven't you heard your messages?*

Delroy   *I called straight back when I saw your calls.*

Mrs Fletcher   *Which you didn't answer.*

Delroy   I don't know how words were getting through her jaw sounded so tight.

How about you just telling me why you were calling? I said, having lost all my authority with Elvis and patience with her.

Mrs Fletcher   *Her waters . . . her waters have broken.*

Delroy   *It's January . . . we're only in January.*

Mrs Fletcher   *Great . . . do you know your ten times table too.*

Delroy   Elvis then bursts out laughing, spitting his drink all over himself. Grabbing the phone and turning off speaker I placed the phone to my ear.

Where is she?

Mrs Fletcher   *If you can, we'll meet you at St Mary's.*

Delroy   I knew she's never had any real love for me, Carly's mum, for obvious reasons, my skin being the main one though, but,

Mrs Fletcher   *If you can,*

Delroy   If I can? This is my kid Carly is having, and her mum is bringing out, '*If you can?*' Wat de rah?

Dat woman facety, man! I turn to Elvis, trying hard not to push his head through the windscreen out of embarrassment, and tell him to 'Drop me off at the nearest tube, QUICK!', I jump out, nearly getting run over during the process. And that was it, me jumping out of the van was the beginning of a very bad day for me. I just didn't know it, but I was going to know it, in about four minutes, I was going to know, fer *trut*. I got my Oyster card, I glide myself through the barriers and I got a serious jog on for the escalators, when I realised, this is the Overground, it's the underground I want. I could hear Carly screaming in me head.

Carly   *You can't even hold my hand on time, that's all I needed you to do, hold my hand and you couldn't even do that.*

Delroy   The orange of the Overground sign scorched my eyes. Overground takes too blasted long! Three stops on the underground to the hospital. I thought, ok, I got time, as soon as I hit the bottom of the escalator, I sharply used the upside ones to take myself back up.

Now considering my panic levels at maximum, I think I was still holding down some street swagger . . . only one bead of sweat perhaps and I was fit so not breathing that heavily . . . I was still smooth. That is when it happened. When the shit got real. Without warning, and I mean without a single bit, I feel a whole heap of hands grabbing me from behind, slamming my face against the side of the wall and keeping it there as the escalator went up. As I went up, that shit hurt, I goes,

What the fuck? What the actual fuck, man.

That's when I started to sweat . . . big time. Some brer with the stinkiest breath ever whispers right in my ear,

Man   *Don't move, keep yer mouth shut.*

Delroy   Straight off I knew this weren't no mugging, or a bunch of white trash lads who fancy a ruck with a brudda, cos they have got it in their minds it's White Boy Day or summin. I was scared cos I knew whoever these guys were, they were hardcore!

Man   *Why d'ya go back up the escalators?*

Delroy   He said like he didn't need an answer.

Why's that any of your mother fucking business?

My eyes bulging with indignation.

Man   Clocked us? Did yer?

Delroy   What?

Man   Trying to make a dash for it.

Delroy   He offered, leaning harder on my chest with his massive forearm. *Clock who, who the living rass are you?*

As soon as I got to the top, I managed to get a look around to see who it was. One of them is flashing his warrant card at me, Old Bill, the fucking police. It was the Babylon troubling me. I should have known. I mean what is this, did someone take me back in time to the nineties or summin? Not just one, but three of them, for me, three! What the fuck is this? So, I ask dem,

What the fuck is this!

What is it about three large white men holding you against a wall, against your will, that makes you realise how small you are? How insignificant you are.

Man   *Shut yer mouth!*

Delroy   One of them snarls, his bad breath swirling its way up my nostrils like smoke.

I just want to know what this is, man?

Policeman   *ID?*

Delroy   He bellowed as his spit sprayed across my now blistering hot face. Don't know why he asked really, cos his hands had already emptied my pockets with force.

You don't understand, I got to be somewhere, I need to get to the /

Policeman   *SHUT UP! OK! SHUT IT! While we check your ID.*

Delroy   He said, our heads now touching.

You got the wrong brer.

Policeman   *For what?*

My mouth now wide open with shock.

What have we got wrong about you?

Delroy   Now, I have been black enough all my life to know this is a fit-up! Some profiling ting, obviously they are on the hunt for somebody, and it happens to be my unlucky day that I fit whoever this fucker is they're looking for, down to a tee . . . i.e. black skin. Normally, I would understand, I would just flex this shit off but this ain't no normal day, this is the day when I become a dad. I don't have time for this. I need to be . . . well, they needed clarity. So, as plainly as I can, I say,

Get the fuck off me, yeah, I ain't done nuttin!

Big mistake. The copper with the rank smelling breath leans in my face again, whilst two of his finest are holding me down tight, in some, mash-up judo 'Got you, nigger boy, but I can't breathe' move!

Policeman   *Swear at me one more time, and you are coming with us.*

Delroy   As I continue to remember that day, that line from PC Stink Breath still does not make any sense to me. I couldn't help it . . . So there I was . . . I felt fifteen again like when I was first tugged by the beast, triggered to fuck I was . . . all humiliated, scared and angry.

'Coming with us'? Looks like that was on your mind from the beginning, But you got the wrong brer, you're holding me up, so if you could be so kind, tell me what this is, so I can go about my business?

Nothing back from him.

Oh for fuck's sake.

I said to myself. I know. He warned me, I heard him loud as clear, I didn't mean for the *fuck* to come out, but my stress level is on an all-time high!

Policeman   *That's it*!

Delroy   He snarled with the petulance of John McEnroe. Then he goes to grab me but I lift my hands and he . . . well, I don't quite know really he just . . . kinda slipped . . . I mean that's why I started laughing . . . cos it was so like . . . well, he just lost all his cool . . . plaps! He fall like a bag of shopping down the escalator, all messy and unrehearsed . . . and I couldn't help but laugh . . . call it gallows humour, call it karma, fuck, call it what you like, man . . . shit was funny for real bedrin. Next minute they're marching me out of the station.

Should I make a dash? No chance, they got me tight, whoever this fucking brudda is that they have me mistaken for, he must have done summin hardcore! I felt shame bwoy, people staring at me hard. It felt as if I'd been sent off at Wembley for breaking Harry Kane's fibula during the World Cup final. My stress level were reaching about eleven out of ten. I weren't swearing now doh, I weren't giving it large, but I was saying,

Carly's waters broken . . . my girl's waters have broken! I'm gonna miss the birth of my kid.

Every chance I got.

She's about to deliver at any time. Don't you care? Don't you realise how shamed you're gonna be, when you see you fu . . . messed up? I'm not your man!

Nothing back from dem . . . Not a word, like talking to a guard outside Buckingham Palace. If that weren't bad enough, when we reach the station, I got their custody sergeant looking down at me. And guess what, he's only a brudda!

Could not make it up! White coppers are one thing, especially the working-class variety, nuttin but *good ole boys* in uniform but a brudda with stripes on his sleeves, deh they're worse, cos they have to overcompensate. Can't be too black for their colleagues, so you believe they're gonna go all white East London on us.

Black Copper   *Name?*

Delroy   I give it to him, in between me telling him about Carly.

Brother, please, this is a mistake I need to be somewhere.

He don't want to know.

Black Copper   *Date of birth.*

Delroy   Fuck it, I give it to him, what else can I do? But he had to say it, he had to ask that question. He had to go there.

Black Copper   *Previous convictions?*

Delroy   *What?*

Black Copper   *What have you done in the past?*

Delroy   I didn't need to ask, I know what I heard, from this coconut!

How can you ask me a question like that? Have you been kissing the white man's arse so long, you starting to like it, brudda?

Black Copper   *Previous convictions?*

Delroy   *I have no previous convictions! As I keep telling you*
people, you have made a rhatid fucking mistake! I managed to get
that in, for as long as it took them to fling me in one of their
cells. All I could think about was Carly, and that she could
drop, any second, my kid, and I am in here. Am I cursed?
Was Zeus looking down at me from Mount Olympus, going,
Oi, Apollo, Let's fuck with Delroy today, I'm bored! Cos it bloody
felt like he was, but I don't know if he knew . . . Zeus that is,
cos I bleeding well didn't know how I'd take to be in there.
In a cell . . . Mate . . . as soon they turned the lock . . . well,
no actually it was when he walked away . . . I felt like, well,
like I'd been hollowed out, like all the things that had been
holding me together mentally just evaporated . . . I started
to sweat in my palms and my armpits not my face, just my
hands and arms were seeping sweat. I don't know if it was
shame over missing Carly giving birth or the claustrophobia
or just that finally they fucking got me, the feds . . . finally I
was just a number, another black man who got fucked by the
police, finally I was another hapless victim to this class/colour
bullshit! . . . I . . . me . . . was on this conveyer belt of hate . . .
I don't know, but I felt . . . shame and rage and a fear . . . a
fear I'd never had before because I knew what these people
was capable of . . . was I gonna be another story . . . was this
it . . . me done . . . finished. It weren't no kinda don't bend
down for the soap kinda fear, it was because . . . I didn't
know if I could make it . . . I didn't know if I was bad
enough, strong enough, tough enough to be held like a . . .
slave, an animal in a fucking cage . . . caged! Me! Fucking
me! Alright, yeah, I'm a bailiff, I take people's tings away
from them, but it's legal, it's a job, it's my job. Someone has
to do it. I pay my tax. I abide by the law. I have never
committed a crime in my life. I voted for Boris, twice. I don't
care that it's fucked up. Is that not allowed? Am I to be told
what I can and cannot do and who I am supposed to be in
my own country?

NO! And then the tears started and I thought already I'd
fucked it as a dad . . . already I was a dad my kid would have

to not wanna be like or be ashamed of. Was I now suddenly unemployable? . . . undesirable?

Unsuccessful? I picked up the paper-thin, spunk-riddled mattress and leaned it against the wall and I pounded it, pounded the shit out of it.

CUNT! CUNT! CUNT! CUNT! CUNT! CUNT!

Over and over and over and over again. Tears making welts on my face.

Policeman   If you don't stop that shit now, boy . . . we'll fucking make you!

Delroy   Boy? I bought my own flat three years ago. I have a mortgage , cha rass, two cats to feed, and yet still, in the eyes of some, I am nothing but a boy . . . I turned to him . . . and I just . . . buckled . . . like a three-year-old standing in the middle of a road staring at a bus hurtling towards them. I buckled and sat and cried all the man tears I'd saved through the years . . . all the shit I'd just buried . . . cried out all the anger I'd hidden, all the hope I'd managed, all the pride I'd held in remission, I wept it out . . . I cried and cried and cried. Four hours, straight . . . the whole four hours that they had me in there, four! Like a baby, and then cell door finally opens, and they chuck me out. Do I get an apology? Do I fuck! Just a,

Policeman   *We'll be pressing charges, pending further investigation. For now on yer way.*

Delroy   Blah blah blah. Normally, I would have loved to have stayed and chatted, and take great delight in telling them about themselves. But needs must, tears wiped, I had a hospital to get to. Carly has probably dropped it by then I thought, not thought . . . I wasn't thinking, I was bloody panicking. As soon as I was out, I clocked my battery was dead, so I couldn't phone anyone. Now I don't know if a record exists for the fastest time there is to run from the local nick to the hospital, but I broke it. In yer face Usain!

Scene Three

Hospital Toilet

As soon as I arrived in the hospital, I saw Mum just sitting there on a chair giving me the look . . . nothing I could say would be good enough for sure, we were never gonna be in 'accord', no matter fucking what . . . I could have rolled in with no legs and she would have looked at me same way . . . Mum's mans . . . but I also knew right then, Carly hadn't dropped it. You think my mum would be just sitting there all calm and serene if Carly had given birth to her first grandchild? No! Cos she'd be in there, fighting with Carly's mum over whose turn it is to hold the sprog. So I told her as we went up in the lift . . . and after being dragged around a police station like some refugee out of Italian waters, I was expecting a little bit of tea and sympathy from me mum but all she had for me, was that

Denise   *It's your fault!*

Delroy   I shall say that again,

Denise   *Your fault!*

Delroy   You should have seen my mout, it was all that!

> *He opens his full wide, like he is in shock.*

Sorry, Mum, can you give that to me again? I ain't sure I heard you right. How was any of that my fault? Then, without skipping a beat, she laid it on for me.

Denise   *It's your fault, Delroy, right from the beginning. Your fault! Because you gave then what they wanted, another mouthy black man. You should know better than that, I raised you better to know that.*

You can't beat those people, not like that, not with noise. You play dem, boy, you play dem at their own game. You kill them with kindness. You don't say a word, you don't give them what they want. You know you didn't do anything wrong, so it is all on them. You cannot beat them by going all loud. Yer nothing but a wurtless fool if

*you think you can. And I didn't raise no fool. So don't go making a
liar out of me, you understand? Use yer head, bwoi.*

Delroy Mums! I bloody hate them. Especially, when they
are right . . . cos, when I ran to the hospital Carly was in,
from the police station, and raced into the ward . . . and
slipped on a gown quicker then a Tyson Fury left hook, and
dived into Carly's room, I was told in no uncertain terms to

Carly *Fuck off, you miserable no-watch wanker!*

By my loving darling mid-contracting girlfriend Carly. *How
the fuck can you be late now! You can't even hold my hand on time,
that's all I needed you to do, hold my hand and you couldn't even do
that.*

Delroy Yeah . . . I had guessed near enough exactly what
she would say. But I'd never have guessed she would go on
to say.

Carly *Get the fuck out of here. I don't want to hear your excuse or
explanation,*

Delroy Her face contorted with the pain of childbirth
and anger.

Carly *I don't wanna hear no 'You don't understand' rubbish.*

Delroy She squeezed through her tight tense jaw.

Carly *Or no 'oh black people got it rough', sick to death of it . . .
you and your 'it's different for us' bullshit, Delroy. All your 'walk in
my shoes' shit or should I say trainers . . . one of your fifty pairs of
trainers! You wear like giving multi-national imperialist racist
corporations money makes you black.*

Delroy She well and truly dug me with that, while wiping
her grease and sweat-soaked hair from her eyes.

Carly *Or your 'white privilege' wank . . . just get the fuck out,
Delroy. You let me down.*

Delroy Her words wrapping round me like a hair shirt.

Carly   *I'll do this on my own, you hear me, on my own. Like I knew I would when we got together, when I got pregnant, you're the same as all of dem. Grow up, Delroy! Just grow the fuck up will yer . . . you're not in South Africa, bruv, you're in Hackney . . . it ain't that fucking 'ard . . . now get out! Out!*

Delroy   I just stood there knowing . . . I can't tell her the rest now, about what happened . . . along with . . . ah what di rass! What the fuck did she just say?! . . . with *'my'* child in her belly. I just backed away with the nurses giving me dead-eye.

Smacking my back into the double doors I exited . . . broken to the core . . . You ever see a black guy go red. I didn't think it was possible either till I saw my face in the mirror when I went to hide in the loos. The shame had managed to bring blood so vehemently to the front of my face it was peaking through my pores like beetroot and chocolate cake. I'm not in South Africa!

Fucking 'ell, man. I thought, All those hours going to anti-natal with this bitch, the only man deh you know . . . all of dem looking at me like a must be her Uber driver or sumink . . . I thought . . . all that back rubbing, all the scraping and fetching and hugging and supporting . . . all the decorating and the managing, hoping and wishing . . . Cooking, cleaning, not drinking, I hadn't had a fucking drink for six months and this . . . this is what she gonna tell while giving birth to 'my' child. ENGLISH PEOPLE!

Fucking 'ell ENGLISH PEOPLE. I thought. How does she think that makes me feel . . . I know I'm not in South Africa but the point is if I was I'd be fucked like them so I feel it, cos we share that knowledge . . . doesn't she understand how small that makes me grow . . . as a man . . . knowing American white men can shoot dead men who look like me out of hate and get away with it . . . and I just need to grow up. ENGLISH PEOPLE, even when you worship the floor they tread they still can say shit like dat . . . can still not see yer. 'All dem', she said I was like all of dem . . . what's that

supposed to fucking mean? The all of who? What kind of
narrow-minded bullshit was that? But in truth . . . I knew
what she meant. I knew she phrased it terribly but I knew
what she meant.

Having just left the police station I knew . . . and the facts
were I now was this racist picture of a black man . . . that was
the fact and nothing now could shake that . . . but that ain't
fair . . . is it? It can't be. *THAT AIN'T BLOODY FAIR.*

Michael   *Delroy?*

Delroy   I know that voice from anywhere. Been hearing it
since I was thirteen years old. Now, it weren't Michael saying
my name that made my body go all cold in that instant. It
was the way he said. It was that tone. The same tone that he
continued with.

Michael   *You. alright, mate?*

Delroy   Now why was he saying it like that? You. Alright.
Mate?   You don't use a tone like that, especially to a mate, to
your best mate. The tone he was giving is the tone you use to
your grandparents, before they are carted off to the nearest
care home. It was then I realised I hadn't been thinking it,
I'd been sounding off like some high-level nutter for all to
hear. Michael heard every word of what I had just said,
every lick. It had to be him, innit? I turned around to face
him.

Yeah, smashing, mate.

He looked good it had to be said. He was true to his word,
when he said was going off the booze for a bit. The last thing
he must have heard from me was me bellowing from
laughter, when he claimed he was giving up the sauce.

Fuck off, mate.

I goes delirious.

Do one!

I ain't laughed so hard since Eddie Murphy's stand-up film *Delirious*, that bit when he's taking the right piss out of his dad, 'My house, you don't like it, you can get the fuck out . . .' But the proof is in the pudding. There he was, my mate Michael, standing there, just standing there all lean and shit, someone put him in a right nice suit, I guess it was the new girlfriend Carly was telling me about,

Carly   *The one who does yoga.*

Delroy   Is how she describes her.

Carly   *She's good for him, she's got him into Pilates and shit.*

Delroy   *Michael Fletcher! On a mat, bending!*

I goes, shook.

Yeah let's see how long it takes for him to fuck that up for himself.

Feeling him move further and further away from me.

Won't last.

I replied trying not to expose my hurt.

Anyhow, he stands there, eyes wide with sympathy.

Michael   *How are ya, mate?*

Delroy   I'd not seen him for some time, well properly anyway, not since his dad's funeral, when his charlie and alcohol ridden body proceeded to dig me and everyone else that he loved well and truly out. That rant was epic. He was giving it.

Michael   *Delroy, my best mate, his parents came over here from Jamaica, but he went and voted for fucking Brexit.*

Fucking leaver, he is, I mean Jesus H, Delroy, I mean what is the matter with you? When they want a curb on immigration, who do you think they are talking about?

Delroy, I love you, like a brother, but you may sound like us, act like us, but you will never be one of us, and deep down you know it, you

have to, cos this is England we are talking about. Banana throwing on the pitch is not regular but, mark my words, that anger is still there, it's coming out in droves, it's making a comeback, or maybe you choose not to.

Delroy   Yeah . . . in a room full of English people too, mate . . . He thought getting Carly to snog me at the wake would somehow make all the shit go away. English amnesia again. I wanted to have nothing to do with him after that. He killed our friendship, there and then, stone dead.

Yes, yeah, smashing, mate.

I said with an age-old black camouflage for when dealing with the English.

He smiles broadly.

Michael   *Only, you're talking to yourself.*

Delroy   He may as well have slapped me round the face with a white glove.

I am just letting off steam, mate, something you should know all about.

Delroy   What?

Michael   I gave him a silent *'nigger please'* with me eyes, that Samuel L. Jackson would have been proud of.

Michael   *Oh . . .*

Delroy   *He said as if he'd just stepped in quicksand.*

Michael   *Really? Now? . . . look alcohol . . . made me /*

Delroy   *Don't blame alcoho, mate, I knew you was selfish from when you nicked Joseph Kiffin's break money for two terms.*

Michael   *Delroy . . . are you ok? I'm eager to be in service of you right now.*

Delroy   *In service?* Eh? What's he eaten, I thought. He stood there, all open and honest, all fucking I don't know what but not Michael Fletcher. Like he wanted to talk about what happened, to say sorry at long bleeding last. But I was thinking, he didn't just deserve the beating I gave him that night, more like he earned it, but if he was willing to put his hands up at last for that, fair dues to the man. But I find with Michael that it is always wise to give him a gentle reminder about such things. You know, forgive but never forget. You gotta watch the English you know. Any excuse to rewrite history and turn on the self-righteous tap, they will bag it. Michael, although I loved him like a brother, was no different.

Look, I'm fine.

He looked to the door and stroked his new 'I'm so wise' beard and offered.

Michael   *I take it Carly ain't dropped it, yet?*

Delroy   *Is this you being in service is it?*

Michael   *Delroy . . . God is watching, mate.*

Delroy   *God?*

Michael   *Delroy . . . give us a break will yer?*

Delroy   Now I don't know if losing weight makes eyes bigger but his never looked bigger and more needy.

No, mate, no air drop of the payload as of yet. She's giving it some welly though.

Michael   *I would ask, why you ain't in there right now, but seeing as I just heard.*

Delroy   *Yes, mate, you heard me talking to myself, you saw me prancing around like I was about to have a seizure, can we just park that now? Do you mind?*

Michael   *Not at all, mate, it's all good, she is my sister remember?*

Delroy   He said trying to make light of things.

Yeah, I remember. All of those years, her calling me black this, black that in front of you and your dad.

Michael   *Yeah I wanted to t /*

Delroy   *And as soon as he was out of the room, however, different story, she couldn't get my shirt off and her knickers down fast enough. Yeah I remember.*

Letting it linger in the room for a bit surprisingly he opened the buttons of his jacket and said.

Michael   *That must have been hard for you, mate /*

Delroy   *I remember her and you having fights, in front of me . . . with fists.*

Michael   *Yeah, Carly had a sweet uppercut that Anthony Joshua would mug her for.*

Delroy   We looked at each other and smiled. He's been my best mate for coming on thirty years, if you can believe that. You can't just brush that off, can yer? But was he going to go and say sorry for what he said to me at the funeral or what?

Michael   *She'll make amends.*

Delroy   *Amends?*

Michael   *She still loves you.*

Delroy   *She has a fucked-up way of showing it though, mate. It must run in the family, eh?*

Michael   *Delroy, she is mad fer yer!*

Delroy   *It's over!*

I said it . . . did I mean it?

I didn't know but it sprayed out of my mouth like a Covid cough.

I've had it with her.

My wet eyes betraying my certainty.

Michael   *You just need to reflect.*

Delroy   *Reflect? The bitch don't want me in there, she wants me under a bus, no offence.*

Michael   *She's giving birth to yer kid, time, yer both just need time.*

Delroy   *Oh.*

I says, in a serious daze, no. Is this really Michael Fletcher? talking to me right now? Going all zen and shit? Was it really him? Or was it that blue-skinned mutant bitch from the *X-Men* films that can turn into anybody that she wants?

It had to be the latter, it had to be, cos whoever was talking to me was not the Michael Fletcher I know. The one who was with me when we nicked the school sign. The one who was shagging some brass on his stag night and the night before his dad's funeral! The one who gave his dad's eulogy off his nut on fuck knows what kind of *charlie*. Now he's sitting there, like he's found religion, telling me, him fucking telling me.

Michael   *Time, Delroy, time.*

Delroy   *Now, I ain't been to church since I was seventeen, but Lawd Jesus fuck!*

Anything else you want to tell me, Michael? Is there anything you would like to lecture me on, seeing as you so sorted now, you straightened yourself, yer cunt!

My hand now shaking in fear of myself.

Who the fuck do you think you are?

Michael   *I don't think I am anything. I am sorry you feel that way, mate.*

Delroy   Straightening himself up to show his size over me.

Mate? Mate? When was the last time you and I have been mates? We haven't bin mates since you shafted me at your dad's funeral. Remember that, you gave me a right seeing too, in front of everyone.

Michael   *I know what I did.*

Delroy   He said closing his eyes in shame.

You know what you did? And?

He then lifted his chin, and his nostrils flared in that Ray Winstone way.

Michael   *And, I am sorry.*

He opened his palms like Francis of bludclart Assisi and then said.

I'd like to make amends . . . I'm sorry, Delroy . . . not just for that /

Delroy   *Amends? How you gonna do that?*

Nothing back from 'im.

Don't worry I'll wait.

Michael   *I don't know.*

Delroy   *No course you don't. The English never seem to know.*

Michael   *But I am sorry.*

Delroy   *All that stuff you said to your dad . . . yeah when he's dead . . . when he couldn't do anything . . . why didn't you say that when he was spinning that racist stuff to me . . . why didn't you say something then . . . to me! You never said sorry about him to me, Michael. You said nothing to me! Was I just meant to take it, huh?*

Live with it, huh? How you gonna make amends for that?

Michael   *I am truly sorry, Delroy.*

Delroy   Now, he said it, he definitely said it, but what I heard, in that one word, 'sorry', was what he said to me back in that church, all over again, all in that one word. It wasn't torture for him, it meant nothing to him then, and still don't. The cunt!

Alright, Michael, what is this? I said cooling my face with some tap water.

Why are you standing there, looking like you've finally read a book in your miserable life? Have you had help? Who have you been talking to? Nothing from him, so I styled it out a bit, dragging the paper towel out with the flourish of a young matador.

And don't say it has anything to do with your bendy bird, the yoga one, cos from what I hear, she ain't that bright. Not unless they're handing out PhDs for knowing how to pull your leg over your head. So what gives? Who is helping you?

Who's your new friend, Michael? Who the fuck is it?

He stood there, looking around the room for the answer but he was still silent. He had an answer, he just didn't want or couldn't tell me. His right, I suppose. But here is my right to tell himself about himself.

Michael, I don't business if you are sorry. Fuck that you are sorry. Tek yer sorrys and ram dem up yer shit hole!

Michael   *I'm sorry you feel that way.*

Delroy   *Michael, are you deaf, did you not hear what I told you what wid yer sorrys?*

But I wanted his sorrys, his friendship, his love, but I wanted action more.

Michael   *Ok, Delroy, just as you like. I didn't come here for this. I just want to go and see my sister.*

Delroy   *No, no, I don't tink so, bitch. You stay right deh, you don't move an inch. I got a whole heap of shit I want to say to you, bwoy.*

Michael   *Ok, Delroy, say what you feel, get it off yer chest.*

Delroy   The more decent he was, the more I wanted to tump him, fer trut.

You know what you said, slagging me off cos I voted Brexit, you wanna know why? Why, I voted Brexit?

I had to say something . . . had to . . . and how much of it I meant, I still don't know, but I had to give it to him . . . I had to let him see me, finally see me, so in an effort to be understood clearly . . . I grabbed his shirt and twisted it in my fist and leaned in so close we could have kissed.

Because all of this, this day that I have had, this shit that we are living in needs to come down.

That's why! Fucking Great Britain, is someone having a laugh here?

Still carrying on like it's the big I am! Rest of Europe is no better, fucking France, rhatid Spain, them saps who come from Germany, like England still treating the have-nots like shit. It's a house of lies, fucking lies. Racist fucking liars, mate. So, I say bring it down, bring it all down! Tear it up, tear it all fucking up!

This is where your old man and the rest of his right-wing nut jobs got it wrong, calling for Brexshit cos they really thought that would mean they would see a few less brown faces on the streets. The same brown faces that was propping up the NHS whenever it is on its knees. Cos the same brown faces will be wiping their arses for them when they wind up in a care home one day. And I don't just want Great Britain on its knees, Michael, I want to keep it there. That's why I voted Brexit! Let's see how great fucking Britain is then, when it ain't got anyone behind them. When it has to rely on the likes of you, the thick as shit working-class Brit like me, who will be on its rhatid hands and knees, cleaning the streets, wiping toilet bowls, sucking cock, wiping up sick, let the British be the people that no one sees, see how we like it. See how it feels to be true niggers of the world. You tink this a joke? Yer gonna find out, yer finding out now. How's it feel? How's it feel now? Still think yer number one? Yer fart! Yer having a laugh. You are the laugh! Whose gonna come for you, when yer down? Who is going to save you? This is it for England, this is the end of the motherfucking line and I can't wait to see it happen, see it right at the bottom, where they can't be seen. Bring it! All of yer, like you're the big I am. Nuttin but a bunch of stupid, arrogant, lazy as fuck, snow-flaking, line-snorting, Fred Perry wearing, red-neck, pecker-wood, inbred jellied eels, fish and chips, gammon-loving, tea-drinking, bacon-eating dumb arse crackers! Wid yer 'God Save the Queen', wrap yourselves around the Union Jack, we survived the Blitz, hands up if you won the war, tek it up the arse from the US of A, Pukka Pies bullshit! Fuck England, RIP!

I said it, how I felt, not what I knew but how I felt . . . not what I thought but what I felt and it felt good to say it, it was like a riot in my mouth and I felt a freedom . . . I felt free. I breathed hard and heavy. Letting go of his now wrinkled shirt I tried to compute what I just said.

Michael   *Right then. I'll see you around, Delroy.*

He said staring at his shirt.

Delroy   *Yes, see you around, Michael, see you, fucking, around. White male privilege, innit Michael? Even you, a fucking third-rate white boy spiv is allowed to change. Not me, not my black arse self, never me, never us. Gotta stay street me innit . . . stay black . . . and silent, right?*

Michael   *This ain't you, mate.*

Delroy (*now raging*)   *This ain't me? Yu tink diss is joke, yu tink diss is how life go? Move yer wurtless self from me, you pussy hole, WHAT YOU GONNA DO, Michael?*

HOW YOU GONNA MAKE AMENDS? What you gonna do? . . . See it deh! Fucking rass clart! Boomba hole! Or should I be more, 'It's alright, geezer . . . no probs, mate'. How about that, Michael? Is that more me? Is that what you want to see? Is that me? You don't know me, Michael, you never knew me, none of yer! You don't know me! You will have to know me to say something like that. So come on, Michael, come on! Get to know me. Get to like me. Get to understand me. Get to love me. Get to respect me. Get to value me.

Get to trust me. Do the work, Michael. It ain't rocket science. (Bellows.) All of you, do the fucking work!

And he just turned away and walked away . . . from me. And something snapped inside me . . . broke off . . . I could feel it and I just had to leave, I had to . . . I couldn't take them any more, any of them . . . it was all ruined . . . the day, the love, the . . . the lot. So I walked out on them. I left them, they were dead to me.

Scene Four

A Courtroom

> **Delroy** *stands up in court from behind his desk.*

Delroy   You may or may not be aware, your honour, that
I've managed to fall out, disagree with, erm . . . to make vex
four different lawyers who had agreed to take on my case, all
pro bono I should add . . . erm by the way 'vex' means anger
. . . as in to make angry in Jamaican patois . . . Thought I'd
clear that up as language is part of the whole point I'm
trying to make here. Anyways like . . . what I'm saying . . .
badly . . . is that . . . they, the lawyers, didn't want me to do
what I'm doing now . . . a closing speech . . . so we parted
ways. Now why? You could ask,

> *He adopts their characters to a T.*

'It's unlikely to curry favour with the magistrate' . . . 'leave to
me' . . . 'trust me'.

> *He shakes his head and smiles.*

You see I think it was all in an effort not to be me. They
didn't want me . . . to be me, your honour.

Cos me isn't good enough to be understood or respected or
taken seriously, by the likes of you.

Now I thought that was kinda off-key . . . you know 'rude'
about you.

About your level of intellect and bandwidth to understand
human behaviour or character . . . also it kinda assumed
you'd be racist and perhaps fall into the same biases as I
believe my case has pointed out. So, I'm gonna be as honest
and myself as much as I can, I'm gonna be me in the hope
you can see me and also understand the point in which it
went wrong with the police. To try to convince you I'm a
good guy stopped on a bad day . . . anyway . . .

Now you've heard already my account of what happened and their conflicting account? Yeah alright . . . I guess you don't need to answer . . . it was kinda rhetorical.

And of course the 'shove' as they put it . . . and the bad language could be seen as crosses . . . as in 'bad behaviour'. But . . . I'd like you to think of this. When man's put under pressure, as you know I was . . . as any dutiful father would feel on the way to the hospital to see the birth of their child!

He tries to compose himself again.

I was prang . . . dented, out of shape, prang . . . so that . . . that's how I felt rushing to the hospital and dat, having got the message late . . . prang . . . excited but . . . prang . . . which is all understandable right? A little nod would do, your honour, just so I know . . . there . . . calm . . . as in, oh nevermind . . . but you see how the way I use language is different . . . right? It's not wrong, it's just different? A swear word to you is an adjective to me /

He hears his mum kiss her teeth.

It's alright, Mum . . . sorry my mum's screwing at me, bwoy . . . 'upset' with me.

Actually my mum . . . my mum . . . bwoy now she is an amazing woman but you lot . . . not you personally but yeah maybe you as you did nothing I bet . . . really hurt her and me . . . The Windrush scandal?

. . . What? . . . erm, yes yes . . . this is about my case actually, it's not quite what I'd written down . . . you could argue it's a detour but . . . well, hear me out still . . . I think it talks of the same ting . . . culture . . . a disrespected culture . . . a misrepresented culture. Cos like, everyone knew she was British right.

. . . She had every right to be here and ting . . . yet you people or to be fair 'your' people . . . the people you'd done put in charge had hatched, concocted a devious plan to rid yourself of us! My mum! Who I'd seen work herself into the

ground, paying her taxes, put her bloody life at risk as a
front-line worker she did, she was to be told come out! . . .
but ere what now . . . I think I felt it worse than she did, cos I
have to stay here, cos I love where I live . . . love what I've
built . . . it's all I know so . . . it's mine . . . so I'm like . . . lost,
cos I'm made complicit . . . I'm made her enemy, coz I'm
powerless to do anything . . . so where do I put that, your
honour? Where? . . . Where do I house that anger? . . .
Where do I get to shoot that anger at? Cos to me it feels like
all of you just told my mum, 'You can't stay here any more
cos we didn't really want you here in the first place'. It makes
a knot in all of us that can't be untied . . . So when PC
knobhead over there . . . hear me OUT! HEAR ME OUT!

. . . When he tells me not to swear like I'm his chattel or
something, standing there, the complete embodiment of the
wankers that wanted to send my mum to a country she'd
never lived in, that wanted to . . . disregard all her efforts to
make something of her life here, to be a model Brit . . . it's
not only hard to take . . . it's bloody hard . . . to do . . . to not
to swear!

It's . . .

He looks over to his mum.

. . . No no don't cry, Mum . . . please don't . . . don't let them
see you cry . . . they love seeing black women cry . . . please
Mum don't . . . they seem to love it innit doh . . . innit doh!
. . . Every drama we're in, 'Get the black woman to wail
maybe she could shout to God'. I mean if I have to watch
Viola Davis crying through her nose again . . . I swear I'll . . .

He smiles broadly.

Dat's it . . . huh! made yer laugh . . . they fucking love dat!

He does an impression of Viola Davis.

So DON'T give dem dat . . . Mum! Please . . . just know I see
you, Mum . . . we see you . . . we love you . . . we know what

you've done and what you're doing . . . so don't cry . . . don't.

He wells up, tears fall from his face.

Your honour . . .

I couldn't help myself . . . I can't help it . . . I couldn't help it . . . it's part of my culture . . . my working-class culture . . . my British culture . . . it don't make me bad, mate, I wasn't even swearing at him, I said 'Oh for fuck's sake' to myself, cos I was gonna miss the birth of my child! A one-time event! Made for me to share with my woman and he was killing that stone dead. Dead! I mean anything can happen in childbirth right? . . . she could have died or something . . . the baby could have . . . I needed to be there . . . so of course I lost my cool! My focus . . . Of course I forgot my . . . place, wouldn't you? The context, your honour . . . everything is about the context! . . . How can we blanketly throw these laws, rules, punishments . . . attitudes down . . . throw these morals down, threaten my livelihood . . . without any empathy . . . without truly understanding and allowing for the context, the context . . . how? unless . . . well unless . . . you're happy to be some kind of . . . cunt?! . . .

We see him being dragged away by the security guard in the courtroom.

Scene Five

Lockdown

Delroy   To say that Carly isn't technically minded is an understatement. She can't even set up a new smartphone without fucking it up. And don't get me started when she switched her broadband package from BT to Virgin.

Carly   *So many cables, all these wires! Where does this one go?*

Delroy   *There and there*, I kept saying. *Cable with the red bit goes into the red hole. Blue bit, blue hole. It's nowhere near as hard* *as you are making it, babe.* Not a clue, common sense right of the winder. So, you imagine my surprise, sitting here in lockdown, when my laptop here was telling me not only do I have an email from Carly, but it's also a folder a file, a video file. I don't know who it was that taught her to do, but I want to shake their hand when I am not kissing their feet. So what gives, I thought? Is she up for apologising for cussing me out like that at the hospital, cos I don't want to know, I don't want to hear. Me and her are done. D.O.N.E.! I'm finished with her.

(*Thinks.*) But it's not going to hurt to hear what she has to say, though is it? Fuck it, I thought. (*Opens the file, presses play.*)

Carly *So, you alright then, knobhead? What's going on?*

Delroy *What do you want, Carly?* I say without thinking, only realising a quick second later that this is a recording. I couldn't help it, it's her face you see? Those annoying, yet beautiful, sexy come-to-bed eyes, Mel from *EastEnders* look on her face. I could have kept her face on pause all day, but I needed to know what she had to say.

Carly *How come you haven't come round? To see us and that? She's yer kid as well, you know? What's the matter with you? Are you thick or something?*

Delroy *You bloody know why!* I say again, knowing full well this was a recording, but not caring, I didn't business.

Carly *You always want attention, innit Delroy? Everyone has to run around and make a fuss about you. What are you, seven?*

Delroy *Yes, bitch, keep it up.*

Carly *Well, I ain't playing.*

Delroy *Do I look as if I care?*

Carly *Well, if you think I am going to tell you how much I miss you, you can dream on.*

Delroy   *Am dreaming now, watch me.*

Carly   *I ain't got the time or the energy to tell you how much I miss you, I ain't got time for that, Delroy.*

Delroy   *Good!*

Carly   *I ain't got time . . . I ain't got time to tell you how much I miss the way you look at me.*

Delroy   Say what?

Carly   *When you stare at me so intense with those gorgeous brown eyes of yours, I find it hard to look back. I ain't gunna say how much I miss looking at you. Your beautiful chiselled face that just makes me want to bite you.*

I ain't gunna say how much I miss the way my skin tingles all over whenever you touch me. Whenever you hold me in your arms. Whenever I think of our weekends together in Blackpool. All of those showers we had together.

Delroy (*beams*)   Damn girl, you went in.

Carly   *No, I ain't saying any of that. What I will say to you, Delroy Francis Tomlin, is fucking call me, you twat!*

Delroy (*to audience*)   I ain't calling her. Like I must do what she says. I ain't calling her. I ain't. I ain't calling her.

Ain't! Fuck her! Fuck 'em all! I ain't calling her.

(*Phone rings.*) Shit, it's her. I know it's her, it's Carly. That's her ringtone video call. Face still scowling, I bet. But still beautiful. Still my Carly.

(*To an audience member.*) Fuck's sake! Alright then, if you're going to go on about it, alright.

(*Answers.*) Yeah, what?

Carly   You alright then?

Delroy   Yeah, I'm fine, babe, how about you?

Carly Yer mum told me what happened to you, in court and that.

Delroy Yeah?

Carly You were found guilty?

Delroy Yeah.

Carly Why you couldn't fuckin well tell me that to begin with, I do not know.

Delroy If you gave me a chance, I would have.

Carly I wanted to see if yer alright.

Delroy I'm goo . . .

Carly *I was giving birth and I wasn't well . . . I wasn't in my right /*

Delroy I know.

Carly *But what I said to you before in the hospital still stands you know.*

Delroy What?

Carly *Yer still a prat, Delroy.*

Delroy Babe, I kno . . .

Carly *A colossal prat.*

Delroy Jesus wep . . .

Carly *Michael told me what you said to him, going all political, fuck England and that, I mean what the fuck, Delroy?*

Delroy Woman never lets me speak.

Carly *Since when did you care about any of that?*

Delroy Since now.

Carly *You've never bin on a single march in yer life, mate. When have you ever held a placard in your hand? Yer twat.*

Delroy   Are yu done?

Carly   *The little people are ones are what matters to you, the little ones.*

You said that. Yer mum and that, my mum and that, friends, family, the little things, well, you've got two little things right here.

Delroy (*sees*)   Oh shit. Shit, man. It's her. My baby. Our baby.

Carly   *Little things, Delroy, she's number one, I'm number two. So, what are you going to do about that then?*

Delroy   How can I hate her now, cos I do bloody *hate* her, I so fucking *hate* her. And seeing her right here, with our baby, my yout, makes me *hate* her even more. It really does. I mean . . . Oh Cha rass, Delroy, say what you mean, man yourself up!

(*To* **Carly**.) I love you, Carly, you want to hear me say it. I love you girl. From the time I was fifteen until now. I love you. I never stopped. Even though you drive me mad wid yer chat, like nails on a chalkboard half the time, I love you! Even though you always show up an hour late whenever we go out, I love you!

Even though you hate my mum's Jamaican patties, but you yam dem down anyway, every last bit, I love you. If you were here right now, I'd fling you down on my bed and show you how much I love you.

Because I do. I love you. I love you. Carly? (*Waits.*) What? Are you just going to sit there, looking all nice, say summin, babe? We're in lockdown, I don't know when I can see you both again. Carly?

Carly   I lo . . . ve . . . y . . . ou. I lo . . . ve . . . y . . . ou.

Delroy   What, what you saying, you are breaking up, I can't hear, the picture's frozen, Carly?

Carly! . . . Shit! This is when I want to go to fucking war with Zoom! Or was it FaceTime she was using, WhatsApp, Skype,

I don't blasted know, I just want her back! I've got no idea
when I can see her again. To have them both in my arms.
This is killing me. Why did I have to leave the hospital that
day? Bloody lockdown, pain in the arse fer trut. If I weren't
found guilty, given this tag, I'd do a DC (*Dominic Cummings*)
by now and go fucking over there. Just wanna see my little
baby girl for the first time. Hold her in my hands for the first
time. All this, if it bleeps you're in brea, shit. (*Sighs.*) Yes,
Delroy, blame the courts, blame Cummings. Blame Michael.
Blame Carly. Blame your mum, blame everyone, but don't
even think about blaming your stupid proud dumb arse
unemployed self. What a total claart you are!

I am a dad. And nothing can ever change that. Nothing, and
Carly is her mum, the woman who I created her with and
that means something. Nothing would ever change that. It's
not an opinion, it's not about faith, it's not about loyalty, it's a
fact, a scientific fact. Unlike all the bullshit in the paper, on
the news about inflation and immigration and Conservative
and Labour and Muslim and Christian, all of those things,
opinions . . . choices . . . desires. I have . . . well, 'we' have
made something factual . . . I guess that's what all the fuss
was about . . . about kids, about family . . . we've made a fact
. . . A living breathing fact. And no matter how long she lives,
nothing can take that away . . . I'm hit, it just hit me in this
moment . . . it's taken all of this time.

Look at 'em, both of them looking like they are frozen in
time . . . oh my days . . . She's got my soft-shaped Caribbean
nose. I'm humbled to the core, man . . . but now I'm looking
at her mouth, and it ain't mine . . . it ain't gonna grow into
my shape either . . . it's frugal in size but perfect but it bares
no resemblance to Carly . . . but I know that shape . . . oh, oh
. . . my . . . it's . . . fucking Alan Fletcher . . . it's Alan's mouth,
Alan fucking Fletcher! . . . Just really bloody small and
brown. I can't believe it . . . he's back . . . he's living on . . .
through me . . . her . . . fuck me . . . what would he have
made of that. See I know what a racist he could be . . . I'd
had to suffer his fucking jokes for time . . . I had to suffer

him forcing Carly to hide me . . . watch Michael cowering from 'im . . . But it's him who took me down the Repton boys' club with Michael . . . him that dropped me home after football. Him who screamed on the sidelines at me.

Alan   Come on, you long streak of piss.

Delroy   And encouraged me to score . . . out of anger, yeah . . . but I scored . . . I got the glory. And there he is on the face of my child we've knitted . . . woven together for ever . . . that is a fact. An irrefutable cast-iron fact. My history was our history and I had to own it . . . without anger or hurt, I have to forgive.

(*In tears.*) What a bundle she is. A sheer bundle of joy. Imagine holding her in my hands for the first time. Wonder how she smells, feels . . .

I'm sorry I was late . . . I'm sorry I didn't stay. Like she cares, considering how early she was, she just wanted to get out here, anxious to start her life and that. Fighting to get out there she was . . . She's a fighter, I can tell. She's my little fighter. She's gonna fight on . . . no matter what you say . . . live on no matter what you do and so am I . . . so am I. I'm gonna fight on and on . . . and on. She is a fact. She is my fact. My everything. Nothing else matters. Nothing can. Nothing should.

Blackout.